I0792696

Like a Mustard Seed

It is like a mustard seed that someone took and sowed in the garden; it grew and became a tree, and the birds of the air made nests in its branches.

—Luke 13:19 NRSV

Like a Mustard Seed

MENNONITES IN PARAGUAY

EDGAR STOESZ

FOREWORD BY ALFRED NEUFELD

Herald Press
Scottdale, Pennsylvania
Waterloo, Ontario

Library of Congress Cataloging-in-Publication Data

Stoesz, Edgar.
Like a mustard seed : Mennonites in Paraguay / Edgar Stoesz.
p. cm.
Includes bibliographical references.
ISBN 978-0-8361-9420-3 (pbk. : alk. paper)
1. Mennonites–Paraguay–History–20th century. I. Title.
BX8119.P3S76 2008
289.7'892–dc22

2008022732

Unless otherwise noted, Scripture is from The Holy Bible, *New International Version* ®, Copyright © 1973, 1978, 1984 by the International Bible Society; used by permission of Zondervan Publishing House; all rights reserved. Scripture marked RSV is from the *Revised Standard Version Bible*, copyright 1946, 1952, 1971, by the Division of Christian Education of the National Council of the Churches of Christ in the USA, and used by permission. Scripture marked NRSV is from the *New Revised Standard Version*, Copyright © 1989, by the Division of Christian Education of the National Council of Churches in the USA, used by permission.

LIKE A MUSTARD SEED
Copyright © 2008 by Herald Press, Scottdale, Pa. 15683
Published simultaneously in Canada by Herald Press,
Waterloo, Ont. N2L 6H7. All rights reserved
Library of Congress Catalog Card Number: 2008022732
International Standard Book Number: 978-0-8361-9420-3
Printed in the United States of America
Book design by Joshua Byler
Cover by Sans Serif

13 12 11 10 09 08 10 9 8 7 6 5 4 3 2 1

To order or request information please call 1-800-245-7894
or visit www.heraldpress.com.

This book is dedicated to

Gerhard Ratzlaff
Peter P. Klassen
Martin W. Friesen

Authors
Teachers
Leaders
Historians
Friends

God Meant It for Good

When their villages in Russia were plundered, and they were beaten
to their knees,
When the Paraguayan "green hell" was one of the few places willing
to receive them,
When they discovered that the grass they had counted on to nourish
their herds was bitter,
When the well water was found to be salty,
When their crops were devoured by grasshoppers,
When plagues left orphans, widows and widowers,
When the land they had bought was claimed also by Indians,
When a border dispute made the Chaco an international battlefield,
When political passions erupted in their midst,
When thousands emigrated back to Canada or left for Germany
or East Paraguay,
When discouragement descended,
When life became so unbearable they questioned their coming,
When they asked, "Is this God's will or a tragic mistake?"
In the stillness of the Chaco night,
Before the nightingale began to trill,
Before the buds appeared on the bottle tree,
Amid cries of anguish, doubt, and fear came a voice:
"I, your God, meant it for good." (Genesis 50:20)

—Edgar Stoesz

Contents

Part 3 How They Are Giving Back

Foreword

Who is a Mennonite? That was not a question one hundred years ago. Mennonites were people from Germanic background, although Swiss and Dutch Mennonites who immigrated to France and North America also had their own identity. But the first five Mennonite World Conferences, held between 1925 and 1955, took place in Europe.

The question of who is a Mennonite become of interest to Mennonites in Paraguay. The first immigrants in 1927 were Canadian citizens of Prussian and Russian Mennonite heritage who came from Manitoba to the central Chaco. They prepared the way after securing the special law that made it possible to renounce military service and allowed for private Mennonite schools strongly influenced by the church. At that moment, the first immigrant group in Paraguay probably represented a minority identity within the larger Mennonite family. They came to Paraguay because they were not convinced that they should integrate into Canadian culture.

Things looked different with the second group, who were refugees from Soviet Russia. They had lost everything and depended heavily on assistance from worldwide Mennonite relief groups, such as Europe's Brüder in Not and Mennonite Central Committee (MCC) in North America.

At the second Mennonite World Conference in 1930 in Danzig, the main issue was how to help these refugees find a new home. The conference's official report is a moving story of global solidarity and Mennonite deaconal theology. Of course there are also some remarkable or even strange portions of the report. Harold S. Bender, the dynamic young leader of MCC who was responsible for Russian Mennonite colonization in Paraguay and would later write his famous "Anabaptist Vision," produced a blooper in Danzig 1930. After praising the beauty and quality of land in the central Chaco, the report quotes him as saying,

> What we had in mind and vision was a future state of Mennonites, where, if possible, all Russian Mennonites would be able to reestablish and develop their life and their culture within a context of unlimited freedom. A very positive aspect of the Paraguayan Chaco in cultural perspective is the fact that there exists no culture at all in that area. So there is no danger that Mennonites with their German culture will be absorbed by a strange culture. The Mennonite nation can continue to exist in Paraguay with its culture and faith, not exposed to any danger but on the contrary under the best thinkable circumstances.

And in the following debate dear Harold S. Bender even dared to say, "The most important question in this area without any culture is the survival of the German Mennonite culture."

Who is a Mennonite? After the Russian and Prussian Mennonites moved to the central Chaco, the Germanic part of the group's identity was strengthened and fostered by the group's two prominent mentors of this settlement: Bender and B. H. Unruh in Karlsruhe and Berlin. But soon a considerable amount of tension arose between Goshen, Indiana, and Berlin. The Mennonite World Peace Conference in Amsterdam in 1936 might have had an important impact. It was a last attempt at an all-Mennonite statement on peace and war at a time when preparations for World War II were well underway.

The German Mennonite delegation had left without signing the statement of July 4, 1936, which was an extraordinarily clear manifesto in favor of nonviolence and against the "sin of war" and compulsory military service. The MCC crew—Bender, C. F. Klassen, P. C. Hiebert, and Orie O. Miller, as well as Emmy Arnold and David Toews, all friends of Mennonites in Paraguay—said they signed the statement in dialogue with the Mennonite churches in Paraguay and other countries. At the same time, Unruh and most Mennonites in Germany went a different way, believing that the future of Mennonitism should be linked to the national history of the German people. Therefore the topic of German identity versus Mennonite Anabaptist identity caused severe tensions in the central Chaco during the war, leaving again the question, What is it that makes a Mennonite?

But at the same time there was already a fascinating debate at the Chaco *Mennoblatt* between Walter Quiring, a fervent Nazi Germanic defender of the ethnic Mennonite cause and Nikolai Siemens, teacher and editor of the *Mennoblatt*. Siemens proposed that a Russian Baptist might be emotionally closer to a Mennonite than a German nominal Catholic, whereas Quiring called this a *seelische Verwirrung* (psycho-spiritual confusion) and insisted that the bonds of racial blood (*Blut und Boden*) have to be stronger than religious loyalties.

Who is a Mennonite? I live in a Catholic neighborhood in Asunción. It's an active parish with a big church in front of our door. Although its members are mostly young people, an elderly man serves as deacon. He's one of our neighbors, and the other day he told me, "I always tell my family and my friends: 'Buy *leche* Trébol' (produced by the Menno colony). Our Mennonite brothers never will pour water into their milk. That is good milk."

In his classes of theology and Anabaptist history, Gerhard Ratzlaff sometimes asks the Mennonite students from Spanish Guaraní, Enlhet, or Nivaclé background if they are Mennonites. They usually respond with a big laugh and say, "No, we are brothers and sisters of the Mennonites." Or they would say that, spiritually speaking, they are Mennonites; their church was founded by Mennonites and has that name. But then again, they are more authentic Anabaptists than most of the Mennonites from immigrant backgrounds. Because some colonies specialize in cheese production, "Mennonite cheese" is well known in Paraguay. So is the "Mennonite smell": some immigrants do not bathe as often as Paraguayans do, and the local temperatures can produce a specific aroma.

For Germanic immigrant Mennonites, it is a somewhat complicated process to realize that they are no longer the only Mennonites in Paraguay. They might even soon be an ethnic minority within the Paraguayan Mennonite family. But important readjustments have been made. Fernheim colony in the central Chaco celebrated its seventy-fifth anniversary with a monument symbolizing ethnic integration and cooperation within the central Chaco, though some terminology still needs to be adjusted: the cooperative agency between the colonies and the native indigenous settlements is called the Association of Indigenous-Mennonite Cooperation Services. But in fact, most of the "Indians" are as Mennonite as the immigrant colony settlers.

In 2006 my wife, Wilma, and I had the privilege of attending the convention of Mennonite Economic Development Associates (MEDA) in Tampa, Florida. Gloria Penayo de Duarte Frutos, a Mennonite and at that time first lady of Paraguay, was the guest speaker. In her testimony, she said that when she identifies herself in Paraguay as a Mennonite, people wonder if she has Germanic background or was born in the Chaco.

Edgar Stoesz has done a superb job telling the story of Mennonites in Paraguay—how they gathered, how they prospered, and how they are trying to give back. Stoesz is a well-received friend of Paraguay, having cultivated friendships among Mennonite leaders over a long period. He might also be one of the best-informed outsiders on the Mennonite experience in Paraguay. He has always shown a keen interest, interviewing and getting the perspectives of key people in leadership. Mennonites in Paraguay are thankful for all he has done for their country, especially for the First Nation people, while an executive at MCC. And Stoesz is one of those who made a Paraguayan chapter of Habitat for Humanity possible, as well as MEDA Paraguay. Both institutions work hard in favor of economic development and social responsibility.

In July 2009 the global Mennonite community is scheduled to come to Paraguay to celebrate at the Mennonite World Conference (MWC) gathering in Asunción. The assembly's theme is "Come together in the way of Jesus Christ," based on Philippians 2:1-11. Eight Mennonite conferences representing various language and cultural groups have formed a national coordinating council to host this event. Around one thousand First Nation people from the Mennonite churches among the Enlhet and Nivaclé, and probably another one thousand from the Spanish Guaraní churches in Asunción and East Paraguay plan to attend together with the descendants of the immigrants and former Paraguayan Mennonites who immigrated to Europe and North America.

Larry Miller, executive secretary of MWC, says, "Paraguay is the Mennonite place where the past meets the future. The historic and ethnic roots of Mennonite identity are there, but also the young emerging churches from the south out of the indigenous and Latino context. Mennonites in Paraguay represent a microcosm of the global Mennonite fellowship of the present."

As a born Paraguayan Mennonite and one who has the privilege to lead the National Coordinating Council for MWC 15, I agree with Miller. This book of Edgar Stoesz helps us in Paraguay toward a gracious and benevolent outsider perspective of our reality. And it surely will help friends of Paraguay to gain a better understanding of the Mennonites of Paraguay.

Alfred Neufeld
Asunción
Author, *What We Believe Together*

Preface

Like a Mustard Seed is the story of Mennonites in Paraguay: how they got there, how they prospered, and how they are giving back. This is a fascinating story that deserves a prominent place in the annals of Mennonite history.

It was a small, inauspicious beginning, like the biblical mustard seed that was called the smallest of seeds. Mennonites came first from Canada in 1927, then from the Soviet Union after the Bolshevik Revolution in 1930, again from Russia as displaced World War II survivors in 1947, from Canada again in 1948, then from Mexico beginning in the 1960s. Also beginning in the 1960s, a dribble of Swiss Mennonites emigrated from the United States. Paraguay has been a twentieth-century gathering ground for Mennonites, a kind of biblical city of refuge.

Why Paraguay, a little-known country sometimes referred to as an island surrounded by land?

"As it was when Juan de Solis sailed up the River Plate four centuries ago, so it was when I entered the land of unknown people and so it is today (1889)," wrote Barbrooke Grubb, an early Anglican missionary in his book *An Unknown People in an Unknown Land.*

Nestled between Brazil, Argentina, and Bolivia, Paraguay declared its independence from Spain in 1811, just thirty-five years after the United States declared independence from England. Paraguay fought a costly war against the triple alliance of Brazil, Uruguay, and Argentina (1865–1870), almost decimating its male population. It had not fully recovered when it fought a war from 1932 to 1935 with Bolivia over a boundary, contributed to by the sudden appearance of Mennonites in large numbers in the Chaco. These costly wars earned Paraguay the dubious distinction of being the most backward nation in South America.

The Paraguay River divides the country in two. The Chaco claims 60 percent of the land area but only 2 percent of the population. East Paraguay, including the capital, Asunción, claims the rest of the country, which had an estimated population of more than 6.6 million in 2007. Its per capita gross domestic product is 1,019 dollars. Paraguay has historically had close ties with the Catholic Church.

The internet-based encyclopedia Wikipedia lists fifty-six presidents since 1844, many of whom did not complete their term of office. This includes the thirty-five-year reign of Alfredo Stroessner, which ended in 1989. A reform followed Stroessner's corrupt and dictatorial rule, including a new constitution that put Paraguay firmly on the road to democracy. Nicanor Duarte completed his term as president in 2008.

So why this Mennonite interest in this inauspicious land? Mennonites needed land and a guarantee of freedom, and Paraguay offered both. It was a perfect match. The land was fertile and plentiful, although it would take several generations to learn how to farm it well. Mennonites were as free as the birds of the air, first in the Chaco and then in the remote parts of East Paraguay. Paraguay needed people to occupy its expanses of land, so the country opened its doors with few questions asked. Young and old, healthy and handicapped, often undocumented, Mennonites were always welcome.

Though free, these courageous Mennonite pioneers were immediately confronted by formidable obstacles. How would they wrest enough food from the pristine but untamed wilderness to feed themselves? How would they navigate through such an unfamiliar place? How would they cope with the oppressive heat and isolation, which often sapped their morale? How should they relate to the native population? How would they deal with their own internal conflicts as well as the external ones? Even in the far reaches of the almost deserted Chaco, they soon found themselves underfoot in the war between Paraguay and Bolivia, in which more than one hundred thousand soldiers died.

The hardy and resourceful pioneers dramatically surmounted the obstacles that confronted them. Their ability to do so was based on an unshakable faith that the God who had directed them to Paraguay would sustain them. Their commitment to mutual aid helped too. At critical points the wider Mennonite community aided them, in a beautiful expression of international fellowship.

As the mustard seed lay in the ground for years, some feared it would die. Then it miraculously germinated and grew. This book covers eighty years during which we see the seed that was "sown in weakness . . . is raised in power" (1 Corinthians 15:43). From an insignificant, almost unnoticed beginning in Paraguay, Mennonites have come to national prominence. When there appeared to be no way, God heard their prayer and opened a way. The land no one wanted has become Paraguay's bread-basket. The members of a once little-known religious sect are admired for their accomplishments. Their voice is heard in church and government circles. The birds are coming to roost in the branches.

Most significant, Mennonites are giving back. The church never exists for itself; it exists for the world. Mission is its fruit. Even when their survival was far from ensured, Mennonites were reaching out to help their neighbors. They gave the cup of cold water and shared the bread of life—their Christian faith.

Paraguayan Mennonites have accomplished what Mennonites in Russia never did: planting an indigenous church whose numbers are growing. Mennonites are moving from enclave dwellers to a multiethnic community that speaks ten languages.

The story of how this happened is rich with suspense and wonder. Laced with contradiction and human failing as well as achievement, it provides abundant opportunity for gratitude and thoughtful reflection.

Acknowledgments

In 1999, Miriam Stackley and I wrote *Garden in the Wilderness: Mennonite Communities in the Paraguayan Chaco*, published by Canadian Mennonite University in Winnipeg. It was quickly out of print. Seeing that the Mennonite World Conference was planning to assemble in Asunción in 2009, Herald Press asked that I write a book that focused on all Mennonite groups in Paraguay.

My first thought was simply to update the material in *Garden in the Wilderness* and add a chapter with the expanded information. But I soon realized that a new book was needed. The result is *Like a Mustard Seed: Mennonites in Paraguay.*

The information in this book is drawn heavily from what Paraguayan Mennonite authors have written. My working library contains 30 inches of books, almost all of them in German. Chief among them are the books written by the three authors, Gerhard Ratzlaff, Peter P. Klassen, and Martin W. Friesen, and this book is dedicated to them. But most of their books concentrate on a particular aspect of this rich history. The value of *Like a Mustard Seed* is that it covers the whole spectrum, including the indigenous people and the emerging Paraguayan church, and makes it available to English readers.

In addition to twenty trips over forty years and drawing on the material others have written, I spent some weeks in Paraguay in 2006 identifying the material, conducting interviews and making my own observations. I was joined by my grandson, Matthew Bauman, who served as photographer and Spanish language translator.

Subsequently I benefited enormously by extensive correspondence carried on by email with people in Paraguay, many of whom are identified in the section on sources. To all of them I extend my sincere thanks. I also want to acknowledge with gratitude their generosity in providing hospitality, helping with transportation, and trusting me with their stories. Not once was I told, "But this is not for the book." They allowed the record to speak for itself.

While *Like a Mustard Seed* tells the Paraguayan story from the Mennonite perspective, Erwin Boschmann's 2008 *Paraguay Tour Guide* is a good companion piece with a wealth of information on Paraguay.

In spite of my good intentions and best efforts to portray both the good and the bad, *Like a Mustard Seed* is my imperfect summary of a remarkable story. In so doing I acknowledge with thanks the contribution of a reader panel consisting of Royden Loewen, Beth Graybill, Gerhard Ratzlaff, and John Roth.

Finally, I want to acknowledge the good work of Herald Press in making it available in this form. Levi Miller was helpful in designing the book; Michael Degan's editing made it more readable. To all my thanks.

Not to be overlooked, I thank my wife Gladys for suffering through yet another project that preoccupied me night and day for more than a year.

Edgar Stoesz
October 2008

Use of Terms

(1) The people in this book referred to as Enlhet were in an earlier period known as Lengua. In like fashion, those now called Nivaclé were formerly called Chulupí. Ayoreo are often called Moro.

(2) In Paraguay the terms Indian, indigenous, and aboriginal are used interchangeably to speak of First Nations people. I have mostly used indigenous to refer to this part of the Paraguayan population.

(3) The abbreviation MG stands for the church called Mennonitengemeinde, which is sometimes also known as Kirchliche Mennoniten. This church formerly had a loose association with the General Conference of Mennonites, which is now part of Mennonite Church Canada and Mennonite Church USA.

(4) The abbreviation MB stands for Mennoniten Brüdergemeinde. This church broke off from the MG in 1860 in Russia. In Paraguay the MG and MB do many things together, especially social-service ministries, but organizationally they are separate.

(5) The term German Mennonite is used to distinguish this group from Latino or Indian Mennonites. It is technically a misnomer because few of its members were ever citizens of Germany. The more correct designation would be German-speaking Mennonites.

(6) Plautdietsch, known also as Low German, is the language of Mennonites who came from Russia. It is or was spoken by Russian Mennonites in Paraguay, the United States, Canada, and Germany. It is

also a written language; I have a Plautdietsch Bible and a frequently consulted dictionary. Plautdietsch is regarded as an informal language; church services and formal education is in German, although Old Colony Mennonites use it in church services as well. There are similarities between Plautdietsch and German, but each is a language in its own right. In general terms, Plautdietsch might be thought of as being to Russian Mennonites what Pennsylvania Dutch is to Swiss Mennonites.

(7) Old Colony refers to Chortitza, the first colony of Mennonites who emigrated from Prussia to Russia beginning in 1789. It is distinguished from Molotschna, which in 1803 was also founded by Mennonites from Prussia and Russia. The Old Colonies in Paraguay came mostly from Chortitza; many came from Bergthal, a Chortitza daughter colony. They were among the first to leave Russia in 1874, which also suggests that they did not experience the renaissance that occurred in Russia after their departure.

(8) *Oberschulze* (plural: *Oberschulzen*) means mayor. *Älteste* and *Ältester* (plural: *Ältesten*) mean elder or bishop.

Part 1
How They Gathered

Like a Mustard Seed is an account of two very different subcultures competing for land no one else wanted and doing it in an unusual way—peacefully. Part 1 contains the dramatic stories of how Mennonites felt miraculously led by God to Paraguay.

In the sixteenth century, Mennonites were driven from Friesland, in the Netherlands, by persecution during the Reformation. Some settled in Prussia's Vistula Valley and soon made it productive. But within six or seven generations they had outgrown it. In 1787 they immigrated to the steppes of Russia, where a similar phenomenon repeated itself. By the 1870s Mennonites were attracted to land available in the North America.

Ten thousand settled on the prairies of Kansas, Nebraska, the Dakotas, and Minnesota, but they figure only marginally in the Paraguay story. The seven thousand that went to Manitoba settled first on eight townships reserved for them in the East Reserve. Later Mennonites came to occupy fifteen townships in the West Reserve, and some also migrated to Saskatchewan. Many endured the harsh Canadian winter in sod houses before they were able to replace them with wooden structures. They broke the virgin sod and soon replaced it with fields of waving grain, reminiscent of Russia.

They surmounted the hardships of the frontier and were eventually confronted by a dispute with Canadian authorities over conducting their schools in the German language. When they were unable to arrive at an acceptable accommodation, some began to look for alternatives. Soon the first group of seven thousand Old Colony Mennonites left Canada for Mexico in 1921.

In 1927 another group of 1,763 left Manitoba and Saskatchewan for Paraguay. There they established Menno colony, which remains the largest Mennonite colony in Paraguay.

By 1930, Mennonites had suffered through the harsh Russian Revolution and civil war, the effects of which were compounded by drought-induced crop failures. Thousands were able to leave for Canada in 1924 and 1925. By 1929 the rest were desperate to leave too, but the doors were closed. Then, miraculously, 5,671 German-speaking people, of whom 3,885 were Mennonites, were permitted to leave Moscow. After a brief stopover in Germany, some got their wish to go to Canada, others went to Brazil, and the rest immigrated to Paraguay and established Fernheim colony, neighbor to Menno colony.

This still left a large community of Mennonites to suffer hardships under Communist rule. In 1941, the German army liberated them temporarily. When the fortunes of the war reversed, Mennonites joined with the retreating Germans, arriving in Germany as the war was nearing an end. After wandering around war-ravaged Europe for some years as refugees, many were able to go to Canada. More than five thousand were gathered by Mennonite Central Committee and helped to immigrate to Paraguay, where half settled in the Chaco and the rest in East Paraguay.

As the decade of the 1940s drew to a close, a fresh breeze was stirring among the Old Colony people who had elected to remain in Canada. Scouts went to Paraguay and purchased a tract of land there. Though they arrived in Paraguay on the same ship, they were actually two separate groups. The Sommerfeld settlers spread themselves out on the south side of what became Highway 7, while the Bergthal colonists settled on the north side.

By the 1960s Mexican Mennonites needed more land. This, in addition to some internal issues, led them to explore their options. Between 1969 and 1983 four colonies, totaling more than six thousand, migrated to East Paraguay.

Also beginning in the 1960s, a trickle of American Mennonites of Swiss heritage discovered Paraguay. They too were looking for land and wanted to avoid the advances of urbanization. They found a welcome awaiting them in Paraguay.

Part 1 concludes with a brief description of the Indians who greeted the Mennonites arriving in the Chaco. For centuries they had hunted this forgotten land covered with scrub bush that they knew like the back of their hand. Their lives had been interrupted occasionally by wars with neighboring tribes. Though the wars had decimated their numbers, they were managing. Then they were invaded by a hoard of white Mennonites, changing their lives forever.

1

Mennonites Search for Paraguay

On Ascension Day 1921, a Mennonite scouting party penetrated deep into the foreboding and inhospitable Paraguayan Chaco. In a clearing surrounded by bush and cacti, with the blue sky overhead and native grass underfoot, the members of the party welcomed the interruption of a religious holiday to reflect on the events of the past years and particularly the past month.

Fresh in their minds were disputes with Canadian government authorities over freedom to operate their schools, though the government had promised such freedom before the Mennonites agreed to come to Canada. Forty-five years later, Canada had passed a law unfriendly to private schools and stated that all instruction must be in the English language. When Mennonites refused to send their children to publicly inspected schools, they were fined heavily, and a few were imprisoned. After exhausting their appeals, the aggrieved Mennonites felt compelled to explore opportunities to emigrate. Martin C. Friesen, an *Ältester* (elder) with the first emigrant group, summarized the sentiment at the time:

> We can hardly believe the government in Ottawa and England knows how badly we have been treated regarding our schools. We gave the English government our unlimited trust to make arable a desolate area here in Canada. It took much hard work to accomplish this. And suddenly we are the enemies in this country because of our language. They invited us and promised to let us have our schools without limitations or interference. The gov-

ernment should see to it that the trust we first had in them is not harmed.

Searching for an Alternative

The delegation to find a new homeland for the community consisted of Bernard Toews and Isaac Funk, representing the Sommerfeld members of Manitoba's West Reserve; Jakob Duerksen, representing the Chortitzer Mennonites of the East Reserve; and Johann Friesen and Jakob Neufeld, representing the Bergthaler church near Rosthern, Saskatchewan. Two were ministers, and all had grown up in Canada. The sixth member was Johann Priez an Altona, a Manitoba businessman, who advised them with legal issues. Priez, though not a Mennonite, insisted on traveling at his own expense.

Accompanying the group were eleven employees of the Casado Corporation, which operated a huge cattle ranch and tannin exporting business in the Chaco. Two of them spoke German, and several indigenous Toba came along to communicate with the indigenous Lengua residing in the Chaco. Together the entire group spoke five languages.

They were equipped with five tall, two-wheel, ox-drawn carts to transport their supplies, which included a variety of dried vegetables and other foodstuffs, mosquito nets, and articles to trade with the indigenous people.

The first expedition into the foreboding Gran Chaco took place in May 1921. Employees of the Casado Corporation accompanied the Canadian Mennonites on the journey.

Twenty oxen were hitched to the wagons, twelve more were along as reserves or as a walking meat supply, if needed. Several of the twelve horses were saddled and available to lead the way for the slow-moving caravan.

As the men meditated on the story of Jesus' ascension into heaven, they felt strangely united with their brothers and sisters, who gathered in far-away Canada, praying for them on this holy day. They recalled their departure from Altona, Manitoba, with hundreds of darkly dressed brothers and sisters seeing them off. They recalled being entertained in the home of Samuel McRoberts in New York, where they sang familiar German songs together.

McRoberts was a wealthy New York banker with large land holdings in South America. His wife was the daughter of missionaries. It was she who had persuaded McRoberts to help Canadian Mennonites with their plight. McRoberts had sponsored Fred Engen's earlier daring expeditions into the Chaco and eventually would devise a financial plan that permitted Mennonites to sell their holdings in Canada and make a new beginning in Paraguay.

Engen, a Canadian of Norwegian extraction, had lost his money in a financial venture. He spent almost a year exploring underpopulated regions of South America, including the Chaco. One admirer said his name should have been Engel (German for *angel*), not Engen. In 1929, when Mennonites heard that Engen lay dying in Puerto Casado, they rushed to attend him. But they arrived too late. They buried him in the Mennonite corner of the Catholic graveyard. The main street in Loma Plata, the Menno colony capitol, the future home of the first Mennonite settlement in Paraguay, is named for him.

The Mennonite scouts exploring the Chaco on that Ascension Day recalled their fourteen-day trip on an ocean liner that to them felt like a floating city. They recalled the sites of Rio de Janeiro, Montevideo, and Buenos Aires, which they had passed through on their way to Asunción. They no doubt reflected on being received in Buenos Aires at the international headquarters of the Casado firm. It was said to be the world's largest tract of land on one deed.

In Buenos Aires, Engen joined them. The scouts had heard much about him, and he would become very important to their expedition. After his 1921 exploration to the Chaco, Engen had cabled McRoberts to proclaim, "I have found the Promised Land."

The marking chisled into a *quebracho* tree: Mennonite Expedition, May 1921.

We can imagine Bernard Toews, the official diary writer, pulling out the handwritten letter José Casado had given the delegation on the morning of their departure, and reading, "It is in your hands to change these lands through your agricultural methods into a garden, a dedication to the founder of your faith and so that you and your followers can be blessed, through your efforts and live in peace and good fortune. For this reason I am prepared to place all my help and knowledge at your disposal."

Their conversation undoubtedly also touched on the indigenous population that appeared to be following them from a distance. They were friendly without exception and even helpful. When in need of meat, Mennonites traded a shirt for a sheep. The indigenous also gave them berries and vegetables, including large watermelons from their gardens, and advised them on where underground water could be found.

These encounters with indigenous nevertheless left the Mennonites mildly uneasy, if for no other reason than the indigenous were naked, or nearly so. Nor did they have a common language. Neither group could have known how intertwined their futures would become.

Early the next morning, refreshed from their day of rest, the Canadian delegation pushed deeper into the foreboding Gran Chaco, with Engen leading the way. On a good day they might travel 10 kilometers (6 miles). Some days it seemed they did little more than provide human food for the largest, hungriest mosquitoes they had ever seen.

They imagined large wheat fields with heavily loaded stalks. Further stoking their imaginations was the sight of their oxen walking in native grass that brushed the bottom of their bellies. The explorers took soil samples for later analysis.

After satisfying themselves that Engen's earlier boast of having found the "Promised Land" was merited, they chiseled into a suitable *quebracho* tree "ME-V-XXI."—Mennonite Expedition, May 1921. Then they headed back to their base on the banks of the Paraguay River.

They were pleased to see how well a sample of wheat they had planted before their departure had grown during their thirty-day absence. What further proof was needed that this sandy soil could be counted on to support their ambitions?

Scouts Return with Positive Report

Casado was anxious to hear their report. He boarded a river steamer with the six-man delegation and headed for Asunción. Immediately upon arrival they dispatched a telegram to their anxious families in Canada:

> Returned to Asunción safe and well—conditions for a settlement promising in every respect—working on the privileges—Mexico and other places not attractive in comparison.

A major hurdle appeared to have been overcome. There was lots of land available. But would the government of Paraguay agree to the "privileges" (that is, conditions) they had received from President Manuel Gondra Pereira when they passed through Asunción weeks earlier and he so magnanimously and prematurely welcomed Mennonites to Paraguay? These conditions included freedom from military service, freedom from swearing oaths, freedom to conduct their schools in German, and the right to self-administer inheritances and fire insurance.

Gondra was eager to receive the Mennonites. In the back of his mind was no doubt the troubling realization that, while literally millions of immigrants flocked to Brazil and Argentina in the period of expansion between 1881 and 1920, Paraguay's immigrants numbered only in the thousands. The country needed to secure its northern border by settling the vast and almost unpopulated Chaco region. Paraguay needed people, which is what the Mennonite scouts had to offer.

Gondra spoke only Spanish, but he was accompanied by the German-speaking Senator Eusebio Ayala, who would later become president. After hearing a detailed report of the visit, the first item for discussion was the presence of the indigenous population. Comparisons were made to Canada, where the government had subdued the indigenous before the Mennonites arrived. The conversation allowed that indigenous could always be placed on reservation later if necessary. Gondra added, "They live a nomadic life with lots of room to move around in."

Gondra also expressed appreciation for the work Anglican missions had done in teaching the South Lengua to read and write not only in their own language but also in Spanish.

A second substantive issue concerned a road or railway connecting the potential Mennonite tract with the Paraguay River, a distance of some 200 kilometers (125 miles). This had implications for the Casado Corporation, which complicated the issue. Casado already had a narrow-gauge railway covering one-third of this distance.

Mennonites left the meeting assuming a gentleman's understanding had been reached that a road would be provided. It never was. The railway issue became very contentious. Many years later, Mennonites still talked about how they came to Paraguay expecting that the road would be provided.

The meeting had taken place in a mood of optimism and accommodation. No serious effort had been made to reduce discussions to binding commitments, much less a written record, which the Mennonites later regretted. Gondra concluded the two-hour meeting with a generous and eloquent welcome:

> I am glad that you have come to look at our country and that you like it. In the name of the Republic of Paraguay I welcome you as settlers. We will receive you gladly. It is our sincere desire that you will settle in our country, that you will like it here, that you will be blessed, that your efforts will meet with success and that you will be able to live your lives here in peace. We will help and support you wherever we can. I will take up your request for special rights with our congress for their consideration and confirmation, and as soon as that is done I will let you know by telegram.

The Mennonites and the president shook hands warmly, and the Mennonites returned home. In New York they had another affirming meeting with McRoberts. Before returning to Manitoba, in an effort to cover all bases, the scouts decided to take another look at the Mexico option. Mexican President Álvaro Obregón Salido and his minister of agriculture received them warmly. The privileges offered by Mexico were not as appealing as those offered by Paraguay, and it appears the Mennonite delegation was already psychologically predisposed to Paraguay.

In Canada, even the largest church buildings were unable to accommodate all who came to hear the delegation's report. Engen, who had by this time become a trusted friend to the group, was included in the reporting panel. He told the eager crowds,

> We are all convinced that the Chaco offers untold business and commercial possibilities and that it is suitable for farming and for farm settlers who are willing to go to work to accomplish something. In this way the hidden secrets of the natural garden will be revealed and the people will be blessed with great riches. Immeasurable blessings will result and will result in a Menno-land.

Paraguayan Congress Debates

Meanwhile the Paraguayan press had another view. It pictured the Mennonites as a "closed society." Some critics felt the negotiations had offered Mennonite foreigners advantages Paraguayan citizens did not enjoy, as this extract from an editorial shows:

> The Mennonites are a rigid people not responsible to any nation. And it would certainly not be to Paraguay's advantage to settle them here because their contributions will be insignificant to the development of our economy. No country or nation seems to be able to get them to adjust. They act out the Ten Commandments in an exaggerated manner. The religion of the Mennonites is a fantasy. They oppose scientific and religious education. The Mennonites want their rights but they want none of the related responsibilities.

Another critic noted, "This Mennonite position—nonparticipation in war—has been proclaimed as something positive. Why then has this religious group not been able to attract more members? Even though Canada is a Protestant country there are fewer than fifty thousand members but there are several million Catholics."

Others defended the Mennonites: "Even though they will not serve in the trenches, they will cultivate the land. The inner Chaco is a giant wilderness. This is the first time that people have indicated a willingness to settle in that wilderness and to make their home there. We need no further guarantees or security."

Still others noted that wherever Mennonites had lived, they had "enriched the country." These defenders called Mennonites "industrious, righteous, vigorous and well disciplined." They noted that the Mennonite community did not practice racial discrimination but was "a religious faith, and that is what sets them apart."

An eloquent and prophetic speech concluded the parliamentary debate: "All the privileges that Paraguay wants to give Mennonites will create negligible difficulties compared to what lies ahead for Mennonites when they tear themselves away from their homes to settle in the wilderness."

Green Light for the Green Hell

Tension was in the air as the Parliament voted on whether to accept the Mennonites and agree to their conditions. The final vote was 13-5 to allow, as one person called it, "a green light for the green hell."

Now a decision was before the families in Canada. The terms offered by Paraguay and Mexico were laid side by side with the scouting reports. It was noted that in Mexico the invitation was signed by the president and minister of agriculture, leading some to question what would happen should there be a change in government? They were bothered by what appeared to be a strong military presence. Paraguay, however, was perceived to be a peaceful country.

Canadian Mennonites were so preoccupied with their own quandary they did not have much time to think about the suffering of their brothers and sisters in Russia. Prayers were no doubt offered on their behalf, but what more could they do? It was a sobering time for Mennonites on both sides of the Atlantic.

Wherever Mennonites gathered, emigration was the topic of conversation. Might the Canadian authorities soften their position so the Mennonites could remain? Did they know enough about Paraguay to make this life-changing decision? The suspense was wearing. Leaders finally set a date in 1922 when families would be required to decide.

The Mennonite communities voted, and when the votes were counted, those on Manitoba's East Reserve were almost evenly divided between Mexico and Paraguay. The West Reserve voted overwhelmingly for Mexico.

The Mexican contingent proceeded expeditiously, and their story is told in chapter 7.

More Obstacles

The group opting for Paraguay faced a knotty problem. To get the money they needed to purchase the Casado tract in Paraguay, they needed to sell their farms in Canada. But they were reluctant to sell until they were more certain how things would work out in Paraguay. It was the well-known "you can't get there from here" syndrome.

So they turned to their old friend, Samuel McRoberts. After analyzing their problem, the indomitable McRoberts organized Intercontinental Corporation Ltd. to purchase their farms in Canada at seven dollars an acre. In Paraguay he created the Corporacion Paraguaya to purchase 125,400 acres from the Casado Corporation at about $1.25 an acre.

With this hurdle removed, the decision to remain or leave lay with the individual families. The elderly remembered well their hard beginning in Canada. Some concluded that the demands of the Canadian government were not so onerous after all, and they elected to remain. Others sold their farms for what they could get and prepared to depart for Paraguay. But when bad reports drifted back to Canada, they changed their minds and remained in Manitoba. Some who decided to remain in 1926 ended up immigrating to Paraguay in 1948. (See chapter 6.)

In the middle of all this uncertainty of the years 1924 to 1927, Canada was experiencing a major influx of Mennonites fleeing Russia in the aftermath of the revolution and civil war. Some of the new immigrants came to occupy farms Paraguay émigrés had left behind. Neighbors and Canadian authorities were confused by all this coming and going. But the Mennonites, both those departing and those arriving, were comforted by the thought that they were guided by God's invisible hand.

2

Menno Colony

On November 26, 1926, 309 people in fifty-one families sailed in the first contingent from Canada to Paraguay. En route one baby was born, and a three-year-old girl died and was buried at sea. As they steamed up the Paraguay River on the *Apipe*, a small Argentine ship that had seen better days, they were travel weary and anxious but hopeful. Their long ordeal with the Canadian government was over; their Paraguay adventure was about to begin.

Saying *Aufwiedersehn* to loved ones they would likely never see again had been emotional and painful beyond words. Memories of those farewells were still vivid as they arrived in Buenos Aires. The emigrants had left behind farms and businesses they had painstakingly built during the community's fifty-two years in Canada. It was a high cost willingly paid by predominantly young parents who were committed to bring up their children according to their Anabaptist convictions, however misguided some of their neighbors thought the venture to be.

In Buenos Aires their trusted friend, Fred Engen, joined them. He had in his possession the valued PL 514 papers guaranteeing their entrance into Paraguay. Engen had also thoughtfully brought apples to help children celebrate Christmas Day "on the water."

While passing through Asunción on December 29, they were honored to have President Eligio Ayala board the ship to give them a hearty welcome to Paraguay—in German!

They progressed along tree-lined riverbanks toward their Puerto Casado destination. An almost full moon illuminated the flat Chaco terrain with the occasional outline of a tall *quebracho* tree in the distance, a type of tree nicknamed "the ax breaker." Mostly it was bush and the occasional appearance of small, skinny people with dark skin. The only sounds, other than the steady hum of the engine, was that of wooden paddles hitting the clear water, propelling them to their destination.

Weeks earlier they had left their farms and friends in Manitoba in the beginning of winter. Now they were arriving in tropical Paraguay in the heat of summer. Excruciatingly hard days were behind them. Harder days were ahead.

Paraguay at Last

Arriving in a new location at night with only a few strangers to greet them seemed foreboding, but the immigrants were buoyed by the assurance that many more Mennonites would follow. Glad to finally have their feet on solid ground, the families found space to spread out under the trees and settled for the night, anxious to see what the morning would bring. Swarms of mosquitoes fed on them.

Morning light ushered in not only a new day but also a new year. It was New Years Day, 1927. Individually and collectively they offered up prayers of gratitude and petitions for strength for the days ahead. Awaiting their use were five crude, partially completed barracks, along with a few earthen baking ovens. Children went exploring while adults busily arranged their baggage and set up tents they had brought along. It was primitive, but they were, after all, intending to be there only temporarily.

On the second day an afternoon shower mercifully broke the heat, followed by a spectacular rainbow. This they interpreted as a much-needed assurance of God's blessing.

Then a Bombshell

Engen announced to a hastily called meeting that the Casado staff had just informed him there would be a delay of "some weeks." It seemed the 216-square-mile tract they had purchased within the much larger Casado tract had not been surveyed. This made it impossible for them to lay out their villages and individual family plots.

It was not what they wanted to hear, especially now, knowing the poor conditions of their temporary quarters. The water supply, cooking facilities, and toilets for a group of this size—and expected to grow—were inadequate, to say the least. This caused spirits to sag and tempers to rise, but what choice did they have?

The faint of heart questioned if perhaps the newspapers in Montevideo were right when they asked critically,

> Why are you leaving your prosperous farms in Canada? Why are you going into this world neglected Chaco desolation? There you have no drinking water or timber to build, nothing but heat and sand and sooner or later you will have to leave anyway. Why don't you stay in Uruguay near the sea and where there is greater business traffic.

Every couple of weeks, the *Apipe* came with another boatload of hopeful Mennonites unaware of the bad news that awaited them. Martin C. Friesen was, with his family, among the one hundred people that made up group number 6. He could not know the heavy burdens that awaited him as Ältester. It was a bittersweet time for all. They were glad that their numbers were growing, and they were glad to see relatives and old friends again. But the growth further taxed the temporary facilities, and still more immigrants were en route.

Martin C. Friesen, whose gentle spirit, many historians concede, helped Menno colony through its difficult beginning.

They looked forward to large wheat fields and fat cows in deep grass. But now this would have to wait until after the surveyors demarcated the boundaries of their land so settlement could proceed.

Engen and five Mennonite men ventured into the interior to check on the surveyors' progress. It was at this stage that Engen became aware that the group was not one homogeneous company of peace-loving Mennonites. It was in actuality three groups: Altkolonier from Manitoba's West Reserve, Chortitzer from the East Reserve, and Bergthaler from Saskatchewan.

All were seeking the same thing: a new homeland. But as historian Martin W. Friesen, son of Ältester Friesen, noted, "Each group now tried unceremoniously to implement its own peculiarities as the correct ones without trying to find out what the other groups thought."

Weeks stretched into months, with no end in sight. The waiting exceeded the tolerance threshold of some of the immigrants, but harder trials were ahead. Health problems had given them trouble from the beginning, but they managed with a generous dose of grit and home remedies. A few deaths occurred, but the settlers reminded themselves that deaths would have occurred had they remained in Canada. However, there were so many deaths that they had to negotiate for a corner of the Catholic cemetery.

Colony leader Jacob Braun, in his little book *Im Gedenken an jene Zeit*, tells lovingly about the death and burial of his daughter. The ground was so hard they resorted to picks to reach the required depth for the grave. In the meanwhile, two more of his children died, and before they could be buried, a fourth also passed away. Braun widened the grave and buried all four children in it.

Health officers in Puerto Casado rendered a dreaded diagnosis—typhoid. The camp was quarantined. Health reforms were introduced, but they were not rigorously observed. Some took comfort in a fatalistic belief that God was purging them for a purpose.

The diagnosis was not surprising. The immigrants' water came from the river unfiltered and untreated. Facilities for bathing and hygiene were woefully inadequate, and the poor diet and oppressive heat diminished the immigrants' resistance. The illness and death indisputably contributed to low morale.

The immigrants found ways to make use of the wait. Some purchased and trained oxen, and their blunders provided entertainment for the camp. Some planted gardens, hoping not to be there to reap the produce. Mostly they sat under trees waiting, complaining, and fixing blame. Others were so spooked by the "angel of death" that they ventured into the Chaco on their own.

No one knew what to believe. With the lack of information, rumor and speculation took over.

Having heard of this floundering, McRoberts came to the Chaco in July 1927. "What worries me most is the delay in the construction of the railway by the Casado Corporation," he wrote in his diary. "This creates a great disadvantage in the transportation of the settlers to the settlement areas. But what can we do? We are not the ones responsible for its construction."

Meanwhile, word of the Chaco plight filtered back to Canada and had a chilling effect on those still poised to come. Two more groups were already underway, bringing the number of Mennonites in Paraguay to 1,763 people in 279 families. This further strained the temporary facilities. It also put the lid on what the planners had hoped would be a much larger migration.

In the middle of this conundrum, Ältester Friesen addressed his people:

> Many have forgotten how we prayed to God to remain true and constant to the end. It was our wish that God would show us our refuge—and He has done it. And yet, instead of being thankful, we are grumbling. You blind people, when will you become thankful?

Not only was the flow of new families to Paraguay interrupted, some sixty families were so discouraged they returned to Canada, only to be faced with another difficult beginning. Returning to Canada was simply not an option for most.

Scouts were sent to explore options in East Paraguay. Their findings were cautiously positive but, bad as the Chaco was treating them, they did not have the energy (or the unity) to make another beginning. Come what may, they had to make it work in the Chaco.

Approval to Possess the Land

In April 1928, sixteen months after the immigrants arrived in Puerto Casado, the surveying was completed. The number of immigrants had shrunk from 1,763 to 1,257. Anxious as they were to leave Puerto Casado, relocating the entourage was a logistical challenge. The first 72 kilometers (45 miles) of the trip would be on Casado's narrow-gauge, slow-moving railroad. The remaining 130 kilometers (81 miles) would be by oxcart and on foot.

In Puerto Casado and along the way, they left behind almost one hundred graves, almost half of them of children under the age of three.

When they arrived that April at what would become Menno

colony, families were assigned to individual plots, and ten to twenty families constituted a village. Menno colony originally had fourteen villages, but by 1950 that number had increased to fifty-two. The plan was to lay out the plots so that each family had at least some cleared land to get started.

Instantly this corner of the vast Chaco was transformed into an anthill of activity. The colonists felled trees and sawed logs by hand into boards. They made bricks of mud and grass, and constructed modest two-room houses with grass roofs. They dug wells, but many were too salty for human or animal use. They cleared land with shovels and axes; they planted gardens and fields of cotton and peanuts.

In the early evening and the peaceful setting of their new homeland, as the families relaxed after their day's labor, they saw campfires in the distance, reminding them that they shared the Chaco with others. They had unknowingly set up their colony in an indigenous hunting ground. (How we would have enjoyed listening in on the conversations the indigenous had among themselves!)

A pioneer house being constructed with adobe bricks and a grass roof. The work was often done communally.

These first years were truly a hand-to-mouth existence. Learning what to plant and when was an exercise in trial and error. Much of what they did in Canada was unworkable in the Chaco and had to be unlearned. They had nothing to clear the brush and break the virgin sod but hand labor and untrained, often uncooperative oxen, which pulled improvised implements. If it was not drought, it was swarms of grasshoppers that destroyed the crops and left little for those who did the planting.

Neighbors from Russia

As Menno colony continued its early struggles, Russian Mennonites fleeing Communist persecution and oppression joined it in 1930. These refugees would later form Fernheim colony. Remembering their own difficult beginnings just three years earlier, Menno colony sent 108 ox-drawn wagons to pick up the 1,481 new arrivals at the Casado train station.

As the springless wagons ambled through the countryside, the Plautdietsch banter between those arriving and those welcoming them was no doubt lively. The Menno hosts were anxious to hear about happenings in Russia, and the new arrivals were anxious to learn about life in the Chaco. Upon reaching their destination, the Menno drivers unloaded the newly arrived families in a clearing, wished them Godspeed, and returned to their homes.

To an outsider, the two colonies of Menno and Fernheim were identical. But below the surface were deep, historic differences that remain to this day. A brief anecdote illustrates this: When a young Menno driver resisted transporting the Fernheim family randomly assigned to him, he was asked why. Shyly, he explained that his father had instructed him not to bring along any man with a mustache, then a taboo in Menno colony because of its association with the military.

Interrupted by War

Mennonites heard rumors of tension between Paraguay and Bolivia, but they were so busy building houses and planting gardens they gave the rumors little heed. Nor were they convinced that war was likely. Then one day, schoolchildren spotted a soldier, and more soldiers were sighted in the following weeks. The children of entertainment-starved Menno colony watched with amusement as soldiers marched through their drills.

The Mennonites were unaware that their presence had innocently contributed to the war. The boundary between Paraguay and Bolivia had never been well established. The colonies were part of the Gran Chaco and therefore thought to be of little significance. But the arrival of Mennonites in large numbers and a rumor of oil in the region changed all that. Bolivia protested to the League of Nations and insisted that Mennonites going to the Chaco should come through Bolivia instead of Paraguay. When that failed, both nations prepared for war. *Christian Century* headlined its story on the crisis "Mennonites: Innocent Pawns in the Chaco War."

On September 8, 1932, Menno colony dedicated its first church/school building in the village of Osterwick. As the service was adjourning, they heard gunfire and the roaring of canons. It was the beginning of the three-year war between Bolivia and Paraguay.

Mennonites were told to evacuate. But to where? Instead of immediately running, these veterans of war and revolution organized an all-night prayer meeting. Their answer came at sunrise with a verse of Scripture, "'Not by might, nor by power, but by my spirit,' says the Lord of hosts" (Zechariah 4:6). They elected to stay.

The Mennonites suffered just one war-related casualty. Paraguay eventually won the war, although it did not gain much territory in post-war negotiations, which were protracted and inconclusive.

Mennonites and the Chaco War

Tragic as the Chaco War (1932-1935) was, Mennonites nonetheless benefited. First, the war brought Mennonites into contact with Paraguayans such as Alfredo Stroessner, who later become president and remained a life-long friend to the community. The war afforded Mennonites an opportunity to shelter indigenous people, who were hunted like animals by both armies, forming an enduring bond. Mennonite families also received some much-needed income by selling surplus food such as eggs and watermelons to soldiers. For a time the doctorless Mennonite colonists received medical care at a hospital the army commandeered in Filadelfia.

The Chaco War left behind thousands of spent rifle shells. Mennonites gathered and smelted these to make doorknobs and shower heads—a modern-day beating of spears into plowshares.

The war also increased the Chaco horse population and left behind wrecked vehicles that the ingenious Mennonites scavenged for other uses. Some Mennonites also earned money hauling freight for the Paraguayan army.

The Transplant Becomes Rooted

Soon families were able to move from their tents to simple houses they had built from native materials. Slowly the bush was pushed back and gardens emerged. Gradually paths to frequently traveled points like the village schools and churches emerged through the tall grass and connected neighbors. While life was hard, the colonists were getting acquainted with the Chaco, and a new life was beginning to take shape.

Menno colony's population doubled between 1927 and 1953. The growth was driven by a high birth rate and the lack of high emigration that other colonies were experiencing. But the social and physical infrastructure needed to serve such a large and expanding population was woefully lacking. The question was how to introduce changes without fracturing the colony.

While pledged to uphold tradition, Ältester Friesen was in his heart of hearts a progressive man. He saw the need for change at three levels: the colony, the church, and the school. Friesen obtained some school materials from Germany and introduced them at a meeting of village teachers. When he saw how coldly the idea was received, he took the material home, only to have teachers get it from him privately.

Bit by bit, driven by necessity, a more progressive way of thinking emerged. The colonists organized a cooperative that became the colony's commercial center. Colony governance was redesigned to add more functions to the *Oberschulze* and the oversight committee with which Friesen worked. Schools were separated from the *Gemeinde* and placed under the control of a special committee.

Progressive Education

By the early 1950s the pioneer teachers had retired, and replacements were hard to find. The colony was in a deep malaise. One parent said prophetically, "If the level of education in school and in the home does not improve, emigration will have done us no good." Some new thinking was beginning to shine through the shadows of tradition. Progressive leaders began to say, "To stand still is to go backward." But change to what? And how to bring it about without fracturing the colony, which had by this time doubled in size?

During the 1940s Ältester Friesen's son, Martin W. Friesen, gathered colony teachers to share with each other in a retreat setting. They were looking for ways to incorporate needed changes without offending the status quo. At first, the sessions lasted a week, but gradually they lengthened to two weeks, then to three and four weeks. Teachers found them stimulating, and something was astir.

This led to a historic meeting on January 16, 1951, in the progressive village of Ebenfeld. Martin W. Friesen modestly declined to say who organized it, but it is safe to assume he was involved, along with the newly elected progressive Oberschulze, Jacob B. Reimer. The organizers were pleased when twenty teachers from nine schools came. In retrospect, many call the meeting "the day Menno colony turned a new leaf."

In 1956 Menno colony built a teacher training school in Loma Plata. While under construction it was mysteriously vandalized, a reminder that not everyone was supporting the reform. The school opened in 1957 with thirty prospective teachers in attendance, including seven women. By 1976 enrollment had increased to 174. A transition was underway in Menno colony.

Life Gets Better

As the decades of the thirties, forties, and fifties unfolded and a new generation emerged, the people of Menno colony learned to make the foreboding Chaco fruitful. Their lives improved, though much was predicated on what they were able to coax from the soil. The following table traces the colony's growth and economic progress:

Growth of Menno Colony

	1927-28	1976-77	2006
Population (in round numbers)	1,200	6,000	8,900
Horses	65	3,353	3,972
Oxen	390	21,862	N/A
Cattle	430	30,770	385,000
Pigs	100	1,976	5,900
Tractors	N/A	N/A	1,050
Plows	120	1,331	N/A
Cultivators	58	1,203	N/A
Ox- or horse-drawn buggies	130	1,104	150
Automobiles/motorized bikes	N/A	1,249	3,149/2,631
Refrigerators	N/A	828	3,226
Air Conditioners	N/A	N/A	4,981

Source: *Kanadische Mennoniten Bezwigen Eine Wildnis* by Martin W. Friesen, 1987. 2006 figures by Walter Ratzlaff.

Poised for the Future

Menno colony worked its way through many internal and external challenges. Layers of tradition and conservatism almost choked it, and the system nearly collapsed on itself. But the traditionalist mentality, prompted by necessity, gradually gave way to a more progressive way of thinking. That this was possible without fracturing is attributable in large measure to the sensitive leadership of Ältester Friesen, Oberschulze Reimer, and their successors. Early on, change was measured not in years but in decades. Then it accelerated, and today some fear that tradition and core values are endangered.

Not only had the Menno pioneers carved out a place for themselves in the inhospitable Chaco, they also had cleared the way for others to follow. The human cost was far greater than they could have imagined. Along the way, expectations had to be revised. But today Mennonites have become known as *Chaqueños* (Chaco dwellers), and the Chaco has become their home. Reimer, the long-time Oberschulze, was asked to explain how all this came about. "It is a miracle of God," he said, "but also of the courage of God-fearing settlers."

3

Fernheim Colony

Beginning in 1923, nearly twenty thousand Russian Mennonites received permission to immigrate to Canada. They were fleeing the civil war, which had broken out in the aftermath of the 1917 Russian Revolution. As the Communists consolidated power, they created a repressive police state. Often the police came in the dead of night to forcibly remove husbands and fathers, who were never seen again. What little food the Mennonite farmers had was taken from them. The desperate conditions were made worse by a drought that left the Mennonite population in Russia weakened by starvation, decimated by a typhoid epidemic, and living for several years at death's door. Many died, yet others were rescued by food sent by Mennonite Central Committee, then in its infancy. Self-sufficient Mennonites had been cruelly beaten to their knees and left pleading for mercy.

Canadian Mennonite relief organizations and the Canadian Pacific Railway helped the thousands who were able to leave for Canada. Others were not permitted to leave, or they chose to stay, hoping political conditions would improve and permit them to resume the good life they had known. But in 1928 in the Soviet Union, of which Russia was now a part, dictator Joseph Stalin issued his first "five-year plan." The document laid the groundwork for collectivization, in which all private property was confiscated. Everything was disrupted. Any hope Mennonites had of resuming their former life was erased. Stricken by fear that they would end up paying with their lives for their gamble to remain, all they could do was wait hopefully and pray expectantly.

Then a rumor began to circulate that visas to leave Russia were being issued in Moscow. But with rumors aplenty, what could they believe? Scouts were sent to Moscow to investigate, but before they returned, the hysteria reached such a crescendo that many families left for Moscow, leaving crops ready to be harvested. The families were thinking of Canada, but destination was secondary. The objective now was to put distance between themselves and the hell they had experienced at the hands of the Soviet regime.

As they waited in their crowded temporary quarters on the outskirts of Moscow, the refugees began each day by petitioning God to open a door, miraculously making it possible for them to leave. The dramatic story is told in detail in *Vor den Toren Moskaus* (Before the Gates of Moscow) and other books. More Mennonite refugees were arriving daily, taxing the temporary facilities. Many days brought word of acquaintances being arrested on the streets of Moscow and deported to Siberia, never to be seen or heard from again.

Days turned into weeks and months as the hopeful émigrés continually encountered the dreaded *neyt* (Russian for no). In desperation they engineered a daring protest, but to no avail. Then one day, without explanation, word was received that Germany was offering temporary asylum for five thousand German refugees trapped in Moscow, many of them Mennonites. The fortunate ones bade

Left Behind

Not all Russian Mennonites fled after the revolution. Thousands of Mennonites stayed to live in the newly established Soviet Union. In 1943 many escaped ahead of the retreating German army and lived for some years as refugees in Europe before being resettled, with help from Mennonite Central Committee, to Canada and Paraguay (see chapter 5).

After Stalin's death in 1953, life got better for Mennonites in Russia. In the 1960s, the governments of West Germany and the Soviet Union entered into a family reunification program and permitted families in Germany to "call out" family members from the Soviet Union. It is reliably estimated that, under the program, as many as two hundred thousand persons of German background were repatriated to Germany. Of these, one hundred and twenty thousand were believed to be of Mennonite background. Today very few Mennonites remain in Russia.

a hurried *Aufwiedersehn* to their envious friends, hoping they would follow soon, and headed for the train station. Their joy was tempered with suspicion that this was just another cruel hoax by a government they had come to hate and distrust.

But it was no hoax. Their prayers had been answered. Several hours late, and to the relief of everyone, their train pulled out of the Moscow station and headed west. The date—November 25, 1929—is still a holiday observed in Paraguay by descendants of the refugees.

Germany at Last

The refugees instantly felt at home in Germany. They understood the German language, which they had used among themselves in Russia. They could read street signs and newspapers. But Germany, they were told, was only a transit point; their final destination was still to be determined.

The refugees were appreciatively moved when Benjamin H. Unruh, who had been studying in Germany, told them how he and others had appealed to the German government for help rescuing them. Their plight was also placed on the agenda of the second Mennonite World Conference meeting in Danzig in 1930. The president of Germany, Paul von Hindenburg, was moved to personally contribute 200,000 Reichsmark (about half a million in today's U.S. dollars) for the evacuation. Unruh remained the refugees' advocate and friend. The fledgling MCC, which had helped to rescue them from starvation nine years earlier, was enlisted to find the refugees a permanent home.

Canada was the first choice for most, but the government was reluctant. It was the beginning of the Great Depression, and the moment happened to coincide with a dispute Canadian authorities were having with the Old Colony Mennonites, many of whom ended up immigrating to Paraguay and Mexico. The government finally yielded to the persistent lobbying of the Canadian Mennonite relief organization and offered a qualified reception to those able to meet its stringent health requirements.

What about the rest of the refugees? The United States also was in the early days of what would become known as the Depression, and its doors were essentially closed. Mexico, Argentina, and Alaska were explored but dismissed as unsuitable. With the deadline Germany had imposed quickly approaching, the options narrowed to Paraguay and

Brazil. Brazil was attractive for several reasons, not the least of which was an offer by Germany to provide transport. There was, however, one serious reservation: Brazil refused to grant military exemption.

MCC dispatched Mennonite missionaries from Argentina to see how the Canadians, who had ventured to Paraguay three years earlier, were faring in the ill-reputed Chaco.

A Way Opens

When final lists were drawn up, about one thousand emigrants qualified for Canada. Ironically, some of these would occupy farms left by families who had immigrated to Paraguay. Another 1,244 opted for Brazil and settled in Santa Catarina near the coast city of Curitiba. The remaining 1,572 refugees accepted Paraguay as a last resort. With assistance from MCC, they crossed the Atlantic, then steamed up the Paraguay River, just as their predecessors had done three years earlier on the ragtag *Apipe*. In their possession they held plans to make this wilderness into their new home, which they would call Fernheim colony.

On arrival at Puerto Casado they transferred to Casado's slow-moving railroad. After passing through an unpopulated wilderness, they arrived at Endstation and were greeted in Plautdietsch by Menno colony pioneers. Soon the refugees and their meager belongings were loaded on more than one hundred ox-drawn wagons for the remaining 100 kilometers (62 miles) to the land MCC had arranged for them near Menno

Families lived in tents brought from Germany until permanent houses could be constructed.

Ox carts carried essentials such as flour and sugar from Puerto Casado to the railroad, a dreaded 100-kilometer journey.

colony. Seeing how skinny, weather-beaten, and poorly clothed their Menno hosts were caused one Fernheim refugee to remark prophetically, "As they are, so we will be."

The two colonies became neighbors in an unfamiliar land. To outward appearances they were similar, but their differences traced back hundreds of years to their origins in the Netherlands. Inexplicably, they had limited interaction in those early years.

The Fernheim settlers hit the ground running. They laid out villages and assigned family plots. Simple adobe brick houses with grass roofs soon replaced the tents that sheltered them temporarily. Almost immediately children were attending classes, using makeshift desks under the shade of a quebracho tree. Before many months they were harvesting vegetables from their gardens and eating berries found with the help of the indigenous people.

A Health Crisis

Sickness and even the occasional death could be expected in a community this size, but soon it became apparent something ominous was underway. Deaths had become so frequent that the colonists were unable to find enough wood to build coffins. A typhoid epidemic was soon diagnosed, and before it was brought under control, ninety-four people had died, sixty-four of them from three villages. The tragedy left many orphans and motherless or fatherless families to continue their arduous struggle with the unfamiliar Chaco.

Some of the indigenous Enlhet came to investigate and immediately helped their new neighbors find water and grass to roof their houses. When Mennonite oxen or children strayed into the bush, Enlhet helped find them. Mennonites and Enlhet approached each other somewhat apprehensively, but gradually a mutually helpful bond formed.

The Harbin Contingent Arrives

The Fernheim colony families were still getting settled when yet another contingent of immigrants from Russia joined them. This group was escaping Stalin's purges and had fled eastward until they were up against the Amur River. When the Soviets followed them there, the refugees looked longingly across the river to the Blue Mountains of China. As the Soviets closed in on them, they organized an ingenious plot by which two entire villages escaped on fifty-six sleds across the frozen river in the dead of a winter night.

But more hardship and surprises awaited them in China. They ultimately found temporary shelter in the inland city of Harbin. When their plight became known, the international Mennonite community came to their rescue. After a journey of many months, literally across half the world, 373 refugees ended up occupying two Fernheim villages that became known as the Harbiner Ecke. Others settled in Canada and California.

A Mission to the Indigenous

Fernheim colonists were not prepared for their encounter with the indigenous population. Some were offended by the natives; some were afraid of them and wanted them removed; others saw them as a source of labor. For others it was an epiphany. In the words of Gerhard Hein, a lifelong missionary to the indigenous, "When we saw the Indians we said, 'Is this what God had in mind when He directed us to Paraguay?' We came to see the Indians not only as workers but as living souls." Together with his wife, Irma, Hein learned the Nivaclé language and eventually completed a Nivaclé translation of the Bible.

Plans to initiate a mission to the indigenous were interrupted in

1932 by the Chaco War. Both the Bolivian and the Paraguayan armies tried to use the indigenous knowledge of the Chaco to their advantage. Both sides ended up distrusting the natives. Many Mennonite families sheltered the indigenous people at some risk to themselves, but in the end the indigenous temporarily vacated the war zone.

The three-year war had barely ended when ninety-seven Fernheim colony families, still uncertain of their own future, followed through on their earlier intention and organized Licht den Indianern (Light to the Indians). (The story is told in chapter 20.)

Fernheim Experiences a Split

Having faced down a typhoid epidemic and a war, the Fernheim colonists had to get acquainted with the Chaco before they could make it productive. Periods of drought were followed by flooding. When the weather was finally favorable, they were visited by a grasshopper plague so severe it hid the sun from them at noon. Helplessly they flailed at the grasshoppers with brooms and dug trenches to bury them, but to no avail. In low moments, after a long drought, some were made to question whether Fred Engen's advisers were right when they opined that the Chaco was not intended for habitation by white people.

Early Mennonite missionaries meet with indigenous families.

From the time of their arrival, there were those who thought life would be easier in East Paraguay. This sentiment festered, especially when crop conditions worsened. Self-doubt reached the point where many wondered if the Mennonite Chaco experiment could survive. Most did not have the resources to relocate to Canada or Germany, so scouts were sent to East Paraguay. When they returned with a positive report, Fernheim families were thrown into a deep quandary. Their first seven years had been hard beyond description. But could they make another start while still owing a debt to MCC for the purchase of land and passage to Paraguay?

The day came when a caravan consisting of one-third of the Fernheim colony families retraced their steps to Puerto Casado, intending to relocate in East Paraguay and build Friesland colony. The families who remained watched sadly as sorrowing friends and relatives left behind empty houses painstakingly built over the past three years. (The complete story is told in chapter 4.)

A Huge Distraction

Emotions resulting from the departure to Friesland had not yet faded when Fernheim was engulfed in another divisive episode. With strong memories of how Germany had rescued them from their Soviet inferno, many were predisposed to join the adulation of Adolf Hitler. An informal referendum revealed that a majority of colonists in Fernheim would in a heartbeat trade in their hard existence in the Chaco and return to their beloved Molotschna colony. They saw a German victory in World War II as the only way to bring that about.

Fritz Kliewer, one of Fernheim's best and brightest minds, had been sent to study in Germany with the expectation that he would return and upgrade Fernheim's schools. He returned to Paraguay in 1939. He was fully indoctrinated in National Socialism, and he had a newly earned doctoral degree and a German Mennonite wife. Kliewer quickly found himself drawn into a controversy threatening to divide the colony. Handicapped by incomplete information, some Fernheim members were offended by the militaristic nature of National Socialism while others chose to look past that in the hopes of being liberated from their Chaco nightmare, then at a low point. After festering for years, the dispute divided the colony and came to a head on March 11, 1944, when there was a violent confrontation that resulted in some injuries but no deaths.

The episode left Fernheim families, churches, and the colony itself in deep distress. Kliewer and Oberschulze Julius Legiehn were expelled. They later immigrated to Brazil, where Kliewer had a distinguished career as a teacher. Fernheim elected a new Oberschulze and new teachers were appointed. A Canadian evangelist held a series of revival meetings that helped restore harmony to the divided congregations. The colony had narrowly escaped a brush with death.

Good News Offsets Disappointment

Amid the hardships and distractions were weddings and funerals, baptisms and farewell, births and deaths. Surely one of the happiest days was on February 24, 1946 when Licht den Indianern, after ten long years, finally had seven baptisms to show for its effort.

In 1940 joy had also came to Fernheim in another form. Dr. John Schmidt, unmarried and fresh out of the Kansas Medical School, came to serve the growing population, which had existed without a resident doctor for ten years. Schmidt returned for a second stint a few years later with his wife, Clara, a nurse, who became his lifelong partner. He returned a third time in 1951 to stay. Together the Schmidts pioneered a leprosy mission known as Km 81. Schmidt died on November 6, 2003, and is buried in the Fernheim cemetery, while Clara in 2008 was being lovingly cared for in the Fernheim retirement village, surrounded by family and friends. (The story of the Schmidts and Km 81 is told in chapter 21.)

On the economic front, good news came in the persons of Robert and Myrtle Unruh. They had just graduated from Bethel College in North Newton, Kansas, and came to live in Filadelfia in 1951 for a three-year MCC term. They ended up staying a lifetime.

Soon after the Unruhs arrived, a weather-beaten farmer asked the youthful Robert what he had in mind. He replied modestly that he was hoping to help Fernheim colonists make a better living. The farmer looked into his young face and asked cynically, “Can you make rain?” When Robert hesitated, the farmer added, “If you can’t make rain, you can’t help us. Rain is what we need.”

The Unruhs did not make it rain, but they helped Chaco farmers make better use of the rain they got. And Myrtle’s degree and experience with the preparation of nutritious meals helped families live and eat better.

One of the saddest days was surely in 1958, when the Mennonite and indigenous community gathered to mourn the tragic death of missionary Kornelius Isaak, who had been speared to death by a Moro warrior while attempting to make contact with the tribe.

There was no mistaking that life continued to be hard in the Chaco. When Fernheim colony celebrated its twenty-fifth anniversary in 1955, it was uncertain whether the colony would survive.

"It was not that we were poor," said Peter Wiens, a pioneer teacher and pastor. "We knew we would be poor. It was that we were poor so long."

Even in the darkest hour, the hope that helped them survive was anchored in an unshakable faith that God had brought them there, and God would see them through.

A Line of Credit Brings Hope

In the 1950s, Fernheim was able to benefit from two loan programs (described more fully in chapter 13). When the effects of these reached the level of the discouraged families, it was, to quote a Chaco farmer, "as though a soft spring rain had fallen on our fields." The loans were repaid in full and on time. The value of credit had been dramatically demonstrated and prepared the ground for other initiatives to follow.

Some colonists nevertheless lost heart and departed. Some went to Brazil, but mostly they went to Canada or Germany. Each year between 1952 and 1958, and again from 1964 to 1967, more than one hundred persons left Fernheim. The peak year was 1967, when 166 members left. It was sad to see them go, but a sifting was also taking place. Many who were not well-suited to life in the Chaco were finding an alternative.

Improved Infrastructure

In the early years of the colony, children would spread news by carrying a *Tsadel* (written message) to their neighbors. It was a remarkably efficient system of communication that united the colony. In 1935 the gift of a used telephone system from Germany provided limited service. It was later replaced by another used system, this one from Canada. The villages were now connected by some 80 kilometers (50 miles) of wire hung from crooked poles. As many as twenty-one parties used one line.

The biweekly newspaper *Mennoblatt* served Fernheim from the first year of its existence. Its first editor, Nikolai Siemens, served in that post

Women and children making adobe brick on the frontier. Grass and water were added to local sandy soil and with bare feet mixed into mud that was then formed into bricks. Though labor intensive to make, adobe bricks were durable and well insulated.

for twenty-five years. Siemens possessed a buoyant Christian spirit that was surely one of the rays of hope in that pioneer generation.

Transportation was still as primitive in 1955 as it had been when they arrived a quarter-century before. Poor roads contributed to isolation and low morale. An ingenious Montana farming and ranching couple, Vern and Violet Buller, volunteered with some machinery to build better roads, linking the three Chaco colonies to each other and with Casado's Endstation. That led to the Herculean task of building, with help from MCC and the United States and Paraguayan governments, a road connecting the Chaco colonies to Asunción.

Filadelfia Emerges as the Capital

With the increased need for centralized services, the village of Filadelfia emerged as the Fernheim colony capital. The colony's schools, hospital, three churches, and a few residences were located there. But soon more activities were centralized there, and it became Fernheim's logistical and administrative center. By the year 2000, the expanding business district included a bank, motel, stores, restaurants, car dealerships, a radio station, a bookstore next to the indigenous mission headquarters, factories, service stations, and more. At its center is the impressive colony headquarters attached to the large co-op store. Gradually more Fernheim residents made their homes there, and in 2008 it claimed more than seven thousand inhabitants spread over several square kilometers.

Filadelfia is also the capital of the department (or province) of Boquerón. The governor's headquarters was for some years located beside the large Mennonitengemeinde church on tree-lined Hindenburg Straße, complete with a Paraguayan flag, before being relocated to another part of the village in 2006.

There is curiosity over the name Filadelfia. The original plan was to name Fernheim's colony capital Hindenburg, after the German chancellor who helped rescue them from Moscow. Orie O. Miller, then representing MCC and deeply involved in early Fernheim history, had reservations, thinking it too nationalistic. In deference to Miller's mild objections, they chose to name it after the City of Brotherly Love (Philadelphia) and used the Spanish spelling. The main street now carries the name Hindenburg. Streets named Orie O. Miller and B. H. Unruh cross it.

A winding path that started in the Ukraine and led through tense stopovers in Moscow and then Mölln, Germany, ended in the Paraguayan Chaco. The Chaco, which initially seemed so foreboding, became in one lifetime home to the members of Fernheim colony. The colonists view the future with an optimism sometimes mistaken for arrogance. Their endurance, hard work, missionary spirit, and faith in God's providence are being rewarded.

4

Friesland Colony

Seven years after the Russian Mennonite refugees left their homeland, a kilometer-long ox-drawn caravan meandered through the Chaco toward yet another new home, this time in East Paraguay. Since leaving their comfortable homes in Russia, the immigrants endured the suspense-filled drama in Moscow that led to their short stay in Germany. The group then separated, with some going to Canada, some to Brazil, and the rest to Fernheim colony as a last resort.

It was part of this Fernheim group that loaded all their possession on wagons and left the houses they had so painstakingly built, where children had been born and played, and where gardens and fields had been wrested from the bush. Harder by far was leaving behind relatives and neighbors they might never see again, people with whom they had traded favors and shared backless church benches.

Seven hard years had left them with doubts about a future in the Chaco. The peaceful setting they had imagined soon became a battlefield. The fields they planted and looked to for sustenance shriveled under the hot sun. While waiting for things to get better, things seemed to get worse. The crowning blow came when swarms of grasshoppers descended on them like the plagues visited on the Egyptians.

So they prayed—sometimes for rain, sometimes to be permitted to return to their former life in Russia, sometimes for grace to survive the "green hell."

A Search for Alternatives

While some were able to accept these hardships, others became convinced that the Chaco had been a huge mistake. Lacking the resources to immigrate to Canada, or anywhere else for that matter, they sent scouts to East Paraguay. The scouts found what appeared to be an acceptable alternative inland from Rosario, halfway down the Paraguay River, but on the east side of the river—not in the Chaco. The rainfall appeared to be greater, and they would be less isolated.

The prospect of an East Paraguay alternative took Fernheim colony by storm. Families needed to decide whether they should turn their backs on seven hard years or to continue to hope that life would get better in the Chaco. Were they willing to again live in tents while clearing the jungle to make a new beginning? A colony survey revealed that of 413 Fernheim families, only 92 wanted to remain in the Chaco.

Leaving also had implications for Mennonite Central Committee, which was expecting to recover the loan it had made to cover travel and the land purchase for the Fernheim colony. But there was an impasse: families who were remaining did not feel they should be expected to assume the debt for those departing; departing families did not think they could bear this obligation in addition to the costs of relocating. When MCC and Fernheim colony officials concluded that departing families would not be excused from the per capita loan payment, it seemed unbelievably harsh and resulted in bad feelings that lingered for many years.

Fernheim leaders finally put the question of leaving to a referendum. Their worst fears were confirmed when fully half of Fernheim families opted for East Paraguay. Fernheim leaders made a conciliatory appeal: "You are one of us. We want you to remain. *Haltet durch* (stay the course). God brought us here for a purpose." It succeeded in reducing the number wanting to leave to 40 percent.

The Fernheim pastor chose as his text for their church farewell 2 Chronicles 16:9: "For the eyes of the Lord run to and fro throughout the whole earth, to show his might in behalf of those whose heart is blameless toward him. You have done foolishly in this; for from now on you will have wars" (RSV).

Many were puzzled about the decision of these families to leave Fernheim. "The families are gone. . . . They were restless. Why they

Fernheim families returning to Puerto Casado to eventually establish Friesland colony in East Paraguay.

relocated to Rosario is still not clear to me," said Fernheim Oberschulze Jakob W. Siemens.

"Why are you separating?" asked Benjamin Unruh, who had such a major role in bringing them there. "God rescued you [from Russia] as one body."

"The Friesland settlers begin for the second time in seven years with a hard pioneer beginning no easier than the one in the Chaco," wrote editor P. P. Klassen in *Mennoblatt*, the Fernheim bi-weekly paper.

Homeless Again

Soon 754 people in 136 families were en route to Casado's Endstation, homeless again. Long days were followed by sleepless nights on blankets under the stars, surrounded by wagons and cud-chewing oxen. At Endstation they loaded their precious belonging onto the train for the trip to Puerto Casado. When they arrived and their cargo was transferred from train to ship, we can imagine some of them venturing to the Catholic graveyard, where more than one hundred of their Menno Colony friends lay buried, a sobering reminder of the price of life on the frontier.

It was just a short, overnight journey down the Paraguay River before docking near Rosario. Paraguayan onlookers watched with amusement as these strange people assembled their wagons and got organized for the 50-kilometer (31-mile) journey to the bare 7,000-hectare (17,000-acre) plot awaiting them. Before departing Fernheim, they chose Friesland as their colony name, in memory of their Dutch origins. In the meantime Fernheim was grieving its loss.

Another New Beginning

At their new territory, the colonists organized themselves into nine villages, using methods they were familiar with from Russia. They gave these villages familiar German names and connected them with paths that would later become roads. Quickly Friesland became an East Paraguay duplicate of Fernheim, and they had done it on their own—with no outside help. They could not know how they had, in God's providence, opened the way for others to come years later.

As time passed, the new colonists acquired more oxen and horses before eventually switching to tractors. Cotton production peaked in 1940 and eventually gave way to kafir and corn, and later to wheat and soya. They planted many fruit trees, and the yield was good, but they were never able to establish a good market. Manioca became an important food crop and remains so in 2008.

How to Motivate an Ox

The bad feeling that lingered between Fernheim and Friesland colonies is illustrated in a mythical story of the Friesland ox who grew tired while on a journey and laid down, harness and all. After what seemed like an appropriate interval, several efforts were made to rouse him to stand up. Gentle nudging gave way to more desperate measures. Evening was coming, and the travelers were still far from their destination, so they resorted to the extreme tactic of literally setting a fire under the ox. But all was in vain.

Finally an onlooker whispered something in the ox's ear. Suddenly he stood up and alone moved the whole load to its destination. The astonished witnesses asked the man what he said to the ox. He responded that he told the ox, in Plautdietsch, of course, "If you do not get up immediately, we will send you back to Fernheim!"

Organizing Themselves

When it came time to organize themselves, the people of Friesland wanted to avoid the Fernheim model, which they thought was too authoritarian and which in their darker moments they likened to communism, the harshest insult imaginable. They nevertheless elected an Oberschulze but required him to serve under the direction of a three-man administrative committee.

They resisted establishing a cooperative for similar reasons, but within ten years they had organized their own. To diminish centralization they separated the cooperative from the colony and made membership voluntary. It did not work well, and they eventually reverted to the Fernheim model.

Friesland families brought strong German loyalties with them from Fernheim. Communication between the two colonies was limited, and information reached them only indirectly. But, as in Fernheim, Friesland churches, and even some families, were evenly divide over National Socialism. Some viewed it as antithetical to Anabaptism while others saw a German victory as their best hope to reoccupy their Russian villages. The effects of these divisions lingered for a generation.

Hutterites Arrive

Germany expelled the Hutterian Brethren in 1937 over opposition to Hitler's Nazi regime. They fled to England, but with World War II in the offing this proved to be a temporary stopover. In casting about for options Orie O. Miller urged them to consider Paraguay. Not only were they assured that Paraguay would admit them, MCC offered them a tract of land neighboring the Fernheim colony.

Fernheim received the Hutterites warmly, but the newcomers insisted on exploring options in East Paraguay before making a decision. Much to Fernheim's disappointment, the Hutterites opted to become neighbors to Friesland instead. They chose Primavera (Springtime) as their colony name. Three hundred twenty-three Hutterian Brethren settled on a 7,850 hectare (19,400 acres) tract in 1941.

The two communities had much in common and complemented each other wonderfully. Whereas the Hutterians were more educated and academic, the Friesland colonists were more agrarian and practical. They also had their differences, none bigger than over German National Socialism.

Sadly, a serious schism arose among the Hutterian ranks. One refers to it as an earthquake that divided them and tragically led to their 1962 dissolution. They sold their holdings to Friesland colony and scattered, mostly to other *Bruderhofs* (farm colonies) in the United States and Canada.

Friesland Gets a New Neighbor

Friesland was still in the process of getting itself together when a new challenge unexpectedly presented itself. Among the thousands of Mennonite refugees in Germany were some who agreed to come to Paraguay on the condition that it not be to the Chaco. This story is told more fully in chapter 5, but suffice it to say here that in the search for an alternative, MCC was drawn to a tract next to Friesland colony. So it was that, as Menno and Fernheim colonies served as forerunners for immigrants coming to the Chaco in 1947, so Friesland generously came to serve as a forerunner for what became known as Volendam colony.

Friesland and Volendam colonies cared for each other and did some things communally. But being separated by 50 kilometers (31 miles) of dirt road made for many limitations. The Friesland colonists shared what they had learned the hard way, making a very difficult beginning easier for Volendam members.

Things were getting easier, but there was no mistaking that life in Friesland was still very hard. This was most apparent in the large number of families who pulled up stakes and left their hopes and years of hard work behind. Eighty-five left in 1958. Then the annual number dropped before again building up to seventy-five in 1970. The people of Friesland colony, like their Chaco cousins, were looking for better days.

The Search for What Works

The settlers who left Friesland benefited from what they had experienced in the Chaco, but East Paraguay was different. There they started new cycles of trial and error. Their land was more heavily wooded, making clearing it more difficult. The trees were initially seen as an obstacle to the fields of wheat they envisioned, but then they discovered a temporary solution in a market in Asunción for lumber and firewood.

In the clearings they planted cotton, manioc, and beans as they had done in the Chaco, but nothing seemed to work well. Some were so discouraged with farming they resorted to hauling freight from the Rosario port. The pay was as poor as the roads. Men were required to be gone for days at a time. This was not what they'd had in mind when they left Fernheim. Freight hauling came to be seen as the distraction that it was, but what was the alternative? Some discouraged families concluded the alternative was elsewhere and left in growing numbers.

In the mid-1950s Mennonites were attracted to a program the Paraguayan government was launching to grow corn for export. They recleared the land that had reverted to bush and planted more than 1,000 hectares (2,470 acres) of corn. The plots were small, and the yields were low. Corn was added to the growing list of failed attempts. In desperation they gave wheat another try. To their amazement, a test plot produced good results. By 1965 Friesland farmers had in the range of 1,000 hectares (2,470 acres) of wheat, leaving them with a new challenge: to arrange the facilities needed to store and ship the quantities being harvested.

Things were beginning to look up for the survivors. But Friesland carried a heavy debt from the Hutterian land purchase, which had never been adequately financed. Alfred Fast, the Oberschulze at the time, appealed to MCC for a loan, which helped him arrange a North American itinerary for his *Geltsuchfahrt* (money-hunting trip). He succeeded in securing twenty-two twelve-year loans at 6 percent interest, for a total of 142,000 dollars.

More Good News

In the 1970s soybeans were making a name for themselves. Brazilian farmers were converting coffee plantations into soybean fields, and the idea caught on in Paraguay. Not only were the yields good, soybeans could be double cropped with wheat, in effect doubling the acreage. Soon the plow was following the wheat combine, running night and day, producing two crops annually with yields equivalent to those of farmers in the United States and Canada.

Meanwhile the quality and size of cattle herds increased exponentially from 3,130 head in 1950 to 7,751 in 1970 and 27,478 in 2000. The hectares of improved pasture increased proportionately. Life was getting better. Wheat, soya, and milk became their bread and butter.

Life Is More than Bread

Friesland, like its Volendam neighbor, has a rural character. Its colony center doesn't even have a name, but is known simply as "No. 3, Central."

The Friesland co-op building houses the colony store and headquarters and serves as the Friesland colony center.

The colony consists mostly of two Mennonite churches, a K-12 school with expansive playgrounds, a large grain-handling system complete with silos, a modern cooperative department store and colony headquarters, a hospital and retirement village, a few privately owned businesses, some residences, and a privately owned motel and restaurant, which also doubles as a colony *Treffpunkt* (meeting place).

I was privileged in 2007 to witness the buoyant spirit that prevailed at an evening program to usher in a new school year. Several hundred informally dressed parents and students gathered under provisional electric lights for the outdoor service. Talented and dedicated teachers took turns making impressive presentations—all in German.

The next day I met with ministers of the Mennonitengemeinde and Mennoniten Brüdergemeinde churches. Here too energy and vision were apparent as they ministered to a diverse membership that included pioneers and youth, most of whom will join the church. Some go to Asunción for further training, and not all return. But the vision of these churches goes beyond Friesland and reaches surrounding villages, where they minister to their Paraguayan neighbors and plant growing mission churches.

Next I met with the newly elected Oberschulze, Hans Theodor Regier, a source of some of this recent buoyant spirit. Though young and not a farmer like most of the colony he leads, Regier earned a doctorate from the State University in Asunción. When I invited him to share his vision for Friesland colony, he reached for an almost one-hundred-page five-year plan, complete with multicolor graphs. He offered me a copy—on paper or memory stick.

From its troubled beginning, Friesland has with perseverance and little outside help won a place for itself on the Paraguayan scene. In so doing, it unwittingly blazed the trail for those who came ten years later in need of a homeland and formed the Volendam colony. Friesland has challenges ahead, to be sure, the greatest of which may not be economic but more in the realm of the creeping secularization that often accompanies prosperity.

5

Neuland and Volendam Colonies

A happy way of life ended for Russian Mennonites when the revolution struck in 1917. Between 1923 and 1930 more than 20,000 left for Canada. In 1930, another wave left for Canada, Paraguay, and Brazil (see chapter 3.)

These emigrations still left a sizable community of Mennonites who remained under harsh Soviet rule. In 1941, they were overjoyed at the prospect of German armies liberating them en route to Moscow. Soon, the Russian Mennonites believed, their Soviet nightmare would be replaced with German rule. They dreamed of once again occupying their farms, reopening their schools and churches, and continuing the good life they had known before 1917.

Their dream briefly came true but did not last. The German armies swept through the former Mennonite villages in Ukraine, permitting Mennonites to again order their lives as they were accustomed. But then the fortunes of World War II reversed. The great Russian bear awoke and drove the German invaders out, with great cost of life. Unwilling to live again under Soviet rule, Mennonites fled en masse ahead of the retreating Germans.

The Great Trek West

With warplanes overhead, snow underfoot, and the sound of gunfire from behind, thousands embarked on what became known as the Great Trek. The refugees included women, children, and old men, who walked or rode in horse-drawn conveyances. They fled west, stopping only occasionally to bury their dead in shallow graves. They had no idea what lay ahead; they wanted only to escape what they had left behind.

Those who survived the ordeal arrived in Germany as it was about to capitulate. Few families were intact. Children were separated from parents as able-bodied men were drawn into the army. An estimated thirty-five thousand Russian Mennonites were among the roughly seven million refugees roaming Germany and Denmark during the postwar years, in search of a new life. Everyone was on their own. Their daily challenge was somehow to scavenge enough food to stay alive and remain undetected by authorities in the Soviet zone. To be discovered by the police resulted in swift removal to Siberia. Stealth was the order of the day.

Normal communications were disrupted, but the Mennonite grapevine survived. Wherever Mennonites met, whether they were former neighbors or complete strangers, a whispered exchange in Plautdietsch quickly established a trusted bond and helped them feel connected amid homelessness. Through this informal Mennonite network, many learned the whereabouts of relatives. It was this peoplehood, as well as faith in God's leading, that helped them survive.

Finding a Permanent Home

Again the global Mennonite community came to the rescue of a group of refugees. While Germany's cities were still smoldering, Mennonite Central Committee sent C. F. Klassen, one of their own who had

Timber being sawed by hand for building houses.

immigrated to Canada in 1928, to conduct a survey and devise a plan to settle the scattered refugees. In introducing his mission, Klassen borrowed from the biblical Joseph: "Ich suche meine Brüder" (I seek my brothers—and sisters).

Finding Mennonite refugees hiding in Germany was no easy task. Rounding them up and finding a country willing to receive them without documentation and without meeting health requirements would be that much harder. Transporting them to that country in large numbers seemed to be a human impossibility. There always seemed to be a link missing in the chain of events. But when faced with what seemed like an impossibility, the indomitable Klassen's confident reply was, "Gott kann" (God can). And God did!

Paraguay Extends a Welcome

When it seemed there was no way, a way was found against great odds and under the moving of God's Spirit. Canada agreed to take those that met its stringent health requirements. The United States had inaugurated the Marshall Plan to help Europe recover from the war, but it was not generous in opening its gates for immigration. Mexico was explored but dismissed as unsuitable. When the government of Paraguay was asked, its immediate answer was, "If they are Mennonites, they are welcome!" No conditions were attached.

The Paraguay option was presented to Mennonites sequestered in European refugee camps. The response was surprisingly strong, considering the limited information available. It may not have been so much the attraction of Paraguay as the comfort of putting an ocean between themselves and their Soviet tormentors.

Having Paraguay as an option was a good beginning. The next challenge was how to get them there. No one even had an accurate count of the refugees. The original estimate was as many as one thousand, and in the end it was many more. Ships were not readily available; many were lying on the ocean floor, casualties of the war.

It was learned that a Dutch ship, the S.S. *Volendam*, with a capacity of nearly twenty-five hundred passengers, could be chartered for 350,000 dollars. MCC did not hesitate. It was confident its constituency in the United States and Canada would respond, and later the International Refugee Organization helped to subsidize the cost of transport.

The next challenge was to get word to the scattered refugees. Some were in camps, but many were in hiding, though the Mennonite grapevine reached them. MCC organized a procedure to screen potential passengers. Several months later the *Volendam* steamed into the German port of Bremerhaven already half-filled with passengers gathered in the Netherlands and Munich. The plan was to add one thousand passengers who had been hiding in Berlin and then to be on their way to Paraguay.

But the Berliners had not arrived in Bremerhaven. MCC workers waited nervously while the hours ticked away. Then a telegram announced that the Berlin contingent would not be coming. Soviet authorities had refused to permit their train to pass through the Soviet Zone. General Lucius Clay, the U.S. commander in Germany, feared an international incident amid Cold War frenzy.

A maddening exchange of telegrams flew among Berlin, Bremerhaven, Washington, D.C., and the MCC headquarters in Akron, Pennsylvania. In a series of quickly called meetings, officials considered a variety of scenarios, all of them associated with huge risks. Should the *Volendam* continue on half full? Should it stay in port and pay heavy penalties for waiting for Berliners who may never show up? The mantra became *arbeiten und beten* (work and pray). *Gott kann.*

Aware of the critical situation, the worried group onboard the *Volendam* called a prayer meeting. Many were anxious to be reunited with loved ones they had not seen since the war began. The suspense built as the meetings, telegrams, and phone calls continued. In their memoir of helping refugees after the war, *Up from the Rubble*, Peter and Elfrieda Dyck recalled the apprehension of the refugees:

> [As] Elfrieda Dyck was making her rounds in the houses where the anxious refugees were sheltered in Berlin, she took note of a Mr. Sawatsky who had set his packed suitcase in the hallway. When she inquired, he replied, "Frau Dyck, tonight we prayed for a miracle. I did too. I never did that before. And then I started thinking: just in case God is going to answer our prayer, why we aren't even ready. So I packed—I just want to be ready."

In the Bremerhaven harbor, the captain of the *Volendam* looked at his watch impatiently. The waiting time allowed in his contract was about to expire, and there would be heavy penalties. The prospect of a train passing through the Russian zone seemed preposterous to him.

But It Happened!

While Peter Dyck was frantically negotiating with officials, Elfrieda stayed near the telephone. On January 31, 1947, she received a call saying the way had been cleared. Twelve U.S. Army trucks had been dispatched to transport the refugees to the Berlin train station for the trip to Bremerhaven.

Within an hour more than a thousand refugees—women and children and a few men—were assembled quietly on a dark street. What official military records in Washington called Operation Mennonite was underway. Soon the Berliners were at the railroad station being loaded, not into comfortable passenger cars but into unheated, benchless freight cars with standing room only. As the wagons were filled to capacity, the click of iron locks broke the eerie silence.

"But why are we not moving?" some asked in whispered tones. "What if the Soviets do not allow us to pass through their zone?" others wondered.

Finally the train began to move. Six hours later it stopped again, this time at the border into the British zone. Suspense built as the minutes ticked away. The conductor explained nervously that they were waiting for a green light. Finally, after what seemed like an eternity, the train lurched forward and proceeded to pick up speed. Overjoyed that their prayers were being answered, first it was just one car, then two, and soon the whole train was singing "Nun danket alle Gott mit Herzen, Mund und Händen" (Now thank we all our God) while speeding through the war-ravaged German countryside.

Once in Bremerhaven, the transfer of a thousand people and their sparse luggage from the train to the *Volendam* took place with remarkable efficiency. The strong helped the weak. Soon long-separated loved ones were in a tearful embrace. The ship's engines started, and the refugees were on their way. Escorting the group were Peter and Elfrieda, who had been so central in making it happen and whose role was still far from over.

Some refugees were healthy; some needed help to board the ship that would take them to their new home. Some were bitter over the hardships that had befallen them while others were at peace, looking forward to a new future in Paraguay.

There were children without parents and parents without children.

There were husbands without wives and even more wives without husbands. The men were either killed in the war, languished in some camp in Siberia, or perhaps were still incognito somewhere in Germany. Almost half of the women did not know where their husbands were or whether they were dead or alive.

While the passengers were discussing their experiences and comparing what little they knew about Paraguay—often more rumors than fact—the dramas continued. The plan was to dock in Buenos Aires and then to transfer passengers to smaller ships to be shuttled to Paraguay. Less than a day before their scheduled arrival, Argentine officials had not yet given their approval, not wanting to end up with a shipload of refugees. The *arbeiten und beten* routine was in motion again.

When Orie O. Miller was informed that the *Volendam*, with its 2,303 passengers, was days overdue for its scheduled arrival in Buenos Aires, and that Argentina had not yet agreed to give them temporary refuge, he quoted Psalm 50: "The cattle on a thousand hills are his." The inference was that they had entrusted the refugees to God's care, and now there was nothing further they could do.

Only after MCC, with the help of Spanish-speaking Mennonite missionaries, had given the Argentine officials convincing assurances were the needed approvals given. When the refugees finally arrived in Buenos Aires, seventy white tents arranged in two long rows awaited them. Also awaiting them was the unwelcome news that Paraguay was engulfed in a revolution and that there might be a short delay. They had seen enough war, but this one, they were assured, would be of short duration, and it was. The first contingent managed to reach the Chaco, where Menno and Fernheim families gave them temporary shelter.

Almost two thousand refugees were delayed first in their Buenos Aires tent city and then in camps in Paraguay. This delay afforded the MCC staff more time to make the necessary arrangements, including making good on a promise that an alternate location would be found for those unwilling to settle in the Chaco. It seemed the refugees had learned of difficulties in earlier settlements, though some of what they'd heard was imagined or exaggerated.

MCC had dispatched C. A. DeFehr, a Winnipeg businessman, to help with the Paraguay reception. DeFehr located a tract near Friesland colony. He and advisers from Friesland surveyed the tract from the backs of borrowed horses and concluded that it was acceptable. DeFehr presented his findings to the waiting families, who agreed to settle on the land. Within months the refugees, the first of four waves, had settled, some in the Chaco, the rest in East Paraguay.

More Transports

After a brief trip to report to the supporting Mennonite constituency in the United States and Canada, the Dycks returned to Germany, where more refugees were surfacing. Less than one year later, 860 more refugees had been rounded up and transported on the ship *Heintzelmann*, escorted by Elfrieda.

Then it was the ill-fated *Charlton Monarch* with 758 passengers escorted by Elfrieda. The ship was chartered by the International Relief Organization, not MCC and never reached its Buenos Aires destination. Questionable equipment and an irresponsible crew endangered the ship on its ocean crossing. It became completely disabled and issued an SOS off the coast of Recife, Brazil. The weary and frightened passengers were eventually shuttled to Recife. The strong helped the weak, and transport planes shuttled them to Asunción for the last leg of their anxious journey. More *arbeiten und beten*.

The refugees kept coming. So MCC chartered the S.S. *Volendam* for a second trip to transport 1,695 passengers, bringing the total to 5,616 refugees relocated in the twenty months between February 1, 1947, and October 6, 1948. All were settled in Paraguay, except 431 who went to Uruguay and several hundred who scattered elsewhere, mostly in Argentina. An additional seven thousand were settled in Canada with assistance from MCC and other Mennonite relief organizations. The largest relocation of Mennonites ever had been successfully completed. Now the sobering question was, How will they fare on the Paraguayan frontier?

Volendam Colony

Two thousand and forty-two "souls," as the Germans are apt to say, took possession of a 30,000-hectare (74,000-acre) tract purchased by MCC in East Paraguay, neighboring Friesland colony. It was divided into 425 family plots ranging in size from 15 to 40 hectares (37 to 99 acres). Friesland families, themselves still in a hand-to-mouth existence, generously hosted the new arrivals for several months, resulting in lasting friendships. The years of refugee wandering had ended; the longing for a peaceful setting in which to live had at last been realized. But hard days were still ahead.

They went about the painstaking task of clearing and planting, erecting houses from native materials, and organizing their common life. Some were better suited than others for the rigors of pioneer life. For some, particularly the many widows, it proved to be a physical impossibility. There are stories of refugees who melted into tears as they stood helplessly, with ax and machete in hand, before an impossible tangle of trees, weeds, and brush. In the first year of the colony, 277 people left. Many went to Asunción and from there to Argentina. Some returned to Germany or found relatives who helped them relocate to Canada.

Struggling to Overcome Obstacles

Food and shelter was the first order of business. MCC provided an antiquated sawmill to convert trees into building material. The settlers planted crops and built houses. Eventually the fields and herds grew bigger while the wooded areas shrank. Each family was on its own, although they helped each other in times of special need. It was a community of both rugged individualism and mutual aid.

On Sundays they gathered at the village church to worship and find inspiration from each other and from preachers who drew from Scriptures that emboldened them to face another week. Their children were in schools taught by teachers trained in Russia. From day one, the strong provided for dependent elders and orphans.

Like Friesland, Volendam had to learn by trial and error. After trying wheat and corn, they tried to grow rice, but the results were always disappointing. Each cycle of hope was followed by disappointment that worsened their morale and led to more emigration. By 1961, 223 families had left, mostly for Canada and Germany, reducing the colony census from 1,800 to 800. Volendam was in a downward spiral that some feared would lead to its demise.

It was a time of testing and sifting. Those who were not well suited for the frontier left. Some were too old, and some had no background in farming. Their departure, while sad, made room for those who survived. MCC was helping on a grand scale, but it had limited experience with resettlement, and it had many other commitments in the postwar era.

Answers to prayer were not yet visible. A men's group in the United States raised money to buy a bulldozer and recruited a skilled mechanic to build colony roads that would reduce the colonists' isolation and improve the marketing of their products. Relatives from earlier migrations to Canada supported them morally and through the Mennonite relief organizations. North American businesspeople founded the Mennonite Economic Development Associates to assist them. But life was tenuous in spite of all the assistance.

Breakthrough

In the late 1950s they gave wheat another try, this time with good results. They soon discovered that they could double crop wheat with soy beans. At long last, the colonists had found an answer to their economic woes. This discovery coincided with a million-dollar loan MCC had arranged for the five colonies (see chapter 13). With the money allocated to Volendam, the settlers purchased tractors, seeding and harvesting equipment, and grain handling facilities. Soon tractors and cars replaced horses and wagons. Eventually modern, air-conditioned, brick houses replaced the first adobe houses, which became storage building. Churches and schools were expanded and improved. Church and mission budgets increased.

With seven hundred inhabitants, Volendam is today one of the smaller Mennonite colonies. In the past, many questioned its future. Will it have the critical mass needed to educate and train its youth? Can it support schools and other essential services its members want and need? Will it be able to support two Mennonite churches? Are its leaders qualified to help the community navigate challenges while remaining meaningfully connected to its Anabaptist roots? Optimists insist that all Volendam needs is a new generation of visionary leadership that will build on its rather remarkable record.

Neuland Colony

The experience of Neuland colonists was similar to that of Volendam. The colonists were sheltered initially by the kindness and generosity of their neighbors in Menno and Fernheim colonies, who built houses for ninety-four families headed by women. The rate of emigration was high. As families were able to arrange more suitable options, many relocated to Canada and Germany.

As in the other colonies, Neuland built a strong cooperative and a system of governance similar to what it had known in Russia. The church-going population of both Neuland and Volendam was divided between Mennonitengemeinde and Mennoniten Brüdergemeinde. Members of both colonies used Plautdietsch as their everyday language while becoming more conversant in Spanish.

MCC continued to assist both Neuland and Volendam for many years. In addition to underwriting the cost of transporting the refugees (with substantial subsidies from governmental organizations) and purchasing the land, MCC shipped thousands of tons of food, clothing, and supplies. Some ask with justification if it would have been necessary to help so long if more help had been available in the early years.

The new Mennonitengemeinde church in Neu Halbstadt, with a seating capacity of more than 800. Most of the pioneer church buildings have now been replaced by modern structures similar to this one.

Neuland colony was fortunate to have in its pioneer group Wilhelm and Anna Rakko. Starting with very limited equipment and pharmacy supplies, they provided the colony with medical care for its first three decades, before retiring in 1978. The hospital has enjoyed numerous upgrades and is now under the direction of Paraguayan physicians.

Education was a high priority in Neuland from day one. In the first year, most villages had a school taught by teachers who had been trained in Russia. Quickly they established a quality secondary school, tastefully tucked behind preserved bush land in the capital of Neu Halbstadt. Neuland quickly became a full participant with the other Mennonite colonies in a uniform system of education with full Paraguayan accreditation.

With credit from the million-dollar loan, Neuland was able to purchase bulldozers to push back the bush and expand its pastures. Indigenous people helped build untold kilometers of fence to contain growing herds. Ranchers imported better breeding stock and built Australian water tanks to ensure the availability of water for the growing herds. Soon Neuland's peanut and cotton warehouses were empty, and milk trucks and beef transports were commonplace.

Neuland colony became an active participant with Menno and Fernheim in a large-scale program to settle indigenous families on their own *chacras* (small farms).

Today both Neuland and Volendam are happy with their lot. Neither would ask to trade places with the other. Members of both colonies are grateful for the freedom they enjoy in Paraguay and have adopted it as their homeland. This sentiment was stated beautifully by Heinz Braun, a Neuland pioneer, on the colony's twenty-fifth anniversary in 1972:

> Bitter grass to where the bush begins and beyond that an unending thorny thicket, under the cloudless sky and the unmerciful hot sun—but our own land under our feet, again a new home land, no more living as refugees! Inexpressible good

MCC in Paraguay

Paraguay is among MCC's longest continuous commitments. Between 1944 and 1999, MCC's cash remittances totaled 10,690,500 dollars, not including the cost of land purchases and transporting refugees from Europe. Between 1946 and 1962 MCC averaged more than twenty workers in Paraguay annually. In 1950 alone, MCC sent 157 tons of food and supplies in thirteen shipments to Paraguay. In 1955, the volume of activity led MCC to establish a special Paraguay Colony Emergency Relief Fund.

Gradually, as conditions improved, the administration of MCC projects shifted to Paraguayans, with MCC continuing to provide supplemental support. MCC closed its Paraguay office in 1970 but continued to work through its headquarters in Akron, Pennsylvania.

Source: MCC Annual Workbook reports compiled by Edgar Stoesz.

> fortune, many feel rich! What gratitude for each plot of our own land. Many then felt more satisfied and richer than today with 300 hectares [740 acres] of land.

Neuland colonists remain optimistic about their future. Years of facing down harsh circumstances have led to deep loyalty. Neuland exists confidently as the smallest of the three Chaco colonies.

6

Sommerfeld and Bergthal Colonies

An hour's drive from Asunción, on Paraguay Highway 7, is road post Km 81. This veritable oasis on the rolling countryside dotted with palm trees has become world renown for the hospital located there, especially among those who work with leprosy. It is named for its location, Km 81 (see chapter 21).

After driving another ninety minutes on Highway 7, one sees black-and-white Holstein cows grazing on the green pastures of orderly farmsteads with modern bungalow dwellings. During harvest time, large red or green harvesters are as prevalent as they'd be in Kansas or Manitoba. On approaching the business district, one sees restaurants, a German motel, a hardware store, a Christian bookstore, a hospital, and more. A modest sign announces the town as Campo 9, a strange name in the middle of Spanish-speaking Paraguay. In truth, it is a town that grew up alongside a road that is now a national highway and that divides Sommerfeld and Bergthal colonies.

On both sides of the road is a string of Mennonite-owned flour mills. There wheat grown by Mennonite farmers and imported from Argentina is milled into flour and marketed widely throughout Paraguay. A little further along the highway is the colorful sign for Lactolanda, a modern milk-processing plant owned by shareholders from Bergthal and Sommerfeld colonies. There milk from surrounding farms is packaged into boxes or processed into cheese, ice cream, and yogurt for the local and Asunción markets. Travelers are invited to enjoy a refreshing ice cream cone in the clean, well-lit, and brightly colored store.

Members of Bergthal colony originated from the East Reserve in Manitoba, Canada, while Sommerfeld colony members came from Manitoba's West Reserve. Both groups trace their ancestry to Chortitza, the original Mennonite colony in Russia. After their seventy-year sojourn in Canada, the settlers arrived in Paraguay in 1948 by way of the S.S. *Volendam*, which also transported Mennonite refugees from Europe.

To outsiders who pass by the two colonies as they travel Highway 7 on the way to Brazil's Iguazu Falls, one of the natural wonders of the world, the two colonies appear identical. But a look at their story reveals a more complex picture.

In the 1870s, Mennonites in Manitoba had spread out in farm village districts on 160-acre homesteads. They came to occupy eight townships east of the Red River, with Steinbach as their unofficial capital, a small city thirty-five miles from Winnipeg. The sod houses the pioneers first lived in were quickly replaced with two-story wooden structures built with native lumber. The settlers added barns, which were often attached to the residences, and other buildings as needed for their thriving farms. A school building that also served as a church could be found in every settlement from the beginning.

Years later the settlers discovered that land on the west side of the Red River was better suited to farming, so many relocated there and eventually occupied fifteen townships. The region became known as the West Reserve, with Winkler as its capital.

In 1921 the ranks of Sommerfeld and Bergthal were thinned as thousands of their relatives and friends immigrated to Mexico (see chapter 7). Six years later they opted not to join the large group leaving for Paraguay. The sizable community remaining on both sides of Manitoba's Red River sympathized with the objections of their departing brethren but were loathe to give up what they had accomplished in fifty years of hard work. They were still hopeful that it would be possible to live in Canada without compromising their convictions.

They feared this compromise because when World War II started, some Mennonite men were drafted into the military, but some volunteered. It was a wake-up call. In spite of all their efforts to separate themselves from the world, encroaching secularization had caught up with their young people. Emigration fever was revived. The burning question was where to go.

Maybe Paraguay?

An inquiry was addressed to the government of Paraguay, and Paraguay did not equivocate. It was at that time accepting shiploads of destitute Mennonite refugees from Europe (see chapter 5), so why not take in the Canadians who could pay their way?

A three-person survey team left Winnipeg in July 1946. Finding conditions among their cousins and former neighbors in Menno colony at a low ebb, they pursued options in East Paraguay. They located a 44,000-hectare- (109,000-acre) tract halfway between Asunción and Brazil that could be purchased at seven and a half dollars per hectare.

The survey team's report was well received back in Canada. The Manitoba farmers sold their farms and packed their possessions into wooden chests, some of which had accompanied them from Russia seventy years earlier. They worked out a mutual-aid plan in which a "tax" was imposed on the wealthy, making it possible for those without resources to join. The departing group consisted mostly of young families, although some were accompanied by elderly parents, some of whom had been born in Russia.

Four chartered trains took 1,641 passengers with their baggage and some equipment from Manitoba to Quebec City, where they boarded the S.S. *Volendam* for the trip south. The twenty-three-day ocean journey was a time to reflect and to anticipate the hard years ahead. When finally they saw birds circling their ship, they knew they were nearing land. After a brief stopover in Buenos Aires, the immigrants arrived in Paraguay, anxious to occupy the land they had bought.

A Costly Misunderstanding

Before they could gain access to their interior tract, it was necessary to construct a 30-kilometer (19-mile) road through swamp and forest. While the men were busy with this backbreaking work, women and children found shelter but no amenities in an abandoned sugar-cane factory. When it came time to lay out their villages, they realized they were victims of a bait and switch. The very attractive land they had been shown and thought they had purchased was not the tract described in their legal purchase papers.

Angered by this deception and other disappointments, 441 souls returning to Canada, shrinking the membership of the Paraguayan contingent by 25 percent. Instead of the gently rolling wheat fields they had imagined, they were surrounded by bush and woods, with some of the most valuable trees already harvested. By 1982 two-thirds of the original Sommerfeld families had returned to Canada. As the anniversary recollection *Sommerfeld: 1948-1998* noted:

> The encounter with a foreign culture, with strange customs and practices, with an unfamiliar language and unfamiliar money was hard. Here the earth is red instead of black, tall trees instead of open prairie, manioc instead of potatoes, oxen instead of cars or tractors. For some the adjustment was too great. They called it quits and moved back to Canada without even seeing the land they had purchased.

The woods the settlers considered an obstacle were in fact what sustained them in the early years. Instead of plows and harvesters in fields of ripened grain, they had sawmills and lumber wagons. The wooden houses they built on little tracts of uncleared land resembled houses they had left behind in Canada. Soon these houses were surrounded by fruit trees, manioca, vegetables, and flowers of all kinds—and many lively children.

The settlers took care to include a newly credentialed Ältesten. One trained nurse handled healthcare. This proved to be a costly oversight, as sickness and death were ever present on the frontier. An early epidemic took twenty of their little ones. Today both Bergthal and Sommerfeld have hospitals operated by Paraguayan doctors. On the same premises are comfortable retirement homes where their aged receive loving care.

Colony members tried to duplicate life as they had known it in Canada, which was much as they had known it in Russia before that. They constructed schools and church buildings. Their emphasis was preservation, not innovation. Bergthal, even more than Sommerfeld, held to tradition.

A ranch hand at work. Production of dairy and meat products has grown since the 1980s.

Things Improve in the 1960s

Like finding their way through a maze, the colonists learned through trial and error. Much of what they brought from Canada had to be unlearned. Eventually their fields and herds grew more productive. Navigating the surrounding Latino culture became easier. Highway 7 was upgraded in 1962, improving transportation and access to the Asunción market.

Fifteen sawmills fueled the colony's economy in those early years. The mills converted logs into lumber for markets in Asunción. As clearing increased, the economy shifted to dairy farming. Imported breeding stock boosted the quality of the cattle. The pastures improved, and provisions for winter feed multiplied.

When the market for raw milk proved to be unreliable, farmers from both colonies established a modern milk plant with equipment imported from Brazil. Today attractively designed Lactolanda milk, butter, cheese, and yogurt cartons grace many Paraguayan tables.

Loans from the United States government through the Paraguayan Development Bank helped the transition from lumbering to dairying and later to crop farming. Farmers had brought some tractors from Canada, but much of the work in those early years was still done by hand or with the help of oxen. Sommerfeld and Bergthal did not participate in the credit programs (discussed in chapter 12). Early experiments with wheat were disappointing. But like their compatriots in Friesland and Volendam, the Sommerfeld and Bergthal colonists discovered the benefits of raising soybeans double-cropped with wheat. After a generation, the Sommerfeld and Bergthal farmers had found their answer.

Soybeans found a good international market, but the wheat market was unreliable and fluctuated wildly. So Jacob Braun, an enterprising Sommerfeld member, began milling wheat into flour. After Braun's untimely death, others nursed his innovation along. When a small mill produced favorable results, they built a bigger one. Today, on both sides of the highway, are six large mills with mammoth storage silos, most privately owned. They operate twenty-four hours a day, six days a week, supplying much of Paraguay with nutritious wheat flour.

Tradition Confronts Innovation

The colonies were thriving, but Mennonites did not come to Paraguay for economic reasons. They came seeking freedom to live according to their religious convictions. Almost immediately differences among themselves raised conflicts. Some wanted to change the education system while others held to tradition. Some wanted to evangelize their neighbors while others preferred a quiet, corporate witness. Some were attracted to worship services that included singing in four-part harmony, which was traditionally forbidden.

In 1981 the colonies obtained access to electric power lines that had previously passed over their heads en route to Asunción. Welcome as this was for some, it introduced a whole raft of technologies that threatened the old regulations. These included radio and later television and the Internet. Outsiders can hardly imagine the strife and bad feelings over innovations modern people take fore granted. In 2007 a conflict raged over whether loudspeaker systems should be permitted in church services. How does a system that values tradition deal with new technologies and ways of thinking without compromise?

On one of my recent visits to Paraguay, I hitched a ride from Asunción to Bergthal. While driving at speeds in excess of 120 kilometers (75 miles) per hour, my driver instructed his son via cell phone on a variety of subjects, including which field to harvest next and in which bin to store the grain, all in Plautdietsch.

Dissent in Bergthal Gives Birth to Tres Palmas

As Bergthal entered its second decade, some were losing patience. One of these was Jakob Braun, a conservative who valued tradition and was at heart a progressive and an entrepreneur but no less Anabaptist. He stepped out of the confines of Bergthal colony to purchase a 2,060-hectare (5,090-acre) tract 20 kilometers (12 miles) north of Bergthal.

Two years later John Janzen joined him, purchasing an even larger neighboring tract. Together they possessed a two-hundred-square-mile spread of land that was subject to flooding but populated by valuable trees. They hired Paraguayans to convert trees into lumber during a period of high demand. Others from neighboring colonies were attracted to the somewhat more progressive environment there. The resulting community grew to three hundred souls and was legally incorporated in 1973 as the Sociedad Civil Tres Palmas.

In 1983 a crisis literally washed over them. The newly constructed hydroelectric dam at Acaray flooded the area, separating the scattered members from each other and disrupting their common life. Some were discouraged, and many left, shrinking the membership by half.

Undaunted and supplemented by the Evangelical Mennonite Conference mission from Canada, the energetic, mission-minded Tres Palmas group, sometimes in partnership with the Sommerfeld Evangelische Mennonitengemeinde, undertook an ambitious mission program. (See chapter 19.)

A Split at Sommerfeld

Similar dynamics were at work on the Sommerfeld side of Highway 7. Älteste Jakob J. Heinrichs, a deeply convinced Anabaptist, was an innovator at heart. Whether in the pulpit or in his workshop, Heinrichs was always looking for better ways of doing things. While serving alternately as Sommerfeld pastor and later Älteste and as a member of the colony administrative committee, a kind of holy discontent was brewing in his soul. Though deeply respectful of tradition, Heinrichs was convinced that changes were needed, particularly in church and school life. He summarized them:

- a library for youth, adults, and Paraguayans
- a youth center
- music and messages with content for their congregation

- a center for church and family festivities
- Spanish classes
- Bible classes
- improvements to the school curriculum
- a paid youth leader

The suggested reforms proved too much for his traditional fellow ministers. When they decided to elect another Ältesten, Heinrichs extended an invitation to all who supported his program to join him in the establishment of a new congregation. So, on March 22, 1994, 140 members established the Evangelische Mennonitengemeinde.

As the energetic group grew, it established its own K-12 school with 212 pupils on a tract across a wheat and soya field from the Heinrich residence. Adjacent is a spacious auditorium where the congregation meets with an attendance of six hundred. Remarkably, Heinrichs and his followers continue to be active members of Sommerfeld colony. I was privileged to witness young, nicely dressed families streaming to the rapidly filling auditorium for the service to begin. The service was much like what one might experience in any rural Canadian community, with some reminders of an Old Colony past.

Jakob and Elizabet Heinrichs. Jakob was a Sommerfeld colony leader before founding Evangelische Mennonitengemeinde in 1994.

Heinrichs does not foresee a day when all the Sommerfeld members will come to his church. "My prayer," he says, "is that the entire colony will experience the fullness of Christ in the Anabaptist tradition and share that message with our neighbors."

Interacting with Paraguayan Neighbors

Bergthal and Sommerfeld, like their Chaco brothers and sisters, had unknowingly put themselves down on territory claimed but not legally owned by indigenous—in this case, Guaraní. This resulted in a dispute between Mennonites who had title to the land and indigenous people who had for generations hunted and gathered there. The dispute was covered in the national press. Mennonites eventually settled indigenous families on their own parcels, much as Mennonites were doing in the Chaco with good results. But their good intentions were not rewarded. The indigenous people preferred employment to farming. An accommodation of sorts was eventually found, including a mission complete with a school, a clinic, and evangelical outreach.

Peering into the Future

Were I to return to Campo 9 in 2028, how will things have changed? Will the children of now nine-year-old Ervie, whose grandfather is my fourth cousin, be studying the well-known German primer *Fibel* and the *Katechismus* (catechism) and doing their numbers and practicing their penmanship as Ervie was doing while I was visiting with his father, and as his great-great-grandfather had done in Russia? Will they be speaking German or Spanish?

I asked Ervie's father, Heinrich, if Bergthal is disadvantaging itself and its children with an education system that does not prepare them for the modern world. I knew his answer before I finished the question. They do not want their children interacting with the modern world that surrounds them. That is exactly the point. His reply, was simply, "Dout leht sich" (They pick it up).

Later we stopped by the Bergthal colony office, where I was given an impressive computer printout of the colony's facts and statistics, prepared by a graduate of their school—a school outsiders regard as substandard.

"And that nice new hospital," I asked, "are your people qualified to staff it?"

Heinrich replied, "We have always had good nurses, some trained in the Chaco, and Paraguayan doctors come here willingly to practice their specialties. We are well served."

"And your impressive Lactolanda, and the colony-operated flour mill," I continued, "do you have persons qualified to manage these multimillion-dollar businesses, sometimes involving international trade?"

With a quiet confidence he replied, "Our businesses seem to run as good or better than some that have these highly paid and educated managers." I was able to corroborate this later from other informed sources and from my own experience.

In twenty years, will Ervie be married to a Bergthal woman? Will

Albert and Mary Hildebrand hold a bag of wheat flour at one of six mills that supply much of Paraguay with flour.

they have the 10 hectares (25 acres) needed to operate a family dairy farm, as his older brothers are already doing? Or will Ervie and his family be numbered among the landless looking for the next frontier?

How will Ervie's generation be seen by its neighbors? Will Mennonites be the objects of jealousy, theft, and occasionally murder? Will they be resented or respected for what they have accomplished for themselves and others? Will their neighbors be attracted to the faith Mennonites practice? If so, will they be welcome in Mennonite churches, or will they be part of a "mission" church?

In twenty years, will Mennonite churches be using microphones for their large gatherings, as is now being disputed, or will this result in another colony split? Will the Älteste with his *Ohms* (pastors) be able to walk that fine line between the progressives and the traditionalist, or will the colonies fracture? What will happen to those who are now on the fringes of what is permissible? Will they be placed under the ban and expelled? Maybe the whole colony will have found another neglected corner of God's shrinking planet to live out their convictions.

I caution myself not to underestimate them. They have managed to survive for generations against all odds.

And they have questions of us and our accommodation with the world. "Is it true," they ask, "that men are marrying men and women are marrying women? Is abortion practiced in your communities? Divorce? Teenage drinking and pregnancies? Pornography?"

Even as I asked if their young people are making a public profession of their faith through baptism, they asked the same of us. They may have a better record of retaining their youth than their modern cousins.

In the words of Ältesten Heinrichs, from the attractive and informative book celebrating Sommerfeld's fiftieth anniversary in 1998 "Sommerfeld has become our home. For that we thank God. But we like our ancestors are only guests and strangers in this world while waiting for a better world not prepared with human hands."

7

Mexican Colonies

Mennonites had left Chortitza colony in Russia in the 1870s and resettled in Canada. After almost fifty years in Manitoba and Saskatchewan, some seven thousand Old Colony Mennonites, as they were called, moved to Mexico between 1922 and 1926. Between 1969 and 1983, four colonies moved from Mexico to Paraguay.

We pick their story up at a pier in Buenos Aires in 1919. Five Canadian Mennonite scouts were awaiting a ship for their journey home. The trip had been filled with frustration and disappointment. Day after day, they visited government offices in Brazil, Uruguay, and Argentina and spoke to land agents, trying to convince them to grant the Mennonites land and certain concessions.

But they kept returning empty-handed. They were well received everywhere, but when it came to granting the preconditions, especially exemption from military service, government officials demurred.

Adding to their gloom, one of their number, Johann Wall, died on the trip. They buried him in an unfamiliar graveyard in Curitiba, Brazil.

Their conversation, no doubt in Plautdietsch, ranged over many topics. Were their families safe? Perhaps the government had in the meantime granted some concessions, making it possible for them to remain in Canada. We can imagine them speculating over the fate of distant relatives and former neighbors in Russia, which was then in the throes of revolution and civil war.

They were so absorbed in their conversation, they were unaware of being overheard by a man also awaiting passage on a ship to New

York. He turned out to be the Canadian consul. After hearing their need, he urged them to consider Mexico.

Upon returning to Canada, they learned that interest in emigrating and the issues driving it had not abated. Mennonites were fed up and wanted to leave, but they were also confused. Canadian government officials were alternately imposing regulations and appealing for them to remain. Scouting reports were contradictory and unreliable. Rumors circulated through the community like a virus, and no one knew what to believe. Florida? Quebec? Alabama? Mississippi? Minnesota? Remain in Canada? Later Paraguay was added to the list of options.

Then someone recalled the consul's invitation to consider Mexico. We do not know if they were aware that Mexico had just been through a revolution, with some unsettling aftereffects. Nor do we know if they were aware of the legendary Pancho Villa, who had terrorized the region earlier and at that time was trying to maintain the revolution.

On the backs of hired mules, a new scouting team surveyed Mexico's sparsely inhabited Eastern Sierra Madre Valley in the state of Chihuahua, where Villa had once been provisional governor. The Copper Canyon in Chihuahua, said to be a geological wonder larger and deeper than the Grand Canyon, rises to an altitude of 2,000 meters (6,560 feet).

Being generally satisfied with what Chihuahua had to offer, the scouts made their way to Mexico City and were received by President Álvaro Obregón Salido and his minister of agriculture. Amid more glitter than they were accustomed to and speaking through translators, they presented their petition with the usual list of conditions, including exemption from military service and freedom to operate their schools. The president gave his approval and confirmed it in writing.

Back in Canada, the scouting report was well received. Some were ready to leave, believing that meeting the Canadian government's conditions would amount to a compromise with the world. Others felt less strongly about the government's conditions and wanted to stay. Congregations and even families were divided.

Those who decided to leave had to convert the farms they had so painstakingly built over two generations into cash so they could purchase land in Mexico. Some of these farms, in a Mennonite irony with few equals, were purchased by families arriving in large numbers from the Soviet Union gulag.

By fall of 1922 the group opting to emigrate had drawn up a passenger list for the first three chartered trains. Of 4,526 Old Colony Mennonites in Manitoba, 3,340 left for Mexico and resettled in Chihuahua. Simultaneously, almost one thousand of nearly four thousand Old Colony Mennonites in Saskatchewan settled in the neighboring Mexican state of Durango. As one writer described it, "The Mennonites were headed south while the Canadian geese overhead were headed north!"

The eleven-day route took them through the Dakotas, Nebraska, Kansas, Oklahoma, and New Mexico, sometimes unknowingly skirting communities where Mennonites lived. On the trains with them were livestock, implements, seeds, and household basics. An onlooker described their arrival in Mexico:

> They are well-to-do, self-assured farmers, come as a solidaristic group with documented privileges to take possession of their lands. Was this the goal? Was the boundless highland that appeared so inexpressibly wild and worlds away in the pale shimmer of moonlight, the new *Heimat* one had exchanged for familiar things in Canada?
>
> And then they were standing about in groups, speaking among themselves as at home, by the hundreds, out there on the wild prairie under a lowering Mexican moon—Plautdietsch. With first light began the unloading. Holstein cows and great Belgian horses, chickens and geese, grain tanks and bundle wagons, farm wagons and great heavy tractors, coils of barbed wire, roofing and corrugated iron, furniture, bedding . . . by noon all was ready, and the long caravan of horse-and-tractor-drawn wagons snaking down the hill of San Antonio, out on the valley floor, where the new villages were to rise.

Canadian neighbors and government officials could hardly believe their eyes. Formerly thriving communities were now nearly empty—with thousands more émigrés poised to follow. "I guess they meant it," some thought. More than one-third of the Mennonite population eventually left Canada. Those that remained accepted the conditions being imposed, including the English language and town life. Some would follow later, and some who left returned to Canada. Manitoba especially was a revolving door for the Mennonite community in the 1920s.

Putting Down Roots in Mexico

In Mexico they subdivided their 440-square-mile tract into village districts and then into 160-acre family plots called *Koagel.* In the land of adobe, they built wooden houses and schools, and planted gardens and fields. They soon discovered that seed they'd brought with them did not do well. They tried a number of crops before finding their answer in corn, beans, oats, and later dairy farming. Mennonites eventually became better known for their cheese than their religion.

As in Paraguay, these ventures in Mexico were carefully planned, even to the point of bringing along hay for the horses. But sadly, the émigrés made no provision for healthcare. It was entrusted to God. In 1925 125 died from malaria, typhoid, or small pox. Sickness, death, and a scarcity of potable water contributed to low morale.

On top of all this, a dispute arose with local government authorities over schools. The federal government honored their appeal, but some Mennonites began to wonder if their sad history with the Russian and Canadian governments was repeating itself in Mexico.

Government officials were, in fact, impressed with the schools and wondered how the Mennonite model might be duplicated. Their only reservation was that Mennonites remained virtually unassimilated into the culture.

A Familiar Problem

The pioneer generation had enough land, but a high birth rate and continuing emigration from Canada doubled the population by 1949. Land was in short supply, and young families immediately bought available tracts. But the Mennonites' ability to make marginal property productive drove up prices, often making land unaffordable. They were victims of their own success.

So they did what their forefathers had done in Russia: they established daughter colonies. By 1944 Old Colony Mennonites had participated in as many as seventeen colonization ventures in five Mexican states and one in distant British Honduras (now Belize). The established settlements always lent aid to new settlements, easing the hardship and risk of a new beginning. As a result, most of these ventures were at least a qualified success.

Internal Conflict

As in other colonies, disputes over modernization often broke out among the Old Colony Mennonites. How much change should be permitted? How much tradition should be maintained? The Mennonites' unique dress (bib overalls and long-sleeved shirts for the men and long, heavy skirts and Russian-style *babushkas* for the women) suggested separation from the world. Yet even in Mexico's hinterland, they were unable to shut themselves completely off from the world. Rubber tires, for example, became an issue. "What," outsiders ask, "is wrong with rubber tires?" Old Colony reasoning is that they are "worldly" and increase mobility, thus distracting from community, one of their bedrock values.

Violators of tradition were admonished by the overburdened Älteste. If that did not produce compliance, the offending party was banned. The ban is a very harsh punishment in a system in which so much revolves around community. A violator is often separated from his or her own family. But banned people continue to live in the colony, injecting a constant discordant presence.

Adding to the dissension, the Old Colony community in Canada and mission interests in the United States became concerned about the spiritual condition in the Mexican Old Colony church. They sent missionaries who called them to personal repentance and new life in Christ. When someone responded to this invitation—and a few did—elders who feared schism banned the repenters.

Most transportation in the Mexican colonies is by horse-drawn buggy or wagon.

By the 1950s, Mexican Mennonite communities were deeply troubled. There was inadequate land for the growing population and the schools had deteriorated to the point that one cynic observed, "Mexican Mennonites are illiterate in four languages." On top of all that, the decade was a time of severe drought. People became restless and receptive to rumors that life might be better elsewhere. Some returned to Canada. Others were attracted to Paraguay. The strongest interest in emigrating was expressed by those who felt their traditions were being compromised in Mexico. Cost what it may, emigration fever was again in the air.

Paraguay, a Place of Refuge

In 1969, fourteen families established Colonia Rio Verde in East Paraguay, 350 kilometers (220 miles) northeast of Asunción. More families followed, and with a high birth rate, the membership had grown by 2008 to more than three thousand.

In 1972, a small number of families from Santa Clara, Mexico, established themselves on a tract neighboring Rio Verde, retaining the name Santa Clara and their way of life, although a little less strictly than their neighbors.

A third group, Nueva Durango, came in 1978 but got off to a poor start. After paying for and possessing a 13,400-hectare (33,100-acre) tract, a protracted and costly legal dispute over the land title erupted. They ended up having to pay for some of their land twice. These misunderstandings contributed to disharmony within the colony and resulted in many families and entire villages moving to Bolivia.

In 1983, Manitoba Colony was the last Mexican Colony to immigrate to East Paraguay.

Colony	Founded	2005 Population
Rio Verde	1969	3,212
Santa Clara	1972	309
Nueva Durango	1978	1,918
Manitoba	1983	726
Total		**6,165**

As Seen Today

The four Mexican colonies in Paraguay followed a uniform settlement pattern. Large families reside on well-kept farms in self-contained communities. They live in wooden, one-and-a-half-story residences surrounded by shade trees, flowers, and large, well-kept gardens and orchards. Holstein cows graze on improved pastures. Large families travel in horse-drawn wagons and enclosed buggies. An occasional car can be seen driving on slightly elevated, colony-built roads, leaving behind a cloud of dust. Dotting the area are plain, rectangular buildings surrounded by shade trees and serving as the school or church, or both.

While the Chaco colonies have a capital where businesses and residences are concentrated, the Mexican colonies remain rural in character. Both the church and the school are under the direction of the Ältesten. The Oberschulze is not as prominent in the Mexican colonies.

Old Colony Mennonites do not have their own hospitals. Births are attended by midwives. Major illnesses are treated in regional Paraguayan hospitals and, in rare cases, in Asunción. Teachers are seldom trained above the level they are teaching. The colony has no police and no bank. Only Durango colony has a cooperative. Many, except the Älteste, carry cell phones.

Like Bergthal and Sommerfeld, the Mexican colonies in Paraguay and Bolivia have a distinct appearance. A visitor driving through a Mennonite colony notices the uniformity of the farmsteads, fences, and fields.

Old Colony Convictions

Rather than compromise their convictions, the Old Colony people have demonstrated their ability to relocate thousands of their members across national boundaries and make a completely new beginning without outside help. Those of us outside the colonies may differ with them over theology and the Christian's place in the world, but the willingness of these Mennonites to uphold their convictions at almost any price speaks to us. It is both their genius and their nemesis.

Old Colony Values

- Because of their dour exterior, quaint dress, and outdated ways, Old Colony people are often misunderstood. Their ideals are not available for examination on the internet but can best be read in the lives of their members.

- They strive to live by God's commands as based on a literal interpretation of Scripture. Their few printed sources include, in addition to the Bible and songbook, the *Fibel*, the historic *Katechismus* (which children are required to memorize), the *Martyrs Mirror*, and the writings of Menno Simons.

- They regard the world as evil and as a distraction from the Christian calling, which is why they live in isolated communities, separated from the world.

- They believe in doing things communally. They practice mutual aid among themselves and look after their own seniors, orphaned children, and physically and mentally handicapped members. Their mantra is "the common good above personal gain."

- They value tradition and continuity. The Älteste promises to uphold the traditions of the fathers. This makes adopting new ways of thinking or new technology difficult, if not impossible. It sometimes handicaps them in their farming and transportation, but the faithful willingly pay this price.

- They value their children as transmitters of the faith. Arguably, they have a better track record of retaining their youth than their more progressive cousins. That is why education is so important to them and why they feel so strongly about controlling their schools.

- They value pragmatism and hard work. There is no place for fantasy, pretense, or laziness. Young and old are expected to contribute according to their ability.

- They value humility. Pride and ostentation distract from community and are antithetical to their values.

- They value discipline. Children are expected to obey their parents; wives are subject to their husbands; pupils obey their teachers. Everyone is subject to the Ältesten and the Ohms.

People outside the community often look quizzically at the Old Colony Mennonites. Through the perspective of their postmodern conformity, they wonder,

- Why this perpetual moving about, leaving small graves behind?
- Why live so isolated in segregated communities?
- Why the quaint, uncomfortable clothing in the tropics?
- Why this stubborn insistence on the German language?
- Why perpetuate an antiquated education system?
- Why the harsh ban, which divides the community and even families?
- Why all this splintering? Why can't peace-loving Mennonites resolve their differences without bad feelings and divisions?
- Where to next? Isn't the world running out of isolated enclaves where quarreling Mennonites fleeing modernity can spread out?
- What is the future? Will the system eventually cave in on itself?

These questions are valid, but they are questions *outsiders* ask. Amid all these seeming threats and contradictions within the Old Colony is a peculiar blend of stubbornness and *Gelassenheit* (yieldedness). This results in an unexplained confidence growing out of simple faith in the providence of God and a long history of overcoming obstacles.

When the Mennonites from every tribe and nation gather for the Mennonite World Conference in Asunción in July 2009, Old Colony people likely will be quietly tending their gardens and fields. They are Mennonite by another definition.

8

Swiss Mennonites and Amish Colonies

Our story of Mennonites in Paraguay has thus far concentrated on two Mennonite streams: those often referred to as Dutch-Low German, and Russian. This chapter reaches into the Swiss stream, whose numbers in Paraguay are comparatively small. But similarities to the Russian stream are apparent.

Persecution drove Dutch followers of Menno Simons first to Prussia, for several hundred years, then to Russia before scattering. Swiss Mennonites, by contrast, led by such young radicals as Conrad Grebel, Felix Manz, and Georg Blaurock, were driven by persecution high into the Alp valleys. Later they came to reside in eastern France and Germany before immigrating to the New World and settling in Pennsylvania.

Both Swiss and Russian Mennonites have had their struggles with tradition and separation from the world. When unable to resolve internal differences, both communities tended to splinter. A major division for Swiss Mennonites occurred in 1693, when a group led by Jakob Amman separated itself from the main branch to become what is today known as the Old Order Amish.

While Russian Mennonites were still expanding their holdings in Prussia in the late eighteenth century, Swiss Mennonites and Amish were among the first to accept William Penn's offer to join the new colony in Pennsylvania. When, after a few generations, land in the new colony became scarce or unaffordable, or perhaps out of wanderlust, some followed the westward frontier to Ohio, Indiana, Illinois, Iowa, and Kansas, then later California and Oregon. In the 1800s, they moved north to Ontario.

Mennonites and Amish always selected the best farmland to support their agrarian way of life. Those who were more progressive eventually found a place within or alongside the American or Canadian mainstream. Today they constitute Mennonite Church USA and Mennonite Church Canada, the Mennonite Brethren, and numerous smaller Mennonite conferences and denominations.

The Amish willingly pay a high price for their convictions and traditional way of life. Whereas Dutch-Low German and Russian Mennonites escaped pressures to conform to their surroundings by emigrating, Swiss Mennonites and Amish found ways to maintain their lifestyle while surrounded by "the world." Both traditions hold onto a distinct language: Pennsylvania German for Amish and Conservative Mennonites, Plautdietsch for Russian Mennonites.

Swiss Mennonites Discover Paraguay

In the twentieth century, urbanization and inflation drove land prices up in the United States, making it unaffordable for many young families to continue farming. Population pressures and zoning restrictions interfered with their quiet, rural way of life. Many put up with it, but other began looking for a quiet corner of the globe, where they could live with less distraction. Their search led them to consider Paraguay.

Though unrest within the Amish community was widespread, the mass migration that some predicted never materialized. Whereas the Russian Mennonites moved in large groups referred to as colonies, Swiss Mennonite and Amish movements to Paraguay were in small numbers. This, some postulate, has proven to be a limitation. Since 1967, there have been essentially three unrelated initiatives.

Old Order Amish

In 1967 eight Old Order Amish families purchased the Fernheim village of Wüstenfeld vacated by families who immigrated to Canada, for fifteen thousand dollars. In 1969 they also purchased the village of Schönau. The Amish families assumed all the obligations and privileges of Fernheim colony except, at their insistence, they retained control of their schools and churches.

It did not go well. Their numbers remained small; they had some internal disputes; and the interface with Fernheim colonists was disappointing. This was due in part to cultural differences and the lack of a common language. The final blow came when the Amish realized that their first objective, to control their youth, had not been achieved. After ten hard years, they sold their interests back to Fernheim colony and relocated, some to East Paraguay and the rest returning to the United States.

Beachy Amish

Beachy Amish had separated from the Old Order Amish in 1927 over differences, including how strictly the ban should be enforced. In the 1960s, the Beachy Amish community in and around Plain City, Ohio, was having a dispute with the state over highway safety requirements. When their dispute reached an impasse, twenty-four families began looking for a new place to live.

The decision coincided with the plans of one of their members, Paul Eichorn, who wanted to find a place to raise Korean orphans in a protected environment. While en route to investigate Paraguay, Eichorn stopped over in El Salvador and met John Mast, who was serving there under the Amish Mennonite Association (AMA). The Mast family later joined Eichorn in Paraguay, drawing AMA into the Paraguay adventure.

Their search for land led them to East Paraguay. A group of Ohio investors purchased a 5,000-acre tract from Sommerfeld colony that they subdivided into 250-acre tracts and invited families to join. A few did, but not as many as anticipated.

To serve the surrounding indigenous and Paraguayan neighbors and to care for the Korean orphans they were expecting, they established the Luz y Esperanza (Light and Hope) clinic. Dedicated and resourceful nurses, some of whom came and continue to come in rotation from supporting AMA congregations, directed the clinic.

The twenty-four Ohio families, it turns out, never immigrated to Paraguay. The agreement with Korea was canceled, so no children were ever received. But in the meanwhile, a clinic had been established that proved to be an excellent way for the Beachy Amish to introduce themselves to the surrounding community. Word spread, and soon patients were arriving. The staff treated all manner of diseases and provided maternity and emergency services. Their facilities and abilities were often overtaxed, but serving people and sharing their faith had its rewards.

Expectant mothers arrived on foot or by oxcart. In one six-month period, six sets of twins were born. A 2004 report reveals that 11,247 babies had been born at the clinic in thirty-five years. To provide a stream of income, this largely self-supporting group created a seventy-four-acre farm and populated it with chickens and cows. Later they added a butcher shop and a small furniture factory. As more families joined, including some of the families from the Chaco, and as they gained converts, they expanded to a neighboring location called Florida. Their method of evangelism is based on living their testimony in quiet and authentic ways. Love transcends language limitations and cultural differences.

The community meets on Sunday for worship in both locations. Services are conducted in Spanish, English, and Guaraní. Seekers are welcome, and converts are invited to become full members. The combined Sunday-morning attendance exceeds two hundred. Of the membership of one hundred, more than half are Latino Paraguayans.

Conservative Mennonites

Paul Hollingshead was the first to move to Paraguay with his family from Snyder County, Pennsylvania, in 1969. Hollingshead, of Quaker background, anticipated that more families would follow from the conservative group that split from Lancaster Mennonite Conference. The physical appearance of this group is similar to the Beachy Amish—some of the men have beards and the women wear head coverings and long skirts.

They "let themselves down" in the Agua Azul area and were joined by some families from Bergthal colony. The mission venture grew through evangelistic outreach and through immigration from the United States, although not as many as initially anticipated. This led in 1975 to the establishment of a daughter colony, Rio Corrinentes. The colonists supported themselves with farming and later by offering mechanical services.

In the early 1980s, internal conflicts led to a split, resulting in an appeal to the Mennonite Messianic Mission (MMM) of the Eastern Pennsylvania Mennonite Church. The mission has been relocated from Agua Azul to La Montana near Encarnacion on the Argentine border.

Sadness came to the La Montana community in 1999 when Benjamin E. Shank, a young father, was murdered. The culprit was apprehended, but the Shank family and church community asked that his life be spared. This totally unheard-of request came to the attention of the press. When asked to explain such undeserved forgiveness, the bereaved family answered simply, "Everything is in God's hand. . . . What has happened has happened. We have forgiven the murderer because we are Christians." This powerful witness to their Anabaptist faith led to a prison ministry.

In 2007 the MMM consisted of three outposts: La Iglesia Arroyo Claro, with five Paraguayan and two American households; La Montaña de la Fe with twenty-two Paraguayan and seven American households; and Varana, with fourteen Paraguayan and five American households. Six families and four singles are on full MMM support, with a few others on partial support.

These three Old Order settlements have some interaction with each other, but they remain separated from the Russian Mennonite colonies. This is partially due to geographic and linguistic barriers but also to cultural and historic differences. They do not belong to Comité Social y Económico Mennonita, although they benefit from some of its services. They frequent the Mennonitenheim in Asunción, which provides some opportunity for interaction. Mennonitenheim, first called MCC Heim, was for many years the spiritual and social center for Paraguay's Mennonites. It was a guesthouse for visitors, and in its early years a residence for colony women working in Asunción.

The Amish and Swiss Mennonites colonies have been unable to grow as large as other colonies in Paraguay. The expected mass exodus of Amish and conservative Mennonites from the United States has not happened. Meanwhile, land prices have increased substantially. Evangelistic efforts have attracted some Latino Paraguayans, but they are handicapped by language and customs unique to the Amish and conservative Mennonites and foreign to Paraguayan culture.

Like the Russian Mennonites, Swiss Mennonites and Amish in Paraguay are buoyed by the conviction that they are doing God's will and contributing to the building of God's kingdom.

9

The Indigenous People

"Generally speaking," wrote W. Barbrooke Grubb in 1889, "these people, since the discovery of South America by the Spaniards, have remained unchanged—a race of savages, a nomadic people, who have left no permanent remains behind them, no cities, temples, or even burial mounds."

Nothing could have prepared the Enlhet people for the sudden arrival of Mennonites. Some had seen white people before, having watched Casado build a railroad many kilometers long to pull valuable quebracho trees out of the Chaco for export to Europe. Some older Enlhet remembered stories about Grubb, a white Anglican missionary who spent years living with them. He too was friendly and talked about God in ways they could not understand. Some had presumably met the blue-eyed Norwegian American Fred Engen, who led several expeditions into the Chaco. But the real-life drama they were now witnessing was beyond their comprehension.

A caravan of more than a hundred ox-drawn wagons brought white Canadians to establish Menno Colony. It must have felt like an invasion to the Enlhet. Before nightfall, these strange people had set up tents, and the next day they were everywhere looking for timber to build houses. They dug for water where the Enlhet knew there was none. Before long there were fences where only several moons earlier they had hunted ostrich, tapir, nutria, or otter.

Just as the Enlhet were adjusting to the first white settlers, a second bigger wave arrived—thousands of them. These were the founders of Fernheim colony. Everything about them was strange—their clothing, their food, and their language.

The colonists were friendly but distant, and they were surprised to find indigenous people on the land they had purchased. Mostly the colonists were busy building houses and planting gardens. What were the implications for Enlhet people, who must have wondered at the intentions of the white people taking possession of land the Enlhet had for generations called home?

The Enlhet had survived frequent wars with indigenous rivals looking to increase the size of their herds or for women to populate their clan. To avenge an old grudge, they left behind ashes where Enlhet huts had stood. But the Enlhet had never been conquered; they were always able to escape into the Chaco, which to their pursuers was a formidable trap.

Mutual Accommodation

Neither the Enlhet nor the *Lencos*, as the Enlhet called Mennonites, had a map to guide their bicultural encounter. They didn't share a common language; they met only on the common ground of their humanity. They viewed each other initially with curiosity, later with suspicion, but never with hostility. Enlhet learned Plautdietsch; some Mennonites learned Enlhet. At Mennonite insistence, the indigenous wore Mennonite clothing and shoes instead of sandals. On Sunday a shirt or blouse came to replace a bare upper. Both communities struggled to survive the hostile environment with which they were surrounded.

The indigenous people helped Mennonites find timber to build houses. They generously invited Mennonites to "shop" in their "supermarket," the bush, where they found berries, honey, and meat to enrich their diet. In turn, the Enlhet acquired a taste for Mennonite food. Bread and potatoes replaced wild fruit from the bush. Enlhet helped Mennonites find lost cattle and, on occasion, children who wandered into the bush.

Though very different, the white invaders appeared to the Enlhet as peaceful, as Engen had promised. By all appearances, they intended to stay. The Enlhet were a semi-nomadic people, but they aspired to do things they saw Mennonites doing.

Mennonites were undecided how to respond to this surprise encounter. Before long, the Enlhet asked the Mennonites for food to feed hungry families. The Fernheim colonists came to see their "brown neighbors," as they called the Enlhet, as part of God's creation and imbued with an eternal soul.

At the first anniversary of their arrival, Fernheim colonists gathered for a harvest festival, though the harvest had been meager. In addressing the gathering, Ältester Isaak pleaded, "Who is prepared to enter this open field [of mission]? Where are the laborers?" An offering of 690 pesos—about five dollars—was taken. A committee of interested people representing all three Fernheim Mennonite churches was elected and given the task of carrying the mission forward. The mission seed had been planted.

W. Barbrooke Grubb (1865-1930), an Anglican missionary in the Chaco.

Mission Delayed

For years Enlhet and Mennonites looked on as the Bolivian army built one *fortine* (base) after another along a presumed but undefined border. Soon Paraguayans were doing the same and stocking the outposts with weapons. Indigenous people alerted Mennonites to the danger of war, but Mennonites were so busy getting established they did not take notice until schoolchildren saw gun-carrying Bolivian soldiers. They were frightened and wondered what it all meant. Before long the forgotten Chaco was the scene of a war that lasted from 1932 to 1935.

Both armies sought to benefit from the Enlhet knowledge of the Chaco. When Paraguayan soldiers asked Enlhet where the Bolivian army was camping, the indigenous people told them. They did the same when Bolivian soldiers asked where the Paraguayan army was located. Eventually both armies came to view the Enlhet as spies and traitors and shot them on sight. Mennonite families sheltered many Enlhet—saving their lives at some risk to themselves. To escape the war, Enlhet retreated to the geographic fringes of the Chaco.

Bolivia suffered 65,000 casualties (2 percent of its population) and spent 228 million dollars on the war. Paraguay had 36,000 casualties (3.5 percent of its population) and spent 124 million. No one knows how many Enlhet lives were lost. To avoid being detected by a crying

An early encounter between Fernheim Mennonites and Enlhet in 1930.

baby and not wanting to raise children under these conditions, Enlhet parents allowed very few children and almost no girls to survive after birth during the war years. Infanticide combined with war deaths and disease almost decimated the Enlhet population. When sitting around their campfires or in their feasts, they began to question if they had a future as a people.

Surviving the war together laid a foundation for more intimate relationships between Mennonites and Enlhets.

Mission Planning Resumes

On the last day of the Chaco War, June 12, 1935, a roomful of Fernheim colonists met to pray and ask for divine guidance. On September 17, 1935, ninety-seven members representing all three Fernheim Mennonite churches organized the new mission, named Licht den Indianern (Light to the Indians). They identified their objectives as

- to acquaint Indians with the word of God;
- to education children and instruct adults about Christian family life;
- to promote better health;

- to help Indians become economically self-sufficient and to be good Paraguayan citizens.

Lord of the Harvest, Send Forth Laborers

The family of Abram and Anna Ratzlaff, along with Abram Unger, all from the Fernheim villages known as Harbiner Ecke, left their little farmsteads to pioneer this new mission. They were joined later by the Gerhard B. and Katharina Giesbrecht family. Responding to the mission call meant starting over, but this time with support from brothers and sisters.

Their first difficult decision was to find a suitable location for the mission. When they were unable to find water at their first choice, Sepe Lhama, who later became their first convert, advised them to consider the open grassland called Yalve Sanga. A lagoon there never dried up, it was said, and Yalve Sanga emerged as the fourth Mennonite capital in the Chaco.

Learning an unwritten language was by far the hardest challenge facing the new missionaries. Gerhard Giesbrecht spent night after night around Enlhet campfires, happy if after some hours he had added one Enlhet word to his vocabulary. Eventually he was able to tell Bible stories in elemental Enlhet, but without visible results. In reporting to supporters on his first ten years, Giesbrecht said, "Preaching to the Enlhet is like talking to a stone."

More Mennonites

In 1947 came what the indigenous people must have seen as another Mennonite invasion. More strange, peace-loving people—Russian refugees. After the Neuland colony spread out, the territory for the indigenous people to hunt and harvest had shrunk even further. Yet they helped their new Lenco neighbors build houses and plant gardens, though the Mennonites were unable to pay them immediately, even with food or clothing.

One morning Anna Ratzlaff was alone in her simple Yalve Sanga house when two indigenous people startled her by appearing at her open window. She knew from their appearance that they were not Enlhet. With the familiar palm on stomach motion and mournful look, they conveyed that they were hungry. She gave them something to eat, and they went on their way. Later it was learned that these two had been Nivaclé, sent to spy out the land.

The Nivaclé people lived along the Pilcomayo River separating Paraguay from Argentina. Whereas Enlhet drew their sustenance from the bush, the Nivaclé harvested fish from the river. They had already been introduced to Christianity by the Catholic Church and through Pentecostal preaching.

The Nivaclé spies reported, "A new kind of white people. They have white skin, even white eyes and hair, and no weapons."

At first it was just a trickle, then whole clans of Nivaclé came in waves, accompanied by herds of sheep and goats. The Mennonites were overwhelmed. They knew it meant learning another language and getting acquainted with another culture. It also meant offering work and food at a time when they did not have enough for their own families. Mennonites might be able to help some families seasonally, but how could they assume responsibility for an entire clan? Breaking the clan up into family units created other problems.

The Mennonites' motivation for reaching the Enlhet with the gospel applied no less to the Nivaclé. They prayed for guidance. They also appealed to and were later joined by the Mennonite Brethren Mission, headquartered in Kansas.

Women's Work

Negotiations between Mennonites and the indigenous people were always man to man. Women were, one report noted, "left to sit on the side and look on like Egyptian mummies." Later it was learned that in indigenous culture, women were accustomed to a strong role in family decision making. Failure to recognize the role of women and other authentic leaders proved to be a serious flaw in the early Mennonite dealings with indigenous people.

A Breakthrough

Ten years after initiating the mission, Gerhard Giesbrecht was riding through the open savannah with his translator, Sepe Lhama, when Sepe asked, "May I be baptized?" Gerhard was dumbfounded. Was this the moment many had long been working and prayed for? After a lengthy pause, Gerhard asked, "When did you become a Christian?" Sepe replied, "Yes, that day when my wife betrayed me, and I was fleeing in disgrace as

Gerhard Giesbrecht baptizes seven Enlhet men in a lagoon near Filadelfia on February 24, 1946. It was the first baptism resulting from missionary work in the Chaco.

my Enlhet culture demands. You overtook me and we knelt in the grass to pray, you in German and I in Enlhet. There I had a change of heart. I told God I would follow him. I believe that since that day Jesus had forgiven my sins. My heart was filled with joy and thanksgiving."

Gerhard was pleased beyond words at the breakthrough, which had come after many years of work by Gerhard and his entire family. Yet, surprisingly, he was not prepared to fulfill Sepe's request. Sepe would be welcomed as a child of God, without a doubt. But accept a "brown one" as a brother in the Lord? An aboriginal Mennonite? That required more processing.

Before Gerhard and the Mennonite church leaders could come to a conclusion, six more young Enlhet men presented themselves for baptism. Gerhard was commissioned to conduct an abbreviated catechism, after which a public baptism was planned. Expecting that many Mennonites would want to attend, the leaders decided to hold an open-air service at the Filadelfia lagoon on February 24, 1946. Nikolai Siemens, secretary of Licht den Indianern, described it with the following picturesque words:

> It was a beautiful Sunday morning. People were streaming in from all directions, beginning already in the early morning hours.

> Even the largest meetinghouse could not have accommodated half the people who were present. There stand the whites in a huge circle, while the brown families are in the center with the seven candidates dressed in white under the blue Paraguayan sky.

Ältester Isaak captured the spirit of the moment by reading Psalm 118:23, "This is the Lord's doing; it is marvelous in our eyes" (RSV). The candidates responded to the customary questions with a clear, affirmative answer, whereupon Gerhard baptized them by immersion. A new era in this uncharted multiethnic journey had begun.

Tragedy Follows Elation

The Enlhet had for years warned Mennonites that the indigenous Ayoreo were dangerous. One noonday in 1947, without provocation, Ayoreo warriors swooped down on the family of Paul Stahl, brutally killing him and his three daughters, and injuring their mother. It drove fear into the Mennonite and indigenous communities.

Mission-minded Mennonites were troubled that in 1958 the Ayoreos had not been reached with the gospel. After earnest prayer, Enlhet warnings notwithstanding, they decided to brave a friendly, albeit risky, encounter. A delegation consisting of Mennonite missionaries and Enlhet pastors, including Sepe Lhama, was organized. Following a brief presentation of gifts, a young Ayoreo warrior speared missionary Kornelius Isaak, fatally wounding him. The entire community was in shock. Many Enlhet joined with Mennonites in a well-attended funeral at which the theme was "Love suffers long." Many years later New Tribes Mission undertook a mission to the Ayoreos that resulted in an evangelical congregation of about three hundred members.

Menno Colony Joins In

Though Menno colony was established in the Chaco three years before Fernheim, it did not respond to its indigenous neighbors in a missional way for many years. True to their Old Colony tradition, their initial relationship was one of peaceful coexistence. When Menno colony purchased the sixty-three leguas of land that became known as South Menno, they encountered Toba and Sanapaná Indians. Kazique (chief) Antonio described the coming of the Mennonites:

> We heard the Mennonites come in large numbers with their wagons, drawn by oxen, horses and mules. They settled in the shade of a tree. Our people went to look. They gave us beans, kafir and flour and other food for which we were grateful. Our people were happy and satisfied that the whites had come. No one was in opposition.

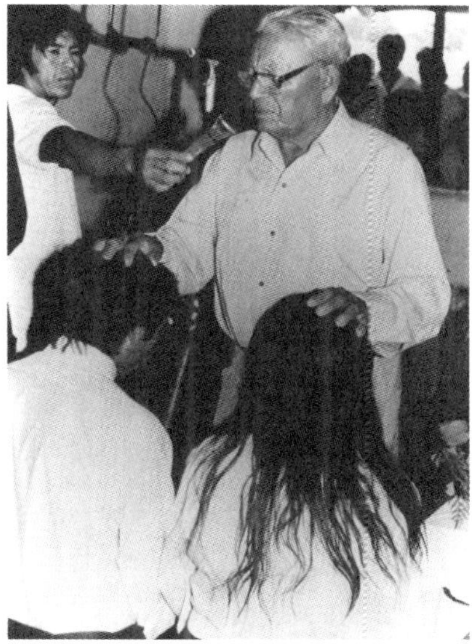

Sepe Lhama, first Lengua Indian convert and long-time pastor.

Two mission-minded members of Menno colony, Johann M. Funk and Bernard W. Toews, felt similarly drawn to undertake a mission. Their work led to the 1955 establishment of the Menno-Indianer Mission (MIM). MIM was joined by the Canadian Evangelical Mennonite Conference for a time, but in 1991 this effort was folded into MIM. The mission initiative led to formation of the Convención Evangelica Unida with fourteen indigenous congregations.

'Twas a Beginning

Both the indigenous and the Mennonite communities progressed in their ability to make a future for themselves in the ill-reputed Chaco. More than coexistence, it was a peaceful relationship of mutual if unequal helpfulness. Both cultures advanced toward a future known only to God.

But both communities would require much more work and forbearance. There would be disappointments and misunderstandings, but the uncharted journey was underway. The indigenous people had, in the providence of God, entered the Mennonite world. Mennonites had entered the indigenous world. The story continues in part 3, where a third stream joins them, the Latino Paraguayans.

Part 2
How They Prospered

Part 1 described how Mennonites came to Paraguay from Russia, Canada, and the United States and how indigenous people they encountered received them. Part 2 concentrates on how Mennonites came to prosper in their new surroundings.

By the 1960s, death, retirement, and emigration had purged the ranks of the pioneer generation. Wrinkled and weather beaten, some took what they could and left for a better life in Canada or Germany. A new generation of Paraguayan Mennonites, with a more optimistic outlook on their environment, was emerging.

But it was not a straight line upward. More families would yet conclude that Paraguay was not for them, leaving behind empty farmsteads, broken relationships, and unfulfilled dreams. This land still wore people down, discouraging them.

But gradually people adjusted their expectations, and sometime in the 1960s, life became easier. At first improvement was imperceptible. But almost five decades later, first-time visitors to a Mennonite colony ask in amazement, "How is this possible?" Some refer to it as a miracle, and they wonder about the "Mennonite secret."

In a year of sabbatical studies at Cornell University, I interviewed Professor Polemann, the resident expert on colonization. I led off by asking him to summarize what he had learned in his lifelong study of colonization. After taking time to light his pipe, he said cryptically, "Only learned one thing. Only Mennonites know how to do it." I was taken aback that he even knew about Mennonites. I asked him what he thought the Mennonite secret was? After a long drag on his pipe, he said, "Answering that would take another lifetime."

The interview was essentially over, but it helped me to see Mennonite colonization through other eyes. If successful colonization is defined by survival, Mennonite colonization in South America, with the Paraguay experience serving as an exhibit, has indeed been inordinately successful.

Is there a Mennonite "secret"? Why were Mennonites able to extricate themselves from what appeared to be the jaws of extinction? Most Mennonites are not comfortable talking about success. This is more than modesty; it is a recognition that, though they have worked hard, the "success" is not their doing alone. The effort rides on the wings of God's blessings.

Mennonites also know that success can be temporary. They are ever mindful of their experience in Russia, where life was so favorable before going sour. Paraguayan Mennonites are only too aware that they live in a nation where few presidents have completed their terms and where inflation and security are constant worries.

In part 2, we examine the factors that helped Paraguay Mennonites prosper and that lay the groundwork for a giving-back stage, which we look at in part 3.

10

Church

A Spiritual Foundation

"Next to the family," wrote J. Winfield Fretz in *Pilgrims in Paraguay*, "the church affects the lives of more colony people than any other organization. It is commonly the first organization to appear in a settlement; in fact, it is generally the organization sponsoring a new settlement."

Church and Christian faith indisputably helped Mennonites overcome the challenges that greeted them in Paraguay. Reasons for this include the following:

- The church is a unifying force and contributes to group solidarity.
- The church lays an ethical foundation for the larger community by teaching biblical values such as honesty, hard work, and above all, love of neighbor.
- The church serves as the conscience of the colony and helps bring balance to the materialistic and secular tendencies inherent in all human institutions.
- The church teaches and practices mutual aid, whereby the strong help the weak, making it possible for all to survive.
- The church serves as a social coordinator where friends meet each other.
- The church brings a transcendental dimension to the harsh realities of pioneer living and invokes a divine blessing on the effort.

Church was important to all the Mennonites who came to Paraguay, although it took a variety of forms. Those who came from Manitoba and Saskatchewan in 1927 and 1948 brought a stable and meaningful church experience in the Old Colony tradition. They mostly continued what they had known in Canada, which was not much different from what their ancestors had done in Russia.

The worship routines of those coming from Russia in 1930 and 1947 had been disrupted by revolution and war. Members of the Neuland and Volendam colonies spent years roaming around Europe as refugees before coming to Paraguay. People under age thirty had never known a meaningful church life. When they arrived in Paraguay, they had to get acquainted with each other before they could create a meaningful congregational life, something with which they themselves were not well acquainted.

Birthing a Church on the Frontier

[The following is based on an account in the Neuland twenty-fifth anniversary book.]

In the Paraguayan autumn of 1947, Hans Rempel and Bernard Neufeld, recent World War II émigrés and now Neuland colony pioneers, were conversing, in Plautdietsch no doubt, about the topics of the day. How is it in your village? Are the families living in their houses yet, or are they still in temporary shelters? Is the school or church building completed? Are there enough teachers to go around? Are they planting gardens? What is the mood of the people? Are they *mootich* (courageous, energetic)? Any deaths, births, accidents, or word from relatives in Russia or Canada?

Then a pause. Both were thinking the same thought but hesitated to say it. Finally one ventured, "Sent wie nu so wiet?" (Are we now that far?) "Has life in our newly established Neuland colony reached that point?" "That point" made reference to the words of their Ältester Heinrich Winter as they were departing from Germany, urging them to establish a church in their midst. But how?

Church had been an integral part of their upbringing in Russia. But all that ended thirty years earlier with the revolution closed the churches and disrupted their lives. They simply did not know how to do church, and they did not know each other, having come from different communities.

Neufeld and Rempel searched their memories for someone who might be able to help. They thought of Klaus Wiebe, who had come from a Russian village where the churches had been permitted to stay open longer. Maybe he could help.

After asking around, they learned where Wiebe lived. On borrowed horses, they rode to his village through the open Chaco countryside. They got lost, but after a few inquiries found Wiebe working on his almost-completed house. After the usual greetings, they stated their mission and asked for his help. Wiebe listened but said nothing. They noticed his eyes fill with tears as he rose and went to his chest of "valuables." He found his German Bible and sought out a verse of Scripture.

Unable to locate it, he closed his Bible, folded his hands on it, and with a distant look paraphrased the verse from memory: "In the establishment of your church, let the word of God be your plumbline."

They knew what needed to be done, but how? Some had Bibles, but there were almost no songbooks. That did not matter; they knew the old favorites from memory. Who were the song leaders in their midst? How many were even interested in church, after all they had been through?

It was clear, they needed to invite the entire Neuland colony to an organizational meeting. But there was no meetinghouse that could hold even a fraction of the people. The village Neuendorf was deemed to be central. Katharina Enns, a widow, volunteered her small, uncompleted house. Fervent prayers were offered for good weather for their open-air meeting and for good participation.

The big day came. The sun had not risen high when people began arriving, some on foot, some in ox-drawn conveyances. It was March 7, 1948. Rempel, Neufeld, and Wiebe welcomed the gathered body, some sitting in the shade of the bush, others standing in the hot sun. After introducing themselves, perhaps singing a song or two from memory, they proceeded to recall the conversation with Ältesten Winter in Germany. Then all three gave testimonies to faith in Jesus Christ and expressed a desire to be joined into a meaningful fellowship. All three signed an improvised membership book and invited the others to do so.

The pause was so long they began to wonder if anyone was interested. Finally Oberschulze Peter Derksen came forward, offered a moving testimony, and added his name to the membership book. Another pause followed.

Then they began to come. Soon a line of men and women formed, some as couples, sometimes just a mother with small children.

"That," the Neuland anniversary book notes, "was the beginning. A holy beginning in the middle of the wilderness, in the humble setting of an unfinished adobe and thatch house [by] people tortured in the time of persecution and flight. A quiet, holy peace rested over the service."

Within months they had a baptismal service, followed by communion. Seven years later the congregation had 694 members.

Affirmation for Pioneer Pastors and Leaders

Beset by their own struggles, pioneer preachers were challenged to find a word of promise and hope in Scripture to share with their congregation. Sometimes this was an admonition not to murmur like the children of Israel. Sometimes it was a reminder to give thanks for the freedom they were enjoying in this new land, with reminders of how their relatives were still suffering under Communism. Sometimes preachers were so hard pressed to find hope in this life, they spoke of longing for Christ's second coming.

These scarred veterans drew strength from each other as they sang the old hymns from memory, with the occasional tear trickling down their weather-beaten faces.

> Oh have you not heard of that beautiful stream that flows through our Father's land?
> Its waters gleam bright in the heavenly light, and ripples o'er golden sand.

And then that picturesque refrain, the music giving wings to the well-chosen words,

> O seek that beautiful stream, O seek that beautiful stream;
> Its waters, so free, are flowing for thee, O seek that beautiful stream.

In the spoken and sung word, in the love and support they felt from each other, they found strength to face another week.

Congregational Life Takes Many Forms

The Old Colony churches of Menno, Sommerfeld, Bergthal, and the Mexican colonies are under the strict leadership of the Ältester, who

At the front of Mennonitengemeinde in Filadelfia during a Harvest Festival in 1998, a horn of plenty displays fruits and vegetables grown locally.

is ordained for life and expected to uphold Old Colony traditions. Assisting him is a bench of Ohms and numerous deacons. Sermons are often read; some have been in existence for many generations. The church sanctuary is a plain, rectangular structure. Membership behavior and practices are prescribed and strictly enforced, through discipline if necessary. The harshest sanction is the ban, the purpose of which is to restore the member to full fellowship.

The progressive churches of Fernheim, Friesland, Neuland, Volendam, Tres Palmas colonies, and Asunción are a carryover from Russia. They have evolved in Paraguay and today resemble a rural church in Canada or the United States. Their church sanctuaries are attractive and functional, some seating more than one thousand people. Most have a salaried pastor who has some theological training or may even have a degree. They have choirs with instrumental accompaniment and Sunday school for children and adults. They engage in a variety of service and mission projects. Church discipline varies by congregation and somewhat by conference, but they do not practice the ban.

The large Menno Colony Chortitzer Gemeinde belonged originally to the Old Colony tradition. It functioned for its first fifty years as one congregation. By 1978, when the colony's population had grown to six thousand, it relaxed its hold on the Old Colony tradition and eased into what is known in Paraguay as Mennonitengemeinde, which had a loose affiliation with the former General Conference Mennonite Church—now Mennonite Church USA and Mennonite Church Canada.

The large Chortitza congregation was subdivided. The prohibition against singing in four-part harmony was lifted. Church governance became more participatory. In 2008 Menno colony had fifteen congregations. Four large, German-speaking churches in Loma Plata have a combined Sunday-morning attendance of almost five thousand. There is one Spanish-speaking congregation serving Paraguayans and, more recently, a growing guest-worker population, plus numerous indigenous congregations.

Since its founding in 1930, Fernheim colony has had three separate and distinct congregations: MG, MB, and Evangelisch Mennonitische Brudershaft, also known as the Alliance, for its failed attempt to reunite the other two. Though separate, the three congregations do things communally, including combined worship two Sundays a month.

Ten congregations in Filadelfia serve the German-speaking, indigenous, and Latino populations. There is also one Catholic Church and a small Pentecostal church.

The German-speaking populations of Friesland, Neuland, and Volendam each has a medium-sized MG and MB congregation. Each has its own building and Christian education and worship routine. They too do things communally. Some have Spanish-speaking daughter churches in surrounding Paraguayan villages.

Sommerfeld and Bergthal continue in the Old Colony tradition, although a quarter of Sommerfeld attends the more progressive Evangelishe Mennonitengemeinde. The Tres Palmas congregations, along with their mission outreach, are in the more progressive tradition.

Church is also an integral part of the mission outreach of churches in the Swiss tradition.

Church in the Indigenous Tradition

The indigenous people of the Chaco had a traditional religion. They lived in tribes, but church was new to them. As they gave up their seminomadic ways and settled in permanent communities and as they came to adopt Christianity, they were baptized and gathered into church fel-

Church and Colony Population by Colony in 2000

Colony	Population	Churches	Church Members	Percent*
Menno	8,812	14	4,871	55
Fernheim	3,947	6	2,244	57
Friesland	696	2	416	60
Neuland	1,637	2	766	47
Volendam	755	2	330	44
Tres Palmas	198	1	85	43
Asunción	1,320	2	582	44
Sommerfeld	2,612	2	1,070	41
Bergthal	2,098	2	867	41
Reinfeld	146	1	60	41
Rio Verde	3,108	2	1,309	42
Santa Clara	332	1	137	41
Neuvo Durango	1,822	1	613	33
Manitoba	628	1	251	40
Total	**28,111**	**39**	**13,601**	**48.6**

***The population figures includes nonbaptized persons, some of whom may not be of church membership age.**

lowships. The first indigenous church was located in Yalve Sanga. Later the settlement scheme included a church and a school in every village.

The church became the undisputed center of their new life. As indigenous people were drawn into the Christian faith, they came bit by bit to own the church. The church became the first modern institution they knew and claimed as their own.

The gospel presented the indigenous with a new ethic. It liberated them from superstitions and fears that were so much a part of their traditional way of life.

It also helped end the practice of infanticide. Mennonites were horrified when they learned that indigenous were suffocating infants they did not want or felt they were unable to care for adequately. It was their form of population control. Mennonites bribed the indigenous people with articles of clothing if they would allow their children to live. Mennonite families raised some indigenous infants, as illustrated in the story of Hans Teichrieb, as told by Wilmer Stahl:

> Hans was born to the family of Monte-í sometime in the late 1930s, in an Enlhet campsite outside of Gnadenheim. He was not received as a family member and, by decision of the women of the clan, he was set outside of the village to die. The father, Monte-í, knowing Mennonite interest in keeping Enlhet children alive and anxious to claim the one-thousand-peso prize offered by the missionaries, went to tell missionary Gerhard Giesbrecht about the infant's fate.
>
> Giesbrecht and Monte-í found Hans with little life left in him. They took him to the hospital, where head nurse, Susanna Isaak, nursed him back to health.
>
> Susy's search for adoptive parents led her to the Teichrieb family, who had 6 of their own children. Hans spent the first seven years, including the first two classes of primary school, in a Plautdietsch-Mennonite environment.
>
> When Licht den Indianern established an orphanage in Yalve Sanga, Hans was transferred there. Then he was adopted by the Juancitos, an Enlhet family without children. Here he learned the Enlhet language.
>
> While still in his teens Hans married a village girl, and became the father of six healthy children. He enlisted in an adult-education program and became proficient in Spanish, and later in mechanics, which helped him find employment.
>
> As an adult Hans was recognized as an Enlhet leader. For some fifteen years, on and off, he was the elected Oberschulze of his community of one thousand seven hundred Enlhet.
>
> Hans passed away in 1997 when he was approximately sixty years of age. In the eyes of his people he had been a great "leader" because he had managed to keep harmony with the surrounding white society.

The practice of infanticide ended as indigenous people adopted Christian ethics, contributing to an indigenous population explosion.

The indigenous church community, including Enlhet and Nivaclé, with a sprinkling of Guaraní and Ayoreo, now number about nine thousand members in thirty-nine churches. These congregations have their own buildings and pastors.

Many indigenous churches are now third-generation congregations. Their leaders have become very capable. The dialogue with other Mennonites is not as one-sided as it once was and promises to become increasingly challenging.

The indigenous people have created Federacion Regional Indigena del Chaco Central (FRICC), a forum in which they decide which cultural practices to retain and how to deal with the influences of modernity. FRICC has helped address a variety of issues, including relationships with the Mennonite community.

Like parents everywhere, parents of indigenous children are concerned about the next generation. Educated children sometimes fail to respect their more traditional and less educated parents. One Enlhet leader complained during an interview that his son refused to work and seemed to want only the "good life" portrayed on TV. As we left his modest house in mid-afternoon, there in the shade of a tree, with an improvised antenna, was his grown son, so absorbed in his TV that he took no notice of us.

Church in the Paraguayan Latino Tradition

Mennonite church-planting efforts in Paraguay began in the second generation. True to the believers church tradition, they did more than evangelize; they gathered converts and seekers into fellowships that

Sunday in the Colony

Sunday morning is a special time in a Mennonite colony. Stores have been closed since Saturday noon. Many churchgoers arrive in modern cars; a few walk, some shaded by an umbrella; a few arrive by bicycle. Some women wear the traditional bun, but most of the young sport modern hairstyles. All are dressed in their finest clothing. As they stream into church, some carry a Bible or a hymnbook. In summer, the church doors and windows are wide open, offering ventilation and an invitation to enter.

The service in the "progressive" German-speaking churches is much like a service in a Canadian or American church. Children sit with their parents; husbands and wives sit together. In the Old Colony churches, men sit to the preacher's right, women with small children to the left. The service includes congregational singing plus special music, often with piano, harp, or guitar accompaniment. There is a sermon, and most or all of it is in the German language.

Announcements help visitors be aware of the many facets of congregational life. The after-service reception is friendly but perfunctory; all have other things to do. They stand around briefly under shade trees—never in the direct sun—to greet and catch up with each other. In summer, drinking water is provided. Then they return to their homes to enjoy a quiet afternoon, perhaps visiting with friends in the evening.

became living organisms. This story is told in more detail in chapter 19, but suffice it to say here that by a recent count there were 126 Latino congregations totaling more than five thousand members with twice that number attending.

Founder	Congregations	Members
MB Gemeinde	69	3,000
MG Gemeinde	38	1,700
EMC	14	210
EMB	5	400
Total	**126**	**5,310**

Latino Mennonite churches are scattered throughout Paraguay, with a heavy concentration in Asunción. Converts are primarily from the working class and have a Catholic background, although Asunción congregations are attracting some middle and even upper-class members. This includes Gloria Penayo de Duarte Frutos, Paraguay's former first lady, who is a member of the Raises MB congregation.

Latino congregations are a valuable addition to the Mennonite mosaic. But theirs is church with a different dynamic. Whereas German and indigenous Mennonites live in colonies, Latino Mennonites are scattered in multiple communities. Their children attend public schools. Their jobs and vocations are varied. Church and a common faith are their main uniting influences.

The emerging Latino churches struggle with their missionary origins and their association with the German Mennonite image. While retaining their own cultural identity, and with a strong evangelical orientation, Latino Mennonites value their Anabaptist heritage and seek to adapt it to their setting. Their leaders have a contagious optimism of the future.

Not Homogeneous

Were it possible to gather all Paraguayan Mennonites in one assembly, they would be speaking ten languages. The members would represent a wide range of vocations and levels of socioeconomic achievement.

Even physically, some blond German-speaking Mennonites would tower over their dark-haired Spanish- and Guaraní-speaking Paraguayan brethren.

Most German speakers are Mennonite as far back as their ancestry can be traced. This is in sharp contrast to the indigenous and Latinos, who are first- and second-generation Mennonites. Some Paraguayan Mennonites eat zwieback, others tortillas. Some prefer lively music with harp or guitar accompaniment, while others draw strength from the *Kernlieder* Mennonites have enjoyed for centuries. Latino Mennonites prefer a lively church service that is in contrast to the German service, which is more staid. Mexican Mennonites move around in horse-drawn buggies while "modern" Mennonites drive expensive, bright-colored cars—all imported, some illegally.

The population of the Paraguayan Mennonite community is about sixty thousand people or 1 percent of the national population. It ranks ninth in Mennonite World Conference membership, ahead of Switzerland and Holland, the cradle of Mennonitism. In terms of national population density, according to calculations made by Gerhard Ratzlaff, only Belize exceeds Paraguay. As Alfred Neufeld has noted:

> The whole Mennonite zoo is present in Paraguay. Our different species are very beautiful and representative of God's creation. But we must find ways to communicate and relate and appreciate each other. For our own future together in Paraguay, we need to learn to say things to each other, based on our common faith.

11

Cooperatives
The Economic Engine

Were you to find yourself blindfolded in one of the three Mennonite colony supermarkets in the Chaco, you might hear Plautdietsch, German, Spanish, Enlhet, Nivaclé, Toba, Ayoreo, Portuguese, and perhaps an occasional word of English, maybe with a Canadian ending, "eh?" Were the blindfold lifted, you could go down a brightly lit aisle and see what you would see in an American or Canadian supermarket, including a refrigerated-meat section, lots of cereals, school supplies, candy, and checkout stations equipped with electronic scanners. You might find yourself in a long line behind a young mother with shorts or a middle-aged indigenous mustachioed man wearing a large sombrero with a chin strap for protection against the strong winds characteristic of the Chaco.

Just around the corner or up the street is a hardware store where you can buy anything from nails to a tractor complete with loader. You might think you were somewhere in California or Manitoba.

Today's cooperative store is a far cry from the *laufki* ("to run,"—the customer presented his or her needs to the clerk, who ran to fill the order) where the pioneers did their shopping. How did these stores progress from the primitive laufki of the pioneer days to the modern cooperative supermarket of today? This is another mustard seed story.

The Origin of Cooperatives

"Individual families stood helpless in front of the obstacles," wrote Peter P. Klassen of the colonies' early years in his book *Die Mennoniten in Paraguay*. Mennonite colonies were well organized. Each village had a *Shult* (leader); the colony had an Oberschulze. The church and school were under the direction of the Ältesten and the Ohms. The *Waisenamt* looked after orphans and widows and estate transfers. On occasions it also served as an unofficial bank, lending money it held in trust from estates. Yet something was clearly missing.

The need in this case was for an economic mechanism to help them do collectively what they were unable to do as individuals. This included a better supply line to and from Asunción. Distance simply made it impossible for the individual families to purchase essentials in far-away Asunción. There were times when the colony was completely out of something as basic as flour! Necessity, it is said, is the mother of invention.

This need was on the agenda when Orie O. Miller visited Fernheim in 1931. Miller was known by some as one of the first three Mennonite Central Committee workers to deliver food to Russia and saved many from starvation. Now he was a shoe salesman living in Akron, Pennsylvania. As Miller told it years later, he and colony leaders went out under the shade of a tree. They surveyed what was needed and then organized what they later learned was a cooperative. MCC sent an advance of five thousand dollars to provide operating capital.

In Klassen's assessment, "It was cooperation facilitated through the cooperative that made it possible for Fernheim to survive the narrow pass of its existence. It was the organ that permitted us to survive economic restructuring within Paraguay."

Functions Performed by a Cooperative

Colony members were not immediately favorably predisposed to cooperatives. Cooperatives reminded them too much of how they had suffered under Soviet centralized planning. But they came to see that cooperatives performed four essential functions for a pioneer community.

1. *Quantity purchasing*. The colonies were by design and necessity remarkably self-sufficient. They grew or made much of what they needed. Nevertheless, basic staples such as salt, thread, cloth stock, and nails could be purchased and shipped only from Asunción. The cooperative became the simple mechanism to purchase and ship these essential supplies in large quantities for resale in the colony.

2. *Marketing*. Mennonites were far removed from a market where

they could sell surpluses of perishables like eggs or cheese. They had to take what a buyer offered, which was not always more than the cost of freight. Only collectively, through a cooperative, were they able to afford the equipment and volume needed to make raw milk into cheese and yogurt and peanuts into cooking oil for the Asunción or export market.

To illustrate the delay in reaching the Asunción market and the heat for which Paraguay is known, it is alleged that what was thought to be a fresh egg in the Chaco was, by the time it reached Asunción, a hatched chick. My hesitation to believe the story was responded to with firm insistence that it is indeed true.

3. *Banking.* The colonies had no banking services in the early years. Currency was rare and optional; it was a barter economy. The cooperative became the colony bank. The value of something sold was credited to the member's account; purchases were debited. Later the cooperatives qualified for bank loans, which they reloaned to credit-worthy families, giving them leverage to better their lives.

This unique, informal banking function extended also to congregations. Instead of using currency, a contributor completed a simple form that was attached to the offering plate or available from an usher. On it the contributor recorded his or her co-op account number and the amount being contributed. On Monday the co-op bookkeeper credited the church account. It was so convenient, the practice continues in some churches even now that currency is available.

4. *Financing social services.* By adding a small margin to each co-op transaction (both buying and selling), the colonies gained funds to pay for their social services, including healthcare (such as it was in the early years), schools, and even a unique social-welfare function. Essentials like flour, lard, and coffee were always available through the cooperative, even for those who were unable to pay. The margin was a consumer tax of sorts.

In his book *El Derecho Cooperativo*, Antonio Bonzi wrote, "The secret weapon of Mennonite colonies is the cooperation between business through ethical principles and living out their religion."

Cooperative Prerequisites

Those leaders meeting under the shade of a tree on that hot afternoon may not have known the technicalities of the cooperative movement as it was then being popularized in the United States and Canada. But they

Abram Hiebert serves customers at the Menno colony co-op in the village of Reinland in 1939.

surely had a wealth of experience with cooperation. Cooperatives have been so successful for Mennonites because of how the two—the church and the cooperative—complement each other.

Caring for each other is central to Christ's teachings. Werner Franz, director of Centro Evangelico Mennonita de Teologia, the Mennonite seminary in Asunción, said in an address to a gathering anticipating the new millennium, "For many the cooperative became the institution that serves to give practical expression to the words of Jesus, 'Thou shalt love the Lord your God . . . and your neighbor as yourself." Or in Paul's words to the Galatians, "Bear ye one another's burden."

Franz observed that cooperatives and churches have similar functions and are organized similarly: both are predicated on strong member participation, both help members realize life's essentials, and both work to eliminate conflict and an excessive profit motive. "Conflict," it is said, "is death. Cooperation is life."

Membership in Mennonite cooperatives is automatically extended to all colony members and is available to serve everyone. This has given Mennonite co-ops the membership mass needed to be successful. Jesus' teachings and promises are similarly available to all—no one is excluded.

Finally, Franz reminded the members that a successful cooperative, like a well-functioning congregation, seeks the good of others. It is the vehicle by which its members practice the oft-quoted slogan *Gemeinnutz vor Eigennutz* (the common good ahead of personal gain).

Cooperatives in the Mennonite Model

The cooperative concept pioneered by Fernheim became the economic engine for Mennonite colonies. Members of Friesland colony objected to the centralization of power that they had experienced in Fernheim and experimented with alternatives. But within ten years they too adopted the Fernheim model. Volendam and Neuland were served by a cooperative from their earliest years. Bergthal and Sommerfeld colony members jointly own the large Lactolanda cooperative. Only one of the four Mexican colonies—Nueva Durango—has a cooperative.

Perpetuating the spirited competition Mennonite colonies have with each other, it is said that Menno colony has the largest co-op store, Fernheim the newest, and Neuland the nicest.

What began so innocently under the shade of a quebracho tree in the Chaco, borne of necessity, has mushroomed into a multimillion-dollar business, employing thousands of workers and serving tens of thousands of people. The cooperative has come to stand at the center of Mennonite economic life in Paraguay. The table below summarizes 2007 activity of the five colonies that are members of CSEM. (Six other Mennonite cooperatives are not members of CSEM, and their figures are not available.)

Cooperative	Members	Annual turnover, US dollars (millions)	Employees
Menno	4,178	$235	1,731
Fernheim	1,711	$153	1,600
Neuland	733	$60	330
Friesland	214	$27	116
Volendam	253	$22	98
Total	**7,089**	**$497**	**3,875**

Source: Berthold Penner of CSEM

An Indigenous Cooperative

When Helmut Giesbrecht retired as Oberschulze of Fernheim colony in 1986, he was appointed president of the Association of Indigenous-Mennonite Cooperation Services (ASCIM), a position he held until 2001. Previously he had managed the Fernheim cooperative. It did not take him long to conclude that if a cooperative was essential for Mennonite colonies, it was no less necessary for the growing indigenous settlements.

Giesbrecht foresaw a rapid increase in both the sales of indigenous surplus production and the purchases resulting from a rising standard of living. Indigenous transactions had to that point flowed through the

Fernheim cooperative based on a normal business arrangement that included a modest charge for handling. Under Giesbrecht's leadership Fundacion Indigena para el Desarrollo Agropecuario (FIDA) was organized to serve the indigenous communities. A loan from Mennonite Economic Development Associates provided the first operating capital.

FIDA's headquarters and large warehouse are located in Yalve Sanga. A warehouse is also maintained in Asunción to facilitate quantity sales and purchasing. Distribution is made to seventeen stores serving the indigenous settlements, which are interconnected by radio and now cell phone. The store records are reviewed and reconciled monthly.

Also at Yalve Sanga, FIDA has a heavy-machine rental and repair service and a tree and plant nursery. Seeds and chemicals can be purchased there at a reasonable price. It is also a place where indigenous farmers can get advice on livestock and crop diseases or other problems facing them.

FIDA administers a loan fund, contributed to by international organizations, permitting indigenous farmers to increase the size of their herds. The center also serves a valuable training function, such as in record keeping. Through FIDA, indigenous members pay less for what they buy, they get more for what they sell, and a small profit margin remains in their control.

Cooperatives for Others

Seeing the role cooperatives performed for Mennonite colonies led Kornelius Walde, then president of the Asunción based Comite Social Economico Mennonita (CSEM) to spearhead the establishment of Federacion de Cooperativas de Produccion (FECPROD), which serves thirty agricultural cooperatives, including five CSEM Mennonite cooperatives. It is a nonpolitical organization dedicated to benefiting farm families. Mennonite leaders view FECPROD as a way to share their experience with their Paraguayan countrymen.

New Challenges

Heinrich Dyck, long time president of CSEM, says, "Impressive as the role of cooperatives have been in history, their role is if anything increasing." Through cooperatives, Mennonites are able to achieve the volume of production necessary to function in an increasingly competitive environment.

In the early years, the Mennonite emphasis was on production. Over time the focus has broadened to include processing the raw product for sale to the public. In their earliest form, cooperatives extracted oil from peanuts and ginned cotton. Then they made milk into cheese and yogurt, and boxed it for sale throughout Paraguay. Now huge investments are being made to process and export meat. If national prosperity continues, light industrialization may develop.

Cooperatives are a multimillion-dollar business in which competition is stiff and profit margins are narrow. Cooperatives are increasingly involved in international trade, which increases their complexity. Inflation and hyperinflation are always lurking dangers. In the future, will the talent be there to manage these large enterprises? The best talent, some say, wants to own its own business, not work for wages.

Service to the wider community does not hold the attraction it once did. Gerhard Klassen, recently elected Oberschulze of Fernheim, decries the rise of egoism and expresses the fear that the motto *Gemeinnutz vor Eigennutz* is being inverted: instead of the common good above personal gain, it is becoming personal gain ahead of the common good.

Informed persons credit the cooperative with being a primary instrument in helping Mennonites to overcome the obstacles that faced them. Essential in that success was a spirit of community.

Whether that spirit will continue, or if individualism and personal ambition will replace it, will be determined in the next decade.

12

Roads

A Way Out of Isolation

When Mennonites arrived on the frontier, the bush greeted them. Beyond the bush was more bush and angry clouds. There were no roads, only paths that became impassable when it rained. There were no schools, stores, banks, not even a post office. The government of Paraguay had given what it had promised—freedom to order their lives—and little more.

The pioneers had a sense of community, but being isolated in the remote Chaco was proving to be a far greater handicap than anyone had anticipated. It is now possible to travel around the world twice in the time it took Mennonites to travel from the Chaco to Asunción. First they had to traverse 70 to 150 kilometers (43 to 93 miles) of bush with oxcarts while fighting off mosquitoes. Then it was 145 kilometers (90 miles) to Puerto Casado on the narrow-gauge railroad, which was intended for freight, not passengers. Finally it was 280 kilometers (174 miles) down the Paraguay River on primitive steamers with irregular schedules. A round trip required anywhere from five days to weeks.

Freight costs on goods to and from the Chaco were exorbitant. When shrinkage and pilferage were added to shipping costs, costs often approached or exceeded the value of the goods being transported.

Isolation was not only a formidable economic handicap; it also had an unanticipated demoralizing effect. The anxiety of a mother attending her seriously feverish child, knowing she was many hours removed from medical care and fearing that the illness would spread to her other children, can scarcely be imagined. Or consider the burden on the families of men who would be gone for weeks while hauling colony freight to and from the railroad terminus.

> **The Road to Nowhere: A Fable**
>
> A man left Neuland Colony with a team of oxen headed for Filadelfia. Wanting to escape the heat, he traveled at night. After putting the oxen on the trail, he laid down in his wagon, hoping to catch a little sleep. He expected to wake up in Filadelfia in the morning. So he meandered through the night in his improvised sleeping car at the will and pace of the oxen.
>
> Toward morning, he became aware of something he imagined might be another traveler. He sat up and in a husky voice yelled "Goade morje" (Good morning). There was no response, so he repeated his Plautdietsch greeting. But still there was no response. Meanwhile, it had gotten sufficiently light to reveal that the road was so crooked he had been shouting at his own back!

Mennonites were comforted in the early years with what they took to be a promise that Casado's railroad would be extended to the colonies. When that did not materialize, discouragement turned to anger. Mennonites were at the same time ambivalent about interaction with the world. Some were in fact attracted to the Chaco because of its isolation. This is still the position of Mexican Mennonites today.

In the late 1960s I asked a Chaco Oberschulze what he regarded as the greatest threat to his colony. I expected him to name drought or the then-critical situation with indigenous neighbors. After a brief pause he answered by pointing to a public bus that happened at that moment to be discharging Paraguayan passengers. Only Mennonites were permitted to reside in his colony.

By the 1950s Mennonites on both sides of the Paraguay River had concluded that something needed to be done to reduce their isolation. But all options appeared to be beyond their reach. They felt trapped.

A Way Is Found

In 1951, John Schmidt, a medical doctor, was addressing the Northern District Conference of the Mennonite Church. He had recently returned from Paraguay, where he had served as the first doctor

Wagons stuck in the mud was a familiar sight in the pioneer days.

in Filadelfia. In addressing the men's organization, Schmidt described the plight facing Paraguayan Mennonites, calling special attention to the need for better roads.

"So long as there are no roads, there is no hope to improve the economic situation," Schmidt said. The men listening were moved to raise money to buy a bulldozer.

Harry Harder, a gifted mechanic with road-building experience, volunteered his services. Volendam colony, then struggling to survive heavy emigration, was selected as the first beneficiary. Within months Harder constructed a 17-kilometer (11-mile) road from the river to the Volendam center. Then he bulldozed a 50-kilometer (32-mile) road from Rosario to Friesland, all the while training local men to succeed him. His nine-month term completed, Harder returned to his family in Mountain Lake, Minnesota, on Christmas Eve 1952, satisfied that a good beginning had been made.

In 1953 the Northern District Conference was again in session, this time in Riche, Montana, the home of Vern and Violet Buller. Again there was talk about Paraguay and the need for roads. Buller, a farmer, rancher, and ingenious unschooled engineer, was unable to sleep that night. "The Lord spoke to me in a kind of peculiar way," Vern, now retired, wrote from his Montana home. In the morning he volunteered their service.

During the following day and into the night the question kept reoccurring, "But with what?" Equipment would obviously be needed. Where would it come from? After prayer and conferring with each other, they heard God ask, "Why don't you give this [Caterpillar] to the colonies?" Later the Bullers upped the offer to include a bulldozer, two graders, a scraper, a Jeep, and twenty thousand dollars for spare parts.

This time the assignment was to connect the three Chaco colony capitals with each other and then with Casado's Endstation, a distance of 135 kilometers (84 miles). Buller, aided by some Mennonite Central Committee Pax workers and by Paraguayan Mennonites, converted wandering paths through the Chaco bush into straight roads with an elevated bed. It required ingenuity to contend with equipment breakdowns and soil that was invariably too wet or too dry. Then came a delay no one had foreseen.

Road construction replaces a path through the bush. The roads connected Chaco colony centers with each other and eventually with Asunción.

The Ayoreos were upset over oil exploration in the territory they claimed as their own. Memories of the 1947 massacre of the Paul Stahl family by a band of Ayoreo warriors were still very vivid. When Buller serviced his equipment in the morning, he noticed what he thought were Ayoreo footprints. Mennonite authorities concluded that continuing the work would be too dangerous and asked that the equipment be parked while they waited.

Buller soon grew restless. The threat was hard to assess and presumably ongoing and the time he had reserved to be absent from his Montana ranch was rapidly running out. He asked to resume road building on the condition that there be no armed protection. The Mennonite authorities reluctantly agreed.

Buller fulfilled his contract, leaving behind more than 100 kilometers (62 miles) of improved roads, his equipment, and a grateful community of admirers and friends. The age of the oxcart was ending, the day of the automobile lay ahead, along with bigger challenges.

Better roads and growing prosperity resulted in a dramatic increase in the number of cars and light trucks. From 1960 to 1975 the number grew from 75 to 431; the number of motorcycles increased from zero to 1,471.

A Way in the Wilderness

One day while Buller was uprooting trees with his bulldozer, he was startled by an airplane overhead. Airplanes flying over was not an everyday occurrence. He didn't know that in the airplane was the recently elected president of Paraguay, Alfredo Stroessner. Having seen from the air what Buller was doing with limited equipment, Stroessner said, "I want to meet that miracle worker." A written message asking Buller to come to Filadelfia immediately was delivered by way of an improvised parachute. Buller jumped into his Jeep, hoping to make himself presentable before meeting a dignitary, but time did not permit. They talked and went their separate ways.

Not many months later, Stroessner surprised everyone by stating boldly in a public meeting, "I promise, no I guarantee, that I will build a road from Asunción to the colonies."

Mennonites were skeptical, and with cause. At the time, Paraguay had few roads anywhere, let alone any through 450 kilometers (280 miles) of unsurveyed territory, populated by puma and alligators. The wild idea landed on the desk of William T. Snyder, later to become MCC executive secretary. Snyder brought the idea to Washington, where it fit some planning underway to construct a Pan American Highway.

Encouraged by Akron and Washington in the north and Asunción in the south, a four-way agreement was signed on July 13, 1955. In the words of the Associated Press, it was "an unlikely coalition" of the Paraguayan Ministry of Public Works (working with the Paraguayan military that administered the Chaco territory), the United States Agency for International Development (USAID), the Chaco Ranching Association, and MCC.

U.S. government engineers completed the road survey. MCC recruited Harry Harder to return to Paraguay to head up the effort, this time accompanied by his wife, Anna, and two teenage children. Harder was the only professional road builder in a motley crew consisting of inexperienced English- and German-speaking Mennonite conscientious objectors and Spanish- and Guaraní-speaking Paraguayan soldiers. The equipment consisted of bulldozers and scrapers, some leftover war surplus. Construction began in the northern outskirts of Asunción in February 1957.

But first, at Stroessner's insistence, the rust-pocked equipment was paraded down Asunción's famous Mariscal Lopez street. It was a public display that Paraguay was at long last claiming the forgotten Chaco, where only twenty-five years earlier thousands of soldiers had died in a senseless war.

Two shifts, from 7 a.m. to 8 p.m., worked through the hallowed siesta break six days a week. They made less than a kilometer of road on good days, of which there were few. Breakdowns and weather interruptions tested the determination of the sponsors, but they persisted, pushing the projected completion date back from two years to four and a half.

Fernheim had built an airstrip in 1948 and worked out an arrangement with Transporte Aereo Militar (TAM) to initiate an air bridge between Asunción and Filadelfia with service three times a week. This service was later extended to Menno and Neuland colonies. In 1956, TAM hauled 1,489 passengers (among them MCC executives) and 112,830 kilograms (1,212 tons) of freight.

The flights were made with a well-depreciated but reliable DC-3. Passengers once complained to the pilot that their ears hurt from a sudden descent. The pilot said he had had a tail wind and found himself over Asunción before he was aware of it, causing him to descend more suddenly than usual. (TAM was not radar-equipped!) To the relief of everyone, the plane was retired soon after the *Ruta Transchaco*, was completed.

With the "Mennonite" crew working its way north, USAID-contracted Williams Brothers, an American oil-drilling company in the Chaco, to work south from Filadelfia. To mark the meeting of the two crews on October 4, 1961, at Km 209, a celebration led by Stroessner included a speech in which he proclaimed that the road plan would make it possible to drive by car from Brazil to Bolivia. Speaking on behalf of ranchers, Robert Eaton, a prominent Chaco rancher, said, "No rancher in the Chaco needs an economist to tell him why he wants a road."

Mennonite colony trucks were ready to roll. Travel time between the Chaco colonies and Asunción was reduced to hours. The road, however, was not an all-weather road. Traffic had to stop and wait when it rained. Stories are told of carloads of people waiting days on end for the road to dry while being mercilessly assaulted by mosquitoes. It was not until eighteen years later that the government got around to blacktopping it.

The cost of transporting freight was cut in half. Loss from spoilage and pilferage almost disappeared. Alfred Hecht, a geographer at Wilfrid Laurier University in Ontario, wrote in a scholarly report, "This permitted the remote agricultural settlements to come under the market area of Asunción and indirectly, the world."

Hecht knew whereof he spoke. The road eventually transformed the Chaco economy from intensive agriculture of gardens and field crops to ranching. Today traffic flows night and day at speeds rivaling those on Germany's Autobahn. Ruta Transchaco was only the latest miracle, paving the way for better days ahead for beleaguered Mennonites.

In his excellent book *Die Ruta Transchaco*, Gerhard Ratzlaff chronicles the courageous undertaking: "If the Ruta Transchaco had not happened, the colonies might have dissolved. When the road became a reality in 1961 it did not solve all the problems, but it brought hope to the economy and improved the living standard."

In a paper presented to the International Geographic Union Regional Conference in Nigeria, Hecht stated, "After access to the market was established by means of a road, the Mennonites called upon their experience of having lived and worked in a commercial industrial world and rapidly changed their subsistence economy to a purely commercial one."

Challenges in East Paraguay

Though closer to Asunción and in a better position to benefit from the Paraguay River, Friesland and Volendam faced similar challenges in the early years. The roads built by Harder in 1952 served a valuable function, but they needed to be maintained and ultimately replaced. Passenger traffic to Asunción was supplemented by relatively inexpensive air charters, but freight costs were substantial and hindered development. It was not until 2004 that the Paraguayan government completed a new all-season road passing within miles of the Mennonite capitals. It was a huge improvement, but I can attest from personal experience that connector roads continue to be a problem in the rainy season.

Bergthal and Sommerfeld colonies too had serious transportation problems in the early years. This is harder to imagine, situated as they are now on the well-traveled Highway 7 between Asunción and the Iguazú Falls. One hundred men preceded their families in their move from Canada to Paraguay in 1948 to work on the 30-kilometer (19-mile), road giving them access to their inland tract. Roads were needed before family plots could be laid out for settlement to begin. In 1962 the much traveled national Highway 7 was upgraded and coated with asphalt, making it an all-weather road.

Ongoing Investment

Today roads are regarded as a necessity. Mennonites have long ago given up waiting on the government to do what Americans and Canadians take for granted. They have spent literally millions of dollars converting wandering oxcart trails into roads. When the kilometers of roads built and maintained by Mennonite colonies in Paraguay are laid end to end, they reach from New York to Vancouver.

In 2006 Menno colony spent nearly 1.6 million dollars on building and maintaining more than 2,600 kilometers (1,616 miles) of colony roads that also service some indigenous and Paraguayan communities; Fernheim spent 584,600 dollars on 1,000 kilometers (620 miles) of road. Figures are not available for others, but roads are a major expense for all the Mennonite colonies, which recognized their importance for both commercial and psychological reasons. In 2008, efforts were under way to hard surface colony roads.

As welcome as these improvements are, there is a downside. Faster roads have resulted in higher speeds and more traffic casualties. Reports of vehicular fatalities appear frequently in colony newsletters. Faster roads also contribute to road dust that is far and away the biggest complaint of Mennonite housekeepers living in the colony capitals. Colony decision-makers are hearing their protests. Soon the streets of the growing colony capitals will be paved.

13

Credit

Leveraging Hard Work

Heinrich Dürksen sat one day in 1953 in his austere Filadelfia office, stewing while his wife and sons were looking after their family *Hof* (farmette). Dürksen was born in Russia and immigrated to Paraguay with his parents when he was nineteen. Now at forty-two, he was in his third year as Oberschulze. He hadn't sought the position; it sought him. The weight of the troubled colony had come to rest on his broad shoulders at a critical time. His thoughts no doubt ranged over a variety of subjects:

- It will soon be twenty years since we arrived with little more than the shirts on our backs, and we are still dreadfully poor.
- How can I give a message of hope when things seemed so hopeless? How do I answer members who look me in the eye and ask in all sincerity when life will get better in this forsaken land?
- I can't ask the people to work harder; they are working too hard now.
- Where will we find qualified teachers? Those we brought with us from Russia are retiring, and others have left. But we don't have the competency to train new teachers.
- Five years after the internal divisions over National Socialism, this colony is still tragically divided. On the surface we are one, but in reality we are two bodies living under the Chaco canopy.
- Every week, families leave the colony—sometimes two a day. Frequently I listen to a young, beaten-down father tell me his

family is relocating to Brazil or Germany or Canada. His voice cracking with emotion, he stares at his bare feet and timidly asks to be excused from the debt in his account.

- When by a stroke of good fortune we end up with some surplus, and we send it to market in Asunción, we don't always get more than the cost of freight.
- How do we meet our responsibility to our indigenous neighbors? God alone knows how many there are, and they keep coming.
- On top of all that, the Chaco is again in a merciless drought. The crops and cattle are dying, and the people are suffering and demoralized. Lord, have mercy!

Dürksen spent sleepless nights wondering about solutions. "Menno Colony on one side of me, Neuland on the other, Friesland and Volendam down the river—they all have it just as bad. It used to be that we heard from Uncle Benjamin [Unruh], our wise advocate in Germany, but that resource has disappeared along with any hope of returning to our villages in Russia now that Germany lies in ruin."

Momentarily Dürksen thought of his cousins and former neighbors still living under Communism in the Ukraine. It had been years since he had received a letter. He offered a quick prayer on their behalf, but soon he was stewing again.

People would occasionally pat him on the shoulder and wish him well when they met in church or at the co-op, but mostly he felt burdened and alone. A prayer was perpetually on his lips: "*Herr hilf mir. Wie soll es weiter gehen?*" (Lord, help me. How shall it go on?)

In his moments alone, Dürksen recalled the three-way split in Germany that resulted in some getting their wish to go to Canada, others opting for Brazil, and Dürksen's group settling for the "green hell."

"Might the fortunate ones who got their wish to go to Canada now come to our rescue?" he wondered. "Mennonite Central Committee helped feed us in the Russian famine and helped us get here. Maybe they could help."

It frustrated and humbled him to admit even to himself that after two decades the colony was still so poor and needing help. In Russia they had been prosperous; now they felt like beggars.

Dürksen had previously discussed the idea of additional help from

Heinrich Dürksen, Fernheim Colony Oberschulze (mayor).

MCC with executive secretary Orie O. Miller and received a lukewarm response. MCC was stretched to the maximum with the newer Volendam and Neuland colonies and a big postwar program in Europe. Dürksen understood, but that did not answer his need.

Hesitatingly but with conviction, the distressed Oberschulze presented to the Fernheim administrative committee the idea of appealing for a loan from *den Brüdern im Norden* (the brothers in the North). They heard him out, but in subsequent debate the risks associated with a loan seemed too great. They were poor, but they still had their pride, and at least they had no debt. The motion failed. Dürksen returned to his stewing and plotting.

Three depressing months later, Dürksen floated his proposal again. By then the men had become more at-home with the idea of a loan. Or perhaps they felt more keenly the pressure of families leaving the colony. This time they reluctantly approved that Dürksen, accompanied by Kornelius Walde, undertake a *Geldsuchfahrt* (money-hunting trip) to the United States and Canada. Their goal was 100,000 dollars "at a low rate of interest."

Their first stop was MCC in Akron, Pennsylvania, where Miller helped them plan strategy and an itinerary. A trial run to Ontario yielded a mere six thousand dollars. They had higher hopes for Winnipeg, but before they could leave, a letter arrived, telling them not to come. Mennonites in Western Canada were giving priority to the new colonies, Volendam and Neuland. They left on their trip anyway, and the response was cool, as predicted.

In recounting the response to their appeals for loan money, Dürksen says in his autobiography, *Das du nicht vergessest der Geschichten*,

"Paraguay was too far away, too unfamiliar and not even an image they could comprehend."

In Winnipeg the group separated. Walde visited Mennonite communities in the United States while Dürksen focused on Canada. When someone was willing to participate, the donor usually wrote it off as charity, not a loan. Donors did not expect to be repaid.

Not only was it hard for Dürksen and Walde to make their case amid all the other appeals, it was humiliating. At the end of the itinerary, they had raised 76,000 dollars from 180 trusting friends. Though short of their goal, Dürksen and Walde now faced the challenge of making it work.

They purchased a steam generator to power a sawmill, a sorghum mill, a press to extract oil from peanuts, and cheese-making equipment—all of it used. The benefits were almost immediate. Fernheim was able to make annual repayments with only one exception, and that was compensated by a double payment in the next year. After thirteen years, the loan was completely repaid.

In reflecting on the effect of the loans, Duerksen postulated that they had for the first time established a foundation that would raise the economic standard and stability of the colony.

A Second Loan

In 1955, U.S. Ambassador Jackson was in Filadelfia, saying goodbye before being reassigned to Washington. In conversation with Duerksen, he asked how he could help. Dürksen replied, "What we need now is credit for the farmers so they can increase the size of their fields and herds." Recalling Paraguay's high inflation rate, Dürksen clarified, "A *dollar* loan with low interest."

Jackson left, and Dürksen busied himself with the routine business of the colony. Almost a year later C. L. Graber, MCC Paraguay interim director, was informed that it appeared a loan had been approved in Washington, though the details were not fully known. Dürksen was first embarrassed that he had forgotten the conversation with the departing ambassador, then he was skeptical.

Soon the rumor was confirmed. Their prayers were indeed being answered in ways they did not know. The U.S. government, in consultation with MCC, included a one-million-dollar loan to Mennonite colonies in Paraguay as part of the Mutual Security Act of 1954. A million dollars—not guaraní—at a "low rate of interest" was almost more than they could comprehend.

The loan was to be administered through the Central Bank of Paraguay. It came with few provisions other than that it was not a consumer loan but was a production credit loan to increase the economic viability of the colonies. It was also understood that it should apply to Friesland and Volendam as well as the three Chaco colonies.

First the five colonies created Comité Económico Menonita (Mennonite Economic Committee) to service the loan. Years later the name was changed to Comite Social y Económico Mennonita (CSEM, translated Social and Economic Mennonite Committee) to reflect a broadened social role. CSEM consisted of the Oberschulzen of the five participating colonies. Its offices were set up and still are in the Mennonitenheim in Asunción. Kornelius Walde was elected to serve as the first executive in 1962. He served in that capacity until 1990.

The million dollars were distributed on a per capita basis as follows:

• Menno Colony	$330,000
• Fernheim Colony	260,000
• Neuland Colony	190,000
• Volendam Colony	115,000
• Friesland Colony	105,000

In the weeks and months that followed, members of the fledgling CSEM became well acquainted with each other as they hammered out details. With discouraged families leaving their colonies daily, there was a sense of urgency to the deliberations. The committee had to clarify questions such as what to do if an individual or an entire colony defaulted. Were their loans going to be in dollars or guaraní? This was no small question in a time of high inflation.

The following purchases, totaling one million dollars, were made based on the agreed-upon criteria:

• 5 bulldozers	$150,000
• Spare parts	60,000
• 50 tractors @ $3,500	175,000

• Spare parts	43,750
• 5 separators @ $7,000	35,000
• Spare parts	5,250
• Horse-drawn implements and parts	283,500
• Wire fencing	55,500
• Cold storage for butter and cheese	95,000
• Rope and burlap plant	42,000
• Oil refineries	30,000
• A starch plant	25,000

When the equipment and supplies began to appear in the colonies, one colony observer noted it was as though a gentle rain had fallen on their fields. Shiny, powerful, smoke-belching bulldozers pushed back the bush, enlarging the fenced pastures and increasing the herds. Tractors replaced horses and hoes. Mechanical harvesters replaced human labor. Hope replaced despair.

Credit Rescues Volendam

From the late 1940s through the 1960s, Volendam colony was the *Sorgenkind* (the child you worry about). This was due in large measure to the number of single-parent households and an unfamiliarity with farming. Even in the first years of the colony, families left as soon as they could arrange sponsorship. By the 1960s, Volendam was a colony of demoralized people without options.

Their cries reached Mennonite Economic Development Associates (MEDA), which was then making a modest beginning in the Chaco. After surveying the situation, MEDA recruited Lloyd Fisher, a professional production credit manager, who went to Paraguay accompanied by his wife, Evelyn, and two teenaged sons, one of whom lies buried there, the victim of inadequate medical facilities. One hundred seventy-four carefully supervised loans totaling thirteen thousand dollars were made in the first year. Most of these loans were for land clearing, the rest to expand herds and pastures.

When the program concluded in 1973, there were just three unpaid loans. Credit had helped Volendam to a better future.

Another Source of Credit

The colonies were still paying off their previous loans when good fortune came their way again, this time through contacts between Alfred Fast, Oberschulze of Friesland, and the church-related development organization German Evangelische Zentralstelle für Entwicklungshilfe (EZE).

The five CSEM colonies—Menno, Fernheim, Neuland, Friesland, and Volendam—were each invited to put forward six economic development projects and collectively to identify two other projects for development. The total value of these projects from 1964 to 1970 was 830,000 dollars. The EZE additionally helped Friesland and Volendam make the transition to farming wheat and later soybeans through loans that reached two million dollars.

Credit to Indigenous Families

Literally hundreds of indigenous families had been helped to settle on their own *chacras* (small farms). Leaders of the rapidly growing indigenous communities felt an urgent need to help these predominantly young families raise their standard of living. If Mennonites were helped by credit, why not also the indigenous? When this need came to the attention of MEDA charter member Erie Sauder, he called a meeting to explore the idea. Credit was a totally new concept for the indigenous. Mission leaders were skeptical, with reason, fearing endless misunderstanding and disappointment: to go from hunting and gathering to the money economy in one generation?

Six languages were in use in the meeting—Lengua, Chulupí, Spanish, English, and two kinds of German. The indigenous asked questions about the difference between charity and a loan and whether they'd be required to make loan payments when there was no crop. Leaders were hard pressed to explain the meaning of such terms as *security*, *guarantee*, and *down payment*. Even interest was a completely unknown concept.

In an experimental program, a credit committee composed of representatives from three indigenous communities was entrusted with an advance of nine thousand dollars. Sauder stayed in close contact with the indigenous committee, always working in close collaboration with settlement staff.

Haltingly the program matured, accompanied by an active education program. When loans were repaid, the money was reloaned. Many were beginning to grasp the leveraging features of supervised credit. By 1977 the loan fund had grown to forty-seven thousand dollars. Approximately 20 percent had to be written off as uncollectible, attributable mostly to crop failure. Credit was proving to be valuable to indigenous farmers.

Sauder took a personal interest in the partnership between MEDA and the Chaco indigenous. In his retirement he was asked which of his many accomplishments gave him the most lasting satisfaction: the large furniture manufacturing business with exports all over the world that bears his name or the popular woodworkers museum that was expanded to include a restaurant and motel? With a wave of the hand he replied, "None of these. The greatest satisfaction of my life was when I was setting up a woodworking shop in Yalve Sanga to help indigenous make basic furniture for their modest houses."

Credit was an essential component to help Mennonites and indigenous people overcome the steep obstacles they faced. Through credit, Mennonites were able to leverage their hard work to achieve greater economic security, making possible a better life for themselves and their neighbors.

14

Scientific Agriculture

From Wasteland to Breadbasket

They planted and hoed; they plowed and prayed. Sometimes they harvested. Sometimes all they could do was hope next year would be better.

These were agricultural communities dependent on what they could grow with the hot sun overhead. Rainfall was sufficient, although not necessarily at the opportune time. The bush and tall grass showed that the soil was fertile, but the grass was bitter and the cattle would not eat it. The farmers wondered what to plant and when, where to get the seed, and how to till the soil when all they had were human hands and unpredictable oxen pulling improvised implements.

Compounding their predicament was the fact that, while some had experience with farming the steppes of Russia or the prairies of Canada, they knew little about farming in the tropics. Many of their members were not even farmers.

Buried in the Mennonite psyche was yet another inhibitor. Sometime in the early 1940s, many were still tentative about Paraguay and fantasized about returning to their former homes in Russia. Their hopes were predicated on Germany conquering Russia, but that option was foreclosed when Germany lost World War II. Some later immigrated to Germany or Canada, but the rest had little choice but to wipe the sweat from their brow and labor on.

A Yearn to Learn

After twenty years, Mennonites, for all their agricultural savvy, were still learning how to farm in Paraguay. One perceptive pioneer observed that people and nature seemed in conflict with each other. They tried different things, but weather variability interfered with drawing reliable conclusions. When asked what they needed, one discouraged farmer replied, "We need everything." Their one consolation—"We are free!"

Fernheim commissioned one of its bright young men, Peter Esau, to see what could be learned and perhaps borrowed from East Paraguay. He was attracted to the grapefruit tree and brought cuttings back with him. In a matter of years, dark green grapefruit trees came to adorn many Mennonite farmsteads. They also added a little variation to an otherwise monotonous diet. But the promising initiative came to a premature end when Esau died of an infected appendix. Fernheim was distracted with internal issues, and Menno colony was still trying to get better results from methods they had brought from Canada.

In 1942, President Franklin D. Roosevelt established the Servicio Técnico Interamericano de Cooperación Agrícola (Interamerican Technical Service for Agricultural Cooperation). STICA was a technical assistance program focused on improving agricultural production in South American countries. A substation was located in East Paraguay close to Friesland and Volendam. Menno Klassen, a single Canadian, was assigned by MCC to serve as liaison to STICA.

It did not take Klassen long to conclude that Chaco ecology was sufficiently unique as to require its own experimentation. He was commissioned to design a modest program, but farmers were skeptical. When Klassen completed his three-year assignment, he concluded, "Only a small start was made in the adventure to discover the secrets to make the Chaco productive." During a return visit thirty years later, he marveled that "the so-called 'green hell' had been made into a paradise."

How was that possible?

Search for What Works

Bob and Myrtle Unruh succeeded Klassen in 1951. Both had been raised on farms, Bob in Montana and Myrtle in Kansas. Both also had grown up in rural Mennonite congregations and had just graduated from Bethel College in North Newton, Kansas. A whole new world greeted the newly married couple.

The Unruhs arrived in Filadelfia on the back of a freight truck after dark. When the truck motor stopped, there was a momentary silence, then out of the night stillness Myrtle proclaimed, "Thank goodness. There remain just 1,756 days before we can return home." This was actually the beginning of what became a lifelong calling for the Unruhs.

While waiting five months for their baggage to arrive, the Unruhs studied German and read farm magazines left behind by their predecessors. Among the ads, Bob noted a reference to Buffelgrass. He determined that it was native to South Africa and that it had done well in Texas's sandy soils, which were thought to be similar to Chaco soil.

It was many months before a response to his information request was received, and many more months before he was informed that a small package awaited him at the colony post office. With the nine-pound package was a bill that came to a quarter of his annual budget. At first shocked and embarrassed and fearing he had made a terrible mistake, Unruh had, it would turn out, made the best investment of his life.

The valuable seeds were planted with care in a living-room-sized plot, and the results were notably better than other grasses being tested. But would the impressive results hold up under field conditions? More seeds was ordered and planted in his 1-hectare (2.5-acre) pasture near the center of Filadelfia, where the hospital and radio station are now located. Again the results were dramatic. A fat cow soon had grass up to her belly! People driving by in horse-drawn wagons stopped to look and inquire where this miracle grass seed could be bought.

Better Grass Deserves Better Cows

Next, better cows were needed to make use of better pasture. The best native cows yielded only one or two liters of milk daily, and it often required a struggle to get that from animals not used to being domesticated. It took as long as five or six years for calves to reach market weight. One farmer described the creolia cow as being mostly hide hung over bones with impressive horns.

Mennonite farmers in Lancaster, Pennsylvania, learned about the need for improved livestock. They selected some of the best from their cows and pigs and in 1961 chartered a plane that became a kind of flying Noah's ark. More followed. Holstein bulls from STICA were crossed with Zebu cows, more than doubling milk production while retaining the hardiness needed to survive the Chaco.

Robert Unruh showing off bulls imported to upgrade the quality of cattle to a gathering of Chaco farmers.

Bulldozers bought with the million-dollar credit program were soon running long into the night, pushing the bush back to enlarge pastures. Indigenous people were engaged to enclose these improved pastures with literally thousands of miles of five-strand fence, held up by hardy but often crooked *pala santo* posts. The flat countryside became dotted with black-and-white cows on green pasture. A ready market awaited their produce at the end of the new road. Many formerly discouraged farmers were beginning to think that there was a future in Paraguay after all.

Bob and Myrtle Unruh closed their first term, which by most standards had been wildly successful, with these words: "We persist with a prayer in our hearts that also through our modest efforts the love of Christ may be made visible." The Unruhs were more than respected; they were loved and became one with the people. They became *Chaqueños* (Chaco dwellers) and devoted most of their adult lives to making the Chaco productive.

Winter Provisions

In their second term, the Unruhs addressed what they saw as the next hurdle—improving nutrition for people and animals during the dry winter months. While Bob experimented with silos and various ways to store hay, Myrtle taught women better home management. She gave cooking and canning demonstrations to a new generation of Chaco women through a course in the local high school. The hot sun that burned their crops was harnessed to dry fruits and vegetables. Always the concentration was on technologies available in the Chaco.

The cover of Myrtle Unruh's cookbook.

To help Chaco women rise to the next level, and as an aid in her classroom work, Myrtle assembled the first Paraguay Mennonite cookbook, *Mit Mamma Gespeist* (Fed by Mama). This modest book came to grace most Mennonite kitchens of that generation. It helped improve the family diet and consequently increased health and morale. Each section included a feature on feeding the soul as well as the body.

Tractors Replace Oxen

Bob turned his attention to the need for mechanical power. Farmers were only too ready to concede the limitations of oxen and hoe and machete farming. They knew the impossibility of getting beyond a hand-to-mouth existence on the backs of obstreperous oxen and skinny horses.

The even-tempered and practical Unruh knew he would have to demonstrate that tractors would increase yields and pay for themselves. His experiments were convincing. Loans were available from the million-dollar fund to purchase a few tractors. Before long, brightly painted tractors and powerful bulldozers were everywhere, expanding fields and pastures.

Things were looking up for Mennonites in the Chaco. People who had been so beaten down and discouraged were smiling more. But the improvement came too late for some. Families left Paraguay in large numbers in the 1950s and 1960s. Sad as it was to see them go, it made room for the survivors to expand their farms.

All this happened at a time of great national instability. The door to the Paraguayan presidency was a revolving one, as one bloody coupe followed another. From 1948 to 1949 six different presidents ruled Paraguay's 1.5 million people. Corruption was everywhere. Inflation eroded the purchasing power of every guaraní.

This was the era of World War II, postwar reconstruction, and mass relocation, phasing into the Cold War. In Canada, many Mennonites were prospering, but thousands of their kin were still trapped behind what was then called the Iron Curtain.

A New Base for Scientific Agriculture

Unruh continued to experiment quietly with technologies that looked promising. He eliminated what was not practical. For example, after years of experimenting with egg production for the Asunción market, he scrapped it in favor of ranching.

In less-than-perfect German, Unruh prepared hundreds of weekly

Myrtle Unruh leads a cooking class.

Robert Unruh inspects cabbage at an experimental farm.

radio programs for airing on ZP 30, the Filadelfia-based radio station. Farmers came to rely on his timely and practical tips, which were always offered in a humble spirit.

The Unruhs were not only interested in production. Bob started a tree nursery and multiplied rose stock to beautify the farmsteads, replicating childhood memories of their beloved Molotschna. Myrtle helped strengthen family life by emphasizing nutrition and homemaking. Bob sang in the choir. Myrtle was active in the women's organization. Their daughter Betty attended the local school.

Though their base was in Fernheim, the Unruhs worked easily across colony boundaries. What they learned was available to all, including the indigenous people.

It eventually became apparent that this agricultural program, so central to the Mennonite economy, needed to be expanded beyond its Fernheim base. In 1972 the program was restructured to include all three Chaco colonies and the emerging indigenous settlements. Loma Plata (Menno colony) was selected as the base for this expanded program, renamed Servicio Agropecuario Program (SAP).

In 2008, SAP employed twenty-five technicians in a variety of specialties, including numerous veterinarians to support the burgeoning livestock industry. It has soil-testing capability and a global positioning system that permits the monitoring of conditions in the vast Chaco. Also located in Loma Plata is a two-year Mennonite agricultural vocational school, where about two hundred fourth-generation farmers from all three Chaco colonies are learning how to take things to the next level.

The Desert Begins to Blossom

A new generation discovered that the Chaco was not meant for field crops; it was meant to be ranched. Crops whither and die if a timely rain eludes them. Cattle can more easily survive a dry spell with hay, silage, or reserve pastures. Dairying and ranching have replaced the dream of wheat their parents nurtured too long.

Milk production increased sharply in the 1970s and 1980s as pastures got bigger and cotton and kafir fields got smaller. Mennonites were milking their way to a better future. Much of this milk is made into cheese and yogurt for the Asunción market. Menno colony in the Chaco and Bergthal and Sommerfeld in East Paraguay have erected large, modern milk-processing plants. The Trebol and Lactolanda brands are known throughout Paraguay. More than half of all the dairy products consumed in Paraguay now come from Mennonite cows.

Almost simultaneously, beef production found a place alongside dairy in this land of *asado* (steak). Before long the number of marketable cattle exceeded the Asunción-based marketing and processing capacities. Shipping cattle hundreds of kilometers under the hot Paraguay sun and hauling some of the meat back to the colonies was not efficient. The colonies needed more slaughter and meat-processing facilities.

The three Chaco colonies studied this problem together and individually. Invariably the discussion stalled over fears that the water supply would be inadequate to support a large-scale eviscerating plant. Colony decision-makers repeatedly backed away from the multi-million-dollar risk, even as the herds and cattle ready for market grew exponentially.

Finally in 2001 Menno colony took the leap. Geological studies convinced them that a tract 10 kilometers (6 miles) from Loma Plata had favorable underground aquifers. They supplemented it with acres of surface lagoons and a water recycling facility, then built a state-of-the-art plant covering 1.35 hectares (3.3 acres), complete with refrigeration. A few years later, the plant had the capacity to process eight hundred cattle daily.

The next challenge was to recruit three hundred workers with the needed skills to operate the facility. It seemed German Mennonites were more interested in growing cattle than in working in refrigerated surroundings. The indigenous weren't much interested in factory work. It became necessary to import workers from Brazil, some of whom speak German. This influx of workers has pumped more money into the Chaco economy and brought a need for more housing.

By 2003 trucks were arriving daily with grass-fattened cattle ready to be made into sausage and other fine cuts for the Asunción market and export to Brazil, Peru, Russia, Angola, Lebanon, Egypt, and Kenya. Russia, where Mennonites had been treated so poorly, is now purchasing large quantities of meat from them!

Menno colony's meat-packing success stimulated Neuland colony, in accord with Friesland colony, to follow suite. Their state-of-the-art facility is on the banks of the Paraguay River near Asunción, along the Ruta. The location guarantees a good water supply and easy access to Asunción markets and labor.

East Paraguay

Similar dynamics were underway in East Paraguay, where dairy and beef herds had also increased in size and quality through imported genetics. Holstein herds numbering ten and twenty cows are commonplace. Milk-can platforms sit at the end of most farm lanes for daily pick-up. Large herds of quality Zebo beef cattle populate lush, well-fenced pastures. East Paraguayan farmers proudly inform visitors that 1 hectare (2.5 acres) of their pasture is needed per cow while 3 or 4 hectares (7 to 10 acres) are required in the Chaco.

East Paraguay farmers have the advantage of supplementing their livestock industry by double-cropping wheat and soybeans, neither of which

Horsemanship at an intercolony rodeo.

do well in the Chaco. Now, twice a year, the plow follows the combine. In one week a field can be harvested of its wheat and planted with a second crop of soybeans. Wheat and dairy have become their bread and butter.

The East Paraguayan countryside has had a facelift. Large fields of ripened grain have replaced the woodlands. Modern combines and four-wheel-drive tractors have replaced beat-up lumber trucks. Herds of Holstein and Zebo cattle grazing on green pastures with a few trees in the fence line have mostly replaced the sawmills, now standing idle with huge mounds of decaying sawdust beside them. Some regret that a program of planting a tree for each tree harvested was not introduced when Mennonites first arrived.

Indigenous Agriculture

The semi-nomadic indigenous people had their own form of extensive (as distinct from intensive) agriculture before Mennonites arrived. They harvested fruits and vegetables, sweet potatoes and watermelons, honey and a variety of berries from the vast but shrinking bush. Their hunting prowess supplied them with meat. The indigenous were dispossessed of land they had hunted for generations when Mennonites, ranchers, and combatants in the Chaco War occupied the fields.

The 1930s and 1940s were a time of radical adjustment for the indigenous community. The indigenous people learned a new kind of farming by working with Mennonites in their fields. Beginning in the 1950s, increasingly in the 1960s, and through to the twenty-first century, thousands of indigenous families have been helped to settle on their own *chacras* (small farms).

Many indigenous people have become remarkable successful farmers, but not all. Their farms are smaller and more labor-intensive. They are geared first to feeding the families. Their principle cash crops are sesame for the international market, cotton, and beans. Indigenous cattle herds are increasing in size and quality. They also have flocks of sheep and goats.

The rapidly growing indigenous population is not only feeding itself, it has surplus production for export. Yet some form of industrialization is needed to increase diversification and employ their rapidly growing population. Land values are also increasing, making farming less affordable for many.

Making the adjustment to farming in the tropics was harder and took longer than Mennonites had anticipated. With persistence, using borrowed and adapted technology, Mennonites and indigenous people have succeeded beyond anyone's predictions. Tractors and self-propelled combines have replaced oxen and horses. Buffelgrass and its successor, Gaton Panic, have replaced native grasses. Scientific agriculture has replaced trial-and-error subsistence farming.

Modern laborsaving devices have replaced the backbreaking work pioneer men and women were required to do. The standard of living of Mennonites now resembles that of farming families in Canada, the United States, and Germany.

Mennonites have played a major role in converting the abandoned countryside into Paraguay's breadbasket. Not only are Mennonites and indigenous people feeding themselves, they are feeding much of Paraguay and people elsewhere in the world. A wandering people, some fleeing Communism, others fleeing encroaching modernity, have made wasteland into a fruitful garden. Paraguay's investment in welcoming the Mennonites is paying handsome dividends.

After the introduction of Buffelgrass, ranchers converted acres of crop land to pasture. They imported better breeding stock, which led to upgraded beef herds. Meat is processed in two large packing plants owned by Menno and Neuland colonies and sold throughout Paraguay. Beef is also exported to more than a dozen countries, including Russia from where many of the Mennonite producers came.

15

Women

They Made It Possible

In the spring of 2007, Mennonites were preparing to receive a visit from Germany's president, Horst Kohler. They submitted a list of people who would participate in the festivities to the embassy. The German embassy reviewed the list and replied, "Wo sind de Frauen?" (Where are the women?)

I found myself asking the same question as I was writing this book. The stories are built heavily on men. And yet, as sure as night follows day, it was women who made it possible. If in part 2 we are identifying those who made a better life possible in Paraguay, surely women deserve a chapter.

The families that came from Russia were refugees; they were forced to leave. Those who came from Canada did so by their own volition, but it was not always by mutual consent. In an article called "Gott es hia uck" (God is here too), published in the 2004 issue of the *Journal of Mennonite Studies*, Patricia Harms tells the story of Helen Froese, whose husband coerced her to leave her six sisters in Manitoba to join the Bergthal group in Paraguay in 1948. He died during the hard pioneer years, leaving Helen to fend for herself and three small children.

The sisters exchanged tapes by mail. In the tapes we hear authentic voices discussing the women's roles in keeping family life and religious identity strong. They also discuss their role in the production and preparation of food and some speak of suffering under male dominance.

These tapes reveal that parents sometimes separated from their children or left older children in Canada while the younger ones went with their parents to Paraguay. Harms tells about one man who was so conflicted about leaving Canada, he prayed while driving his truck to the train station that he might have an accident and miss the train.

A Window on Family Dynamics

Not everything that transpired under those temporary tents portrays matrimonial harmony, as illustrated in the following story.

After eighteen months of living in woefully inadequate facilities and conditions, Menno colony women had had it. Trying to find shelter for themselves and their children from the hot sun by day and mosquitoes at night, tired of being made to wait in long lines to cook a meal or go to the toilet, they insisted that their husbands meet with Ältesten Friesen and impress on him "so geht es nicht weiter" (this cannot continue).

The meeting between the men and Friesen lasted several hours. Otherwise reasonable and gentle men vented their frustration on the saintly but overburdened bishop. When finally given a chance to reply, Friesen reminded them that they had all undertaken this endeavor thinking it was God's will. He pleaded with them to persevere. "We have by far not reached the end of our endurance," he said.

When the weary husbands returned, their wives were not satisfied with their report. They took the unprecedented step of meeting with Friesen on their own. He received them kindly, but no doubt with some apprehension. After listening to them patiently and respectfully Friesen pleaded with the wives to "haltet durch" (stay the course).

The women heeded the bishop. It was hard, but they persevered. If Friesen had capitulated or even wavered, and if the women had not been able to rise to the occasion, the entire story of Mennonites in Paraguay might have melted into the dry ground.

Women Shared the Load

The ordeal of living on the frontier fell heavier on women than on men. Women participated in making bricks, plastering walls, and roofing houses. While trying to nourish and clothe their families, they helped with the fieldwork, often while they were pregnant or nursing, or both. Milking was always a task assigned to a woman.

In summer, families had vegetables from gardens the women had planted. In the dry winter months, there was little more than flour and beans and an occasional egg to nourish large families. Even water was scarce, and it often had to be carried a great distance.

There is one story about a mother who had arranged to obtain from a neighbor one cup of milk every day for her baby. When she went to pick up the agreed-to cup, another of her children accompanied her, begging to be permitted to drink any milk that might spill into the saucer while they were walking.

Women anxiously attended their seriously feverish children without professional help to fall back on. Too often they had to surrender a child they had birthed and carried in their arms to an early grave. Women were on occasion lonely, afraid, and continually weary. Yet the women were admirably courageous and resourceful. One report, which I was unable to verify, was that these pioneer women were able to make scrambled eggs without eggs. They also discovered dozens of ways to fix beans.

While the men are recognized for their role in building strong organizations and had the lead role in preaching and teaching, it was the quiet, behind-the-scenes strength of women that made life in the colonies possible.

Widows—A Special Category

Life was hard for families that were intact, but it was decidedly harder for widows. The first Volendam transport in 1947 had 950 women and only 444 males over the age of sixteen. To compensate for this lack of men, an attempt was made to assign an adult male, called a *Goodman*, to each widow. But this sometimes strained family relationships and resulted in common-law unions.

In Neuland colony, forty-six widows asked to be assigned to one village. They named it *Friedensheim* (home of peace), but it became known as *Frauendorf* (women's village). Men thought it impossible for the women to make it on their own. The women replied, "In Mennonite Central Committee, we did as we were told but we were told that once we were in Paraguay, we could do as we pleased." These resourceful women had become accustomed to fending for themselves.

In her book *Women Without Men: Mennonite Refugees of the Second World War,* Marlene Epp quotes one women's description of life in the Chaco:

> They used to sit in the Frauendorf after a hard day's work, outside their mud houses, all the women in a circle around a smoky fire to keep away the mosquitoes. Somebody would have a guitar and they'd sing. They would sing and share, they would cry and they would also laugh a lot. They were all the same. Nobody was rich, nobody had advantage over the other, they were all going through the same experience, everyday the struggles of pioneering would knit them closer together, and they would all be waiting information from their missing husbands.

An elderly woman peeling a manioc. At her side is a system to capture rainwater, a valued commodity in the Chaco.

When asked how they expected to deal with such physical tasks as digging a well or chopping down big trees or clearing a thick tangle of brush before planting their gardens, they told skeptics that they would help each other. And they did. One widow, upon completing her house said, "Never have I been so poor. Never have I been so happy." It was the happiness of accomplishment.

A Widow's Story

But for some women (and men), life on the frontier was simply impossible. Here is one such an account as written by Anni Neufeld Duerksen, formerly of Volendam and now living in Winnipeg.

> I am (Anni) the youngest of three sisters, (Kaethe and Alice) born in Einlage, Zaporosh'ye, Ukraine. My father was taken from our home when I was only two years old at the end of 1941 or beginning of 1942. My mother did not hear from him until about 1960 when we learned he had died in a Russia

prison. We left Russia in 1942, with the retreating German army (The Big Trek). We stayed in Poland before moving to East Germany, where my mother got a job as a translator for the German army, since she spoke Russian as well as German. One evening a German official told her secretly that if we wouldn't leave that night we would be sent back to Russia.

We left for Berlin, where we stayed in the refugee camp. On January 31, early in the morning we left the refugee camp via truck and train (as by a miracle —1.115 people) and arrived at Bremerhaven where the Volendam was waiting to take us to South America. On February 22, 1947, we landed in Bs. Aires. Because of the revolution in Paraguay we stayed in a tent camp in Bs. Aires for about three months. We arrived in Friesland in March 1947 and stayed with [the] family [of] Abram Kroeker.

A few months later we were told to settle in the vicinity of Friesland, which later became Volendam. My mother was given an ax, shovel, a saw and some other tools, and assigned to a piece of land that was to become our home. She had left us children in Friesland, where we went to school. My mother told us later that she worked and cried at the same time. It was impossible for her to cut the trees and clear the land.

After working hard for some weeks she returned to Friesland, knowing that she could not manage alone in the jungle. My aunt and uncle invited us to live with them in Asunción, where my mother worked very hard holding different jobs to get us girls through school.

In 1953 we moved to Bs. Aires. Here my sisters worked as dressmakers and I continued to go to school. My mother worked hard alongside a hired man to build a house for us. We lived many happy years together in that house.

A Boost for a Few

With few exceptions, women were confined to the home. Families being large, there was an abundance, even an excess, of family labor. This surplus caused some courageous young women to venture out of the colony to work as domestics in a city. This was especially true of women after they completed school and before marriage.

Parents welcomed the income this provided, but they were understandably anxious over single girls in the big city. MCC took this on as a cause, and for some years operated supervised boarding facilities and provided pastoral care in Asunción, Buenos Aires, São Paulo, and Montevideo. Many of these young women returned to the Mennonite colonies, married, and took their place in family and in colony life. Some, sadly, confirmed the validity of their parents' fears.

Changes in Gender Roles

Gender dynamics in Paraguay are similar to those in the United States and Canada. Except for those in Old Colony settlements, where traditional definitions continue to apply, Paraguayan women are venturing out of the home and finding a place for themselves in the professions. More are continuing their education beyond high school. This has resulted in a number of changes.

Women have assumed a major role in healthcare. In the absence of doctors, pioneer women were resourceful in their use of home remedies. Midwives without formal training attended births with a remarkably low mortality and infection rate while working in very compromised conditions. This is still the case in Old Colony settlements today.

Clara Schmidt took it to the next level in 1943 when she conducted the first school for nurses in Filadelfia. Other formal and informal nursing programs followed, serving also the East Paraguay colonies. Today nursing and teaching remain the main outside-the-home occupations for women. A few women have also became fully qualified medical doctors. Of forty-eight Paraguayan Mennonites who have trained as doctors in Asunción or Buenos Aires, twelve were women.

Women became accepted as teachers. Historically, teaching had been open only to men, and this male dominance continues in Old Colony settlements. This changed when professionally trained women teachers were among the post-World War II refugees in Neuland and Volendam. With male teachers in short supply, the exception became the rule. Today women teachers outnumber men, although supervisory roles are still held predominantly by men.

The church came to welcome an expanded role for women. Women's roles were for many years restricted to caring for children and teaching children's Sunday school classes. For a woman to speak from behind the pulpit was expressly forbidden. Today in the Chaco and Asunción churches, as well as in Friesland and Volendam, women have an active part in congregational life, although none are pastors. They lead singing, serve on committees, and teach Sunday school. Most women feel more or less fulfilled in the roles available to them. Of nearly two hundred students enrolled in the two Mennonite seminaries in Asunción in 2007, more than a third were women.

Women are entering business. Many international travelers travel on tickets issued by the thriving Viajes Canada bureau, managed by Eveline Hiebert, originally from Menno colony. Her office is directly across the street from the Mennonitenheim. A sister in Eveline's large family is a medical doctor.

Intergenerational Conflict

The tensions resulting from women working outside the home, particularly mothers, are illustrated by the following fictional piece written by Beate Penner, a married woman who is a teacher in Friesland colony.

> Sabine thinks, in several minutes I will be there. Feeling totally exhausted after a long day of work she looks forward to hold her children in her arms again. Jan, six, and Betti, three, were still asleep when she left the house. Today it was almost dark as she arrived at her mother's place to collect her children.
>
> Sabine turned off the motor and prepares herself psychologically for the discussion with her mother, whom she knows will remind her again of her responsibilities as a mother. "Mama, Mama," the children come running into her arms. For the moment Sabine is the most fortunate woman anywhere. When she is with her children she forgets all her problems.
>
> Sabine listens as her children talk about the day. She is also keenly aware of her mother coming from the garden. Recently she became a widow but still continues to care for her property. Sabine loves and admires her mother even though she does not see eye-to-eye with her on some matters. With a quick hug Sabine greets her mother. "Hello, mother, and how was your day?"
>
> "Quite well. The children behaved, if that is what you are asking."
>
> Between the lines Sabine hears her mother's silent accusations. They love each other dearly but her mother simply cannot understand why Sabine is working outside the home. For her, a mother's place is in the kitchen.

"And how was your day?" mother asks.

"Good. I accomplished everything that needed to be done."

After a brief silence, mother asks, "How long do you plan to continue this way, Sabine? Do you think about your children?"

"Of course, I think about my children, mother. I love them above all else. But I feel more fulfilled when I am also able to work in my field of interest. If I had to spend all day in my kitchen, cooking and baking, I would probably become so irritable that the children would have less of me than they have now."

As she is speaking, Sabine observes tears in her mother's eyes. "Please understand me, Sabine. I love your children and care for them gladly. They are, after all, my grandchildren! But I have concern about you and your family. I want you all to be happy together."

Sabine has nothing else to say but, "It will all be well, mother!"

In a reflective mood Sabine begins her way home. Her mother has never spoken this strongly. Sabine observes her children smiling at her in the rear view mirror. They are happy—their mother is with them again. Sabine returns the smile. Is she doing wrong? Should she stay home with her children? Working full time has given her an opportunity to witness for the Lord. Child care to her is more about quality than quantity. She can, in contradiction to the older women, do both, work and care for her family. Why did God give her talents if she cannot put them into practice?

Sabine is conflicted. Before she accepted the job she weighed the pros and cons carefully and prayerfully. Women in those early years had to work hard and found their way through. It wasn't simple for them. To build up an existence out of nothing—to keep the family alive and to nurture the children. They were high achievers. But times change, and Sabine is convinced that she too will find a way through even though it might appear difficult. God will help her!

Changes for Indigenous Women

The changing role of women was more traumatic in the indigenous communities. Women had a defined and significant role in their aboriginal settings: men did the hunting and gathering while women were in charge of cooking and tending the gardens. Women had a strong voice in family decision making. Their role was unknowingly undercut when Mennonite men negotiated with indigenous men for seasonal employment, leaving the women unconsulted.

The first seven baptized indigenous converts were all men; conversions of women came later. Acting out of their own culture, Mennonite leaders looked to indigenous men to provide leadership in indigenous churches. Early training programs were all geared to men.

Mission leaders eventually became aware that indigenous women were not participating in the evolution underway. While indigenous men were becoming literate and wearing Mennonite-style clothing, their wives continued to wear traditional clothing and nurse their babies as their mothers had done. Mission leaders belatedly recognized that if the indigenous family was to progress, women needed to be included in the process.

A beginning was made in the 1960s when Ann Klassen, a Canadian missionary nurse, was added to the executive team of Association of Indigenous-Mennonite Cooperation Services. She organized a series of activities that helped indigenous women participate in the transformation underway. Anne died young and, at her request, lies buried in the Yalve Sanga graveyard.

Edith Neufeld, Anganetha Eitzen, and others are continuing the work. In a recent year 1,315 women participated in fifty-six group meetings, where they sang, studied the Bible, and discussed topics of interest to women. One participate said, "I was pleased with the teachings. We are to teach our children to pray. . . . We should be more patient with our children. . . . We should not have marital disputes in front of our children."

The program includes forty-eight schools with 854 preschool children, taught by fifty-two teachers, forty-eight of whom are indigenous women. One hundred and seventy-two young women attended a course on home and family management, taught by eight indigenous women with three German Mennonite advisers.

Caomi, a Nivaclé women, speaks of her conversion, as told to Edith Neufeld, and in so doing provides a glimpse into how gender roles have also changed for indigenous women.

> I grew up by the Pilcomayo [River]. In the 1950s Nivaclé people found the Mennonite colonies. We listened to the missionaries as they told us about God and asked us to change our

> hearts. I had my own sinful ways and I drank. I wanted what the missionary said about God. I had a very hard struggle in my heart. Then I confessed all and rendered my whole being over to him. I wanted very much to be baptized together with my husband. Jesus had changed my heart, but I was unable to stop smoking. All the women smoked. We just smoked and smoked. We turned skinny and sick. Then God saved me from my sins. I was free not to smoke anymore, and I got baptized. I became very happy to follow the Lord.

Appreciation Amid a Restricted Role

Women had an indispensable if under-recognized role in this rich history. By today's standards, pioneer women were terribly restricted, but they were loved and appreciated. Not all men had the ability to say it as eloquently as did Abram Fast of Friesland colony in the 1950 poem below. Some nuances are lost in the translation from German, but his message of love and respect remains.

To Our Women

Today I want to tune my harp
and sing a song for a woman;
I want to sing about a heroine,
you all know her very well.

Of course you know her,
you just don't see the heroine in her.
Unfortunately men often think,
that they alone are significant.

Only what a man does is important,
and he's the only one worthy of praise.
What a woman does is insignificant,
because all she does is attend to the kitchen.

But who can fully measure and appreciate
what our women do, day after day?
Quite apart from the food on the table
the tasks she performs cheerfully in every way.

In the morning, very early,
begins for her the day of activity.
She will not shirk any responsibility,
just forward, forward, without stopping to rest.

First, she must get the breakfast on the table,
often the wood she needs, is not there;
however, without spending time to argue about it,
she goes outside herself to get it.

Then she has to see that the children get to school;
her husband is off to his work in Santani;
And now she notices that a button is lost,
from the blue dress of her daughter Mary.

She may not dare lose her nerve now,
as others have done rather often;
she dare not even think about it
because her husband won't like that.

Satisfied, her husband goes to work,
and the children are off to school;
now it is time to start cleaning the house
and this, too, is quickly done.

Meanwhile the cows have arrived,
with their calves pulling on the ropes;
the milking is no small task,
but she does it fast and with skill.

Now is the time to take the milk to be separated,
which she can do at her neighbor's place;
everything is done according to plan
and with experience, joy and skill.

The laundry is waiting to be washed;
by hand, of course, with the wash board;
Why do we have to be so busy all the time?
When will we come to rest at last?

Now she heard the whistle blow 11:30.
This is her signal and high time
to start getting dinner ready,
But what shall she serve her family?

She grabs a pail and hurries into the garden,
and knows exactly which manioca to pull up;
the children do not want to wait,
they are hungry when they come home.

For them there is no rest at noon
since they came into this land.
How lovely the memories of their parent's home,
where once their cradle stood—

With hundreds of small details
the day ends at last, and night is coming.
Work and more work waits everywhere,
but at last, at long last the night is here.

Exhausted she stretches her tired body,
her legs and arms on the straw-mattress;
gently her eyelids close her eyes.
While she longs for her eternal home.

Many heroines on this earth,
unfortunately are not recognized by others,
but what she accomplished in quiet peace,
God rewards when she comes to her eternal home.

Poem by Abram Fast; translated from German by Peter J. Dyck, 2007

16

Health

A Human Prerequisite

Rudolph Dyck opens his interesting autobiography, *Aus dem Leben eines Arztes im Chaco*, with a quote from philosopher Arthur Schopenhauer: "Health is not everything: but without health, everything else is nothing."

A community is only as healthy as its members.

Ironically, Mennonite colonists, who were in other things so thorough in their planning, were inexplicably negligent where health was concerned. They went to great lengths to ensure that new settlements were supplied with what would be needed on the frontier. Care was taken to include a preacher and an Ältester. Those emigrating from Canada to Mexico took implements and feed for their horses. But healthcare was taken for granted; it was in God's providence.

The story of Gerhard and Tina Schartner provides an illustration. They were among those who, while in Germany, gained visas to enter Canada. The night before their scheduled departure, colony planners asked them to go to Paraguay instead. Gerhard's services as preacher and teacher were needed in Fernheim colony. Their immediate answer was, "Yes, if we are needed in Paraguay, we are willing to go." They put their Canadian visa aside and redirected their travels to Paraguay, where they lived a full and productive life with no regrets.

That Tina was a trained midwife was of no account. As it happened, she was one of three Russian-trained midwives who delivered a generation of Fernheim babies. Overwork contributed to the fact that she was able to bring only two of her own pregnancies to full term. Gerhard, after long-time service on the Fernheim hospital committee, led in the founding of the leprosy program at Km 81. All the while he pastored the EMB Gemeinde in Filadelfia.

Many Little Graves

By today's standards, settling thousands of refugees hundreds of miles from accessible healthcare would be unconscionable. Pioneer life exacted a price in human life, and the result was many little graves. The growing numbers of widows, widowers, orphans, and adults unable to work because of illness contributed to low morale and made these pioneer days harder than necessary.

Neuland colony was more fortunate. For its first thirty years, it had the untiring services of Dr. Wilhelm and Anna Rakko.

Volendam required each member family to contribute two hundred bricks for the construction of a hospital in its first year. A succession of doctors served the colony, but continuity as well as most deliveries were managed by Schwester (sister/nurse) Betty [Helmel], who had studied midwifery in Germany. All Volendam physicians since 1966 have been Paraguayan.

The German Red Cross outfitted each Fernheim village with a first-aid kit, but they were soon depleted. It was ten years before a resident doctor was found. There were many births, most of them attended by midwives without formal training.

Healthcare was almost exclusively the domain of women. In Sommerfeld it was Schwester Anna [Heinrichs], who was perpetually on call, working out of her home until 1952, when the colony built a modest hospital. Just weeks before moving with her family to Paraguay, she had graduated first in her class at Concordia School of Nursing in Winnipeg. By the time Sommerfeld celebrated its fiftieth anniversary, the colony had been served by fifteen doctors, none of whom were Mennonite, and thirty-eight nurses, all of whom were Mennonite and three of whom served for more than three decades.

Many Mennonite colonies had in their midst *knibble doctash* (untrained chiropractors). They served a much-needed and appreciated, though limited, function. Mostly the people were hardy and resourceful in the use of home remedies. Indigenous neighbors enriched their treatment repertoire and pharmacy. When illness or accidents occurred, they prayed for grace to accept it as God's will. When death occurred, the community rallied, and somehow life went on.

The pioneer generation was plagued by malaria, trachoma, and stomach parasites resulting in anemia. A survey conducted by a Brazilian doctor in 1938 concluded that 70 percent of school children suffered from trachoma, an infectious eye disease that leads to blindness. Water was not reliably available for drinking, cooking, or bathing. Diets were woefully deficient, especially for pregnant and nursing mothers.

In contrast to modern diets based on meat, the pioneer's diet consisted mostly of flour, sugar, rice, and potatoes—long on carbohydrates and lean on protein and vitamins. In an early year, according to a Fernheim publication, the annual per capita meat consumption was 19 kilograms (42 pounds), compared with 145 kilograms (320 pounds) for the Paraguayan military.

Men engaged in hard physical labor that was often hazardous. Immunizations were not available for children. In summer, the climate was unbearably hot; in winter, chills fostered respiratory diseases. The colonists pushed themselves to work while burning with malaria-induced fever.

Premature Deaths

Before taking possession of the land that would become Menno colony, the first Canadian émigrés in 1927 left ninety-six graves in the Mennonite section of Puerto Casado's Catholic graveyard, victims of typhoid epidemic. Fernheim colonists also suffered a typhoid epidemic while still living in tents, resulting in ninety-four deaths that devastated three villages and left dozens of widows and orphans in its wake. Before their colony was even organized, Sommerfeld members buried twenty people, most of them children, in a temporary graveyard. Four hundred and forty-one Sommerfeld colonists abandoned the pioneer effort and returned to Canada.

But They Managed

Each colony has its own stories and heroes. In Fernheim, it was the legendary Tante Suse. Born in the Ukraine, Suse remained behind in Mölln, Germany, to attend her ailing mother when her father and the first Fernheim settlers left for Paraguay. After her mother's death, Suse followed to Paraguay, arriving, as Peter P. Klassen says in his book *Frauenschicksale*, "with open eyes and an open heart." Fernheim families called on her night and day, year after year, when faced with health-related crises.

With help from the German Red Cross and Mennonite Central Committee, Fernheim colonists were able to construct a modest building that served as a hospital years before it had a doctor. Next to it was a simple, two-room pioneer house that served as a pharmacy and consultation room. Mostly patients recuperated (or died) under the shade of a tree, sometimes sheltered by an improvised umbrella.

When the Chaco War broke out in 1932, Paraguayan army doctors commandeered the modest Mennonite facilities in Filadelfia. When they became aware that Tante Suse was in the process of relocating her practice, they suggested that the army hospital serve both wounded soldiers and Mennonite patients. Tante Suse learned some Spanish; the Paraguayan doctors learned some German.

This unique partnership worked well, and Mennonites were sad to see it end when the war ceased in 1935—although happy the war was over. The physicians left with the army, but Tante Suse continued with very limited resources.

While leaving the Chaco, one Paraguayan doctor remarked that "white Indians" cannot survive in the Chaco. "Your people have no future here," he said. Tante Suse was shocked, both at his dreary prediction and that he referred to Mennonites as white Indians, although he meant no offense. When the doctor returned ten years later, he was astounded to see the progress Mennonites had made.

The hospital closed for a time after the war. When Fernheim was able to engage a doctor, it was not always with good results. Tante Suse was suspicious about the credentials of one who had been employed "off the street." He turned out to be a third-year veterinarian student.

Finally, a Resident Doctor

In 1941 MCC's long search for a doctor found John R. Schmidt, who was just about to complete his medical training. Within a few months the young, single, adventuresome doctor was on the high seas, en route to Filadelfia. Not only did he come with the latest in medical training, he also was able to converse in Plautdietsch. Schmidt even enjoyed cookies baked from the same recipe his mother had inherited from her parents, who had

A 1960 gathering of nurses and doctors from the three Chaco colonies. The men in the front row are the three colony doctors. From the left, Wilhelm Kaethler of Menno colony, Fernheim's Gerhard Dollinger, and Neuland's Wilhelm Rakko.

moved to Kansas from Russian Mennonite communities two generations earlier. Schmidt liked the challenge of pioneer medicine, and Fernheim colonists were overjoyed to finally have a resident doctor.

In his concluding report, Schmidt wrote that he treated about 1,450 patients in a two-year term The most common diagnoses were trachoma, brought along from Russia; hookworm, contributing to nutritional inadequacy; and malaria. Schmidt also wrote that "as far as climate goes, the white man can easily live in the Chaco." That this affirmation was necessary speaks to the doubts some people were entertaining.

Schmidt returned to his home in Kansas, where he married Clara Regier, a recently graduated nurse. Days after their wedding this remarkable couple returned for another stint in Filadelfia. As mentioned earlier, Clara saw the need for better nursing care and organized the first school for nurses in 1943. Menno colony organized a similar school some years later. These schools also trained nurses from the East Paraguay colonies. Schools in Asunción eventually replaced these training programs, but in the meantime they served a much-needed transitional function.

Some years later the Schmidts pioneered leprosy work, which became their life calling. (See chapter 21.)

Mennonites Enter Medicine

A new generation of Paraguayan Mennonites was attracted to the medical profession. The first was Wilhelm Kaethler, who received much of his training in the United States before rendering a lifetime of valuable service with his wife, Frieda, in several colonies. Their son, William, was the resident physician in Yalve Sanga for some years before immigrating to Winnipeg.

Next was Rudolph Dyck, who met his wife, Erika, also a Russian immigrant, while both studied medicine in Argentina. Together they rendered valuable service in numerous colonies and Km 81 before retiring in Filadelfia in 2007.

Hans Epp was the first Mennonite doctor to train in Paraguay. A descendant of the Harbiner adventure, Epp grew up seeing his midwife mother leave at all hours to attend a birth. Upon completing his training in December 1963, Epp was employed as the first full-time Paraguayan-born doctor for the growing indigenous communities. He and his wife, Ingrid, have served the Mennonite community in multiple roles and are today retired in Filadelfia.

As German Mennonites became more proficient in Spanish, more entered medical training, with some graduating with honors. I was supplied with a list of forty-eight Paraguayan Mennonites who've obtained medical degrees since the beginning of the colonies, most in Paraguay but a few in Argentina. Fewer Mennonites are now entering the medical profession because, as a member of a colony high school recently remarked, "It doesn't pay."

Paraguayan Physicians

Paraguayan doctors deserve recognition for their contribution to Mennonite health. When a typhoid epidemic threatened Menno colony in its first days, and when three years later the same fate befell Fernheim, Paraguayan doctors came to the rescue.

Friesland, Volendam, Bergthal, and Sommerfeld all have colony-owned hospitals staffed by Mennonite nurses and Paraguayan doctors. The Mexican colonies do not have their own hospitals but use Paraguayan medical services.

During the Chaco War, as noted earlier, Paraguayan army doctors served Mennonites along with soldiers. Friesland colony was for some years assisted by doctors from the neighboring Bruderhof colony. Difficult cases were referred to Asunción hospitals. The Asunción Baptista hospital was for many years a familiar site for Mennonites. The problem was getting there in time.

Health in the Indigenous Community

Mennonites were disturbed by the lack of hygiene and poor nutrition along with a high rate of infant mortality among the indigenous people. Tuberculosis-induced coughing also alarmed them, because they feared contagion but also because they knew it could be fatal to these neighbors. As a result improved health was one of four objectives in the founding of the Licht den Indianern mission. In 2008 more than three hundred thousand dollars was designated in the Association of Indigenous-Mennonite Cooperation Services' annual budget for health-related projects. Additionally indigenous are always welcome at the Mennonite health facilities, where they sometimes occupy as much as one-third of the beds.

In 2008, ASCIM was soliciting contributions to expand the Yalve Sanga hospital, which also serves outlying clinics. Services also include an active immunization and prevention program, along with dental and eye care. The German charity Deutsches Aussätzigen Hilfswerk has joined in an assault on tuberculosis, which remains a serious health problem.

While substantial improvement have been made in the health of the indigenous people, including lower infant mortality and longer-life expectancy, many health issues remain. Gertrude Hiebert, a medical doctor who has devoted more than fifteen years to serving the indigenous community, is especially concerned about persistent high incidence of tuberculosis.

The Broadening Meaning of Health

A higher standard of living in German Mennonite and indigenous communities has led to a demand for expanded healthcare. High infant mortality is no longer common. People are no longer willing to suffer with an offending tooth until it can be extracted, sans Novocain. No longer are they satisfied to look at the world (or read their Bibles) with poor vision. They wanted and deserved better medical care.

In the mid-1940s MCC assigned Gerhard Klassen, a dentist from

Katharina Hildebrand celebrates her 105th birthday in Sommerfeld colony. She was born in Russia and lived much of her life in Canada before immigrating to Paraguay in 1948 at age 56.

Hillsboro, Kansas, to the colonies. Klassen not only filled cavities and removed teeth, he also trained two Paraguayan Mennonite paraprofessional dentists to succeed him. Today most German Mennonites and indigenous have access to fully qualified dentists with the latest equipment.

Eyesight was a huge problem, owing first to the prevalence of trachoma. It was many years before stigmatism could be corrected with eyeglasses. Some were able to help themselves provisionally with "dime store" glasses. Today fully qualified and equipped Mennonite ophthalmologists in the colonies offer the same services and frames as those available in the United States and Canada.

Many had long been troubled over an inability to better care for those with emotional struggles. The trauma these pioneers suffered left more than its share of emotional wounds that cried out for professional treatment. The Chaco and East Paraguay colonies, with help from MCC, introduced a mental-health facility in 1962. Though headquartered in Filadelfia, the program serves the entire Paraguayan Mennonite community. Marlene Hänel, a German, became the clinic's first psychiatrist in 1959.

After Hänel's contract expired in 1965, the program sank to little more than residential care. It was later redesigned and restructured under the leadership of Heinz Ratzlaff, with support from the U.S.-based Mennonite Mental Health Services. Now known as Eirene/SMSM (*Eirene* means "peace"), it cares for 120 patients annually. The professional staff also conducts educational programs on a variety of mental health issues.

Care for the Elderly

Attached to most Mennonite colony hospitals are modest facilities to care for the elderly. Menno colony Oberschulze Cornelius Sawatzky spoke for all the colonies when he said to me, "We owe much to the pioneer generation. Cost what it may, our intention is to honor them by providing them with good care as long as they live."

The cost is substantial. Menno colony allocates 30 percent of its colony budget to pensions and medical care. Other colonies do similarly. With good care, people live longer, increasing the cost. Some worry that this level of cost will not be sustainable, a phenomena familiar to North Americans.

Today

Rudolf Dyck observed in his autobiography that the nature of illness in the Chaco has changed. Hookworm, malaria, and trachoma, and an occasional case of leprosy plagued the pioneers. The modern medical problems of the pioneers' descendants are obesity, high blood pressure, hypertension, and cancer, especially skin cancer from exposure to the sun (like their cousins in the United States, Canada, and Germany). Tuberculosis remains a problem in the indigenous communities.

The Mennonite birth rate has declined in the German-speaking colonies to just above the replacement level. In the Old Colony settlements, however, *kinderreiche Familien* (large families) are still common.

Paraguayan Mennonites enjoy a quality of healthcare equivalent to and at points superior to what their Canadian and American cousins receive. They see doctors qualified in a variety of specialties. Their hospitals are equipped with modern diagnostic and pharmaceutical facilities. Special cases are referred to Asunción or Argentina, much as North American cases are referred to university hospitals.

17

Education

Preparing the Next Generation

Julius Legiehn, who was a teacher in Fernheim before becoming Oberschulze, once remarked, "Wherever a group of Mennonites let themselves down there, they start a school already in the first year." This was true of Mennonites in the Chaco and East Paraguay.

The availability of land and the freedom to educate their children according to their convictions were two prerequisites for Mennonite immigration. The loss of either was the major contributor to emigration.

"If we can't control our schools, we lose our children, and if we lose our children, we have no future," noted a Menno colony parent. "And is that not why our parents left Russia in the first place?"

Education was also a major component in the German Mennonite mission strategy. It was one of four objectives identified by the Licht den Indianern mission. Mennonite-run schools are arguably the most visible part of the mission thrust to Latino Paraguayans, especially in Asunción.

As we will see in this chapter, education was an essential part of Mennonites' sustainability and prosperity in Paraguay.

Divergent Approaches

Mennonites may be unanimous in the importance of education, but they are decidedly diverse about its purpose and how it should be conducted.

For example, in the Old Colony settlements of Bergthal, Sommerfeld,

A Menno colony village school in 1928. Schools like this were common in the pioneer years.

and the Mexican colonies, education is seen as a carrier of tradition. Its purpose is to pass on the faith as it has been handed down through the generations. Children are taught to conform. Students are divided not into traditional classes but into four categories: *Fibler* (beginners), who learn reading, writing, numbers, and penmanship; *Katechismer*, who must comprehend 202 prescribed questions in the Katechismus and the Ten Commandments; *Testamentler*, who must memorize the Katechismus (three errors are allowed!); and finally *Bibler*, who practice extensive reading and memorization of the Old and New Testaments.

While Testamentlers or Biblers perform their recitations, Fiblers and Katechismers are required to sit with their hands folded on their desks and listen. On occasions a child as young as nine may know the entire catechism.

The Old Colony school system is under the tight control of the Älteste and the Ohms. The system has therefore seen little change for more than one hundred years, dating back to Prussia. Teachers have little latitude for variation. Classroom discipline is strict and sometimes harshly enforced. Education is compulsory for girls from ages six to twelve and for boys from ages six to fourteen.

The teacher is always a man. He has no formal education above the level he is instructing. Some teachers are blessed with natural talent, but some are selected because they are unable to do physical work. The pay is poor, and teaching, surprisingly, is not a prestigious position.

When Menno colony parents asked in the pioneer years that the curriculum be broadened and new ways of teaching be adopted, church leaders responded by insisting, "Let's stay with the old, as we have always done things and keep ourselves separate from those who want to move ahead or who want to go along with the world."

The Progressive Approach

The progressive approach to education traces its roots to reforms that took place in Molotschna colony of pre-revolutionary Russia, after Old Colony people had left for the United States and Canada. A prominent figure in this story is Johann Cornies, who was born in Danzig in 1789 and immigrated with his parents first to Chortitza colony, then to Molotschna after its founding in 1803. He worked a few years as a laborer and later as a huckster. Cornies was denied a good education, but books on a wide range of subjects accompanied him wherever he went.

Through frugal living, Cornies was able to save enough money to purchase a small farm. He soon recognized the favorable opportunities the steppes offered for raising cattle, and he constantly worked to upgrade the quality of his herds and land. By the time of his death at age fifty-nine, he had built a model estate of 25,000 acres with 500 horses, 8,000 sheep, 200 cattle, and a large tree nursery.

Cornies's revolutionary vision extended also to education. He established a readers circle. In 1843 he worked with other reformers and succeeded in wresting control of colony schools from the church and placing them under the newly created Society for Christian Education. The large and growing Molotschna colony was divided into six school districts. Inadequate teachers were dismissed, and attendance became compulsory.

Cornies drew up eighty-seven rules for the instruction and treatment of children. The curriculum, which had previously emphasized memorization of the Bible and a few historic writings, was expanded to reflect a broader worldview. Business and vocational training were added, giving rise to increased industrialization and what is sometimes referred to the Golden Era of Mennonites in Russia. By one account, Mennonite factories before the revolution manufactured about 15,000 mowers, 3,000 threshing machines, 105 windmills, and a variety of farm-related machinery per year.

To further increase the quality of instruction, a teachers college with professors trained in Germany was established. The Mennonite education system was considered a model by all acquainted with it, including Russian school officials.

This was, to be sure, interrupted by the Russian Revolution in 1917, but they brought this education background with them to Paraguay. Many of the immigrants were graduates and proponents of this progressive system of education.

Fernheim Brings Progressive Education to Paraguay

While the families were still living in tents, Fernheim teachers gathered children to begin their studies. With little material, in the shade of a tree, with improvised desks or balancing what few books they had on their knees, the children began their education. Teachers felt an urgency to make up for time lost during the years as refugees. They soon drew up a curriculum based on the Russian system.

Subject	**Hours per week**
Religion	3
German language	4
Spanish language	3
Arithmetic	5
Geography	2
History	2
Nature study	2
Music	2
Art	1
Total	24

Jakob Warkentin, respected Neuland teacher and author is an eloquent spokesperson for this more progressive approach to education. He sees the teacher as both preserver of tradition and innovator. In his view, schools and teachers function to recover what is being lost, preserve what is worthwhile, and explore what is new. He expects education

Jakob and Sina Warkentin, who as children were refugees with the Neuland group. Jakob was nine years old when he immigrated to Paraguay with his widowed mother in 1947. MCC helped him complete several years of advanced studies in Germany. He was a major influence on progressive Mennonite education as a teacher, school administrator, and writer. In 1995 Philipps Universitat Marburg in Germany conferred on him a PhD, and in 2007 Germany awarded him the prestigious Bundesverdienstkreuzes.

to prepare students for the world in which they will be living. His philosophy is stated in the following Kahlil Gabran quote, which he included in addressing a conference called Mennonites in Paraguay—On the Threshold of the Third Millennium, held in Asuncion May 25 and 26, 2000:

> Your children are not your children. They are the sons and daughters of life's longing for itself. They come through you but not from you, and though they are with you, yet they belong not to you. You may give them your love but not your thoughts. For they have their own thoughts. You may house their bodies but not their souls, for their souls dwell in the house of tomorrow, which you cannot visit, not even in your dreams. You may strive to be like them, but seek not to make them like you. For life goes not backward nor tarries with yesterday. You are the bows from which your children as living arrows are sent forth. The archer sees the mark upon the path of the infinite, and He bends you with His might that His arrows may go swift and far.

The traditional and progressive approaches to education stand in juxtaposition to each other. They are a product of the systems that employ them. At the same time they reinforce and perpetuate themselves.

Redefining Boundaries

The Old Colony school system is tightly under the control of the church. In the progressive colonies, authority is divided among the colony, the church, and the school. Occasionally, there are boundary disputes. One of these arose as Fernheim colony was preparing to celebrate its tenth anniversary (details are stated in chapter 3). Fritz Kliewer, a charismatic headmaster educated in Germany, was advocating National Socialism and speaking in support of its militaristic overtones, contradicting the biblical teachings of nonresistance and love of enemy historically taught in the congregations.

Peter Wiens, a lifelong Fernheim teacher and preacher, stated flatly, "The preachers can preach themselves to death if they are contradicted by what is taught in the school." Peter P. Klassen, later the headmaster of the Filadelfia secondary school, argued that to make the church the validator of the school would be the death of both.

This classic church-state conflict led the colony leaders to declare that "church, school and colony must go hand-in-hand. Schools shall be grounded in the Holy Scriptures in full harmony with the Mennonite confession of faith, including the biblical teachings on peace." Some years were needed to bring this clarification into alignment. New teachers were recruited and trained. The issue was resolved without extinguishing the flame of idealism.

Students at the vocational school in Loma Plata.

A New Orientation for Mennonite Education

With the link to Germany interrupted by the war, Mennonite educators sought to establish closer ties to with the Paraguayan educational system. More Spanish was introduced into the curriculum. More Mennonite teachers earned credentials at the State University Asunción. Mennonite schools redesigned their curriculum with Paraguayan accreditation in mind. This made it easier for Mennonite students to matriculate to the state university.

Mennonite educators from different colonies also realized the advantages of working together on an inter-colony basis. Menno colony succeeded in relaxing the grip of the Old Colony, allowing it to participate in the renaissance underway. Neuland colony, with teachers from the heralded Molotschna Teachers College, joined in, as did Friesland and Volendam schools as geographical separation permitted. German-speaking Mennonites in Asunción organized the Concordia school, with German as the primary language of instruction.

While this was happening, Old Colony members continued to adhere to tradition, though splinter groups emerged in both Sommerfeld and Bergthal. When their leaders were lax in the enforcement of traditional regulations, some members immigrated to Bolivia, where tradition was being upheld.

With the passing of time, Mennonites needed new skills to compete in the world around them, and the curriculum of progressive Mennonite schools reflected this. In 2008 more than four hundred German Mennonite students were studying nursing, medicine, business, and other subjects leading to professional degrees from Asunción universities. This includes teachers who will be teaching in Spanish.

Asunción-based higher education was expanded through the Universidad Evangelica del Paraguay (UEP), a recent collaboration by the Insitituto Biblico Asunción (IBA) and Centro Evangélico Mennonita de Teologia (CEMTA), and several other evangelical denominations, along with the Disciples of Christ and the Anglican Church. UEP had a student body of 1,583 in 2007 at several campuses, and about three hundred of these students were Mennonite. The school is a significant resource for the wider evangelical community operating in a predominantly Roman Catholic culture. The leaders of this promising movement made a statement about the future when they designed a six-story main building. The school's graduates will, it is hoped, build strong churches and institutions and provide a Christian influence in the new, emerging Paraguay.

Post-Secondary Education

To satisfy the need for higher education and vocational training based in the colonies, the three Chaco settlements instituted a collaborative program with provision for students from East Paraguay to attend. The program offers three tracks:

- *Vocational and agriculture*. Based in Loma Plata, it includes a two-year program with two hundred students studying agriculture, mechanic, electronics, carpentry, administration, bookkeeping, and business.
- *Teacher training*. Based in Filadelfia, the Instituto de Formación Docente, has an enrollment of forty-six students preparing to teach in the German-language Mennonite schools.
- *Home economics*. Based in Neu Halbstadt, Neuland, fifty-five women are enrolled in a two-year home management course that includes nutrition and uses classroom theory and practical learning techniques.

Theological Training

In the early years of the colonies, a few German-speaking pastors were able to study in the United States, Canada, Germany, or Switzerland. Starting in 1954 and to its closing in 1974, some attended the Mennonite seminary in Montevideo, Uruguay. Some also attended the Baptist seminary in Buenos Aires.

In the 1960s the colonies realized a need for better-trained German-speaking pastors and for Spanish-speaking pastors to serve the growing Latino Paraguayan churches. With help from the Mennonite Brethren Mission, they purchased a choice lot in Asunción. It became the base for a number of Mennonite Brethren activities, including the IBA.

In 2008, eighty-one were studying at IBA. The full-time student body comes from Paraguayan and German-speaking congregations.

A second Mennonite seminary came to Asunción after the Mennonite seminary in Montevideo, Uruguay, closed in 1974, when the political situation there became unstable. Many believed the semi-

The 2001 graduating class of Colegio Loma Plata in Menno colony; schools are in transition from traditional to progressive education.

nary should remain in Latin America, and Paraguay was selected because it had the largest Mennonite constituency. It was also thought to be politically stable. The reborn seminary opened as CEMTA in Asunción in 1977 and relocated to a spacious new campus in 1980. IBA leaders gave serious consideration to joining CEMTA but in the end decided otherwise. As a result, the relatively small Mennonite population in Paraguay is supporting two seminaries in Asunción.

CEMTA's degree programs include a bachelor's of theology, a six-year program for pastors, a diploma program for service-minded students who have not completed high school, and a three- or four-year music degree. CEMTA's library has more than ten thousand volumes, some brought from Montevideo. The school is also known for its excellent music program.

Schools for the Indigenous

The importance German Mennonites placed on education for themselves was extended also to the indigenous, for whom book learning was as foreign as a Canadian snowstorm. It took many years, but Western-style education caught on, and within one generation the demand exceeded what the missions were able to provide.

Village by village the Chaco became dotted with schools for the indigenous people. Whenever a new settlement was established, a modest school was part of the master plan. By 2006, almost four thousand indigenous children were enrolled in the school system Gerhard Giesbrecht had started for six Enlhet children under a tree in Yalve Sanga three generations earlier.

The increase in education also permitted indigenous people to climb the employment ladder. In the early years of the colonies, they had been relegated to weeding, picking cotton, and gathering and chopping wood. Next they became tractor drivers and expert bricklayers, laying the bricks for dwellings that only German Mennonites could afford. Before long, indigenous people were apprenticing and eventually pastoring churches, teaching in a growing number of classrooms, and serving as health auxiliaries. Education was the key.

Education as Mission

Mennonite missions also spread the gospel to the Paraguayan Latino population through education. God alone knows the lives that have been changed by Mennonite-sponsored mission schools, including three large schools in Asunción with more than 2,300 students. (These are described in greater detail in chapter 18.) Mennonites have not only educated their own children, they have also helped to raise the literacy rate nationwide from an abysmally low rate to 91.6 percent in 2008. This is above many of the country's South American neighbors.

Paraguay has given Mennonites what they wanted most—freedom to educate their children—and Mennonites have risen to the challenge. Through education they have helped succeeding generations to face their challenges while upholding the biblical values that brought Mennonites to Paraguay in the first place.

18

Asunción

A Role Born of Necessity

When Mennonites first set foot on Asunción's dusty streets in 1921, they stepped into one of the hemisphere's oldest cities, founded in 1537. Their intent was to determine if the Paraguayan Chaco was a suitable place for them to resettle. In his book *Neue Heimat in der Chaco Wildnis*, Martin W. Friesen describes Asunción:

> Asunción had a population of about 100,000 at that time. The plant life of this city impressed our delegates immensely. How beautiful the flowers, the ornamental shrubs and trees were. Asunción was a green city, friendly and inviting. No one seemed to be in a hurry and everything seems so peaceful. It was obvious the people felt tomorrow was another day. "Mañana!" (tomorrow).
>
> Traffic on the cobblestone streets was normal. Streetcars, some cars, many two wheel carts pulled by oxen, mules or horses rolled through the streets. Included in this rattling and squeaking and creaking traffic, and where the animals were driven forward with a loud voice, were women wearing white shawls riding donkeys and smoking big cigars. Strung across the back of these donkeys were sacks of all kinds of fruit.
>
> So this was the Asunción from which so much was expected.

The pioneer generation saw Asunción as little more than a city they had to pass through en route to the Chaco. Most had no desire to live there. As the Paraguay Mennonite story unfolded, Asunción grew in

Paraguay's new parliament building, where numerous Mennonites have served over the years.

importance, and today it is an essential part of the Mennonite Paraguay scene and is looking forward to hosting the Mennonite World Conference in 2009.

With a population approaching a million, but sans skyscrapers and a panoramic skyline, Asunción is proud of a new modern airport, a new parliament building, *Parque de Museo de Historia Natural,* (National Museum of History) and a swelling business district. The new intermingles with the old. Modern bungalows surrounded by tropical plants with iron burglar bars and tile roofs adorn a new residential district. A young, barefoot mother, with a baby strapped to her back with a brightly colored blanket, winds her way on the crowded cobblestone sidewalk. The young population bears physical traits of Paraguay's aboriginal past. Throughout the city are monuments to war heroes, but the name Alfredo Stroessner, so prominent until he was deposed in a bloody coup in 1989, has been expunged.

While you wait for a green light, hordes of street boys offer to clean your windshield in exchange for a few guaraní or to sell you one of Asunción's five daily newspapers. In a unique feature, garbage is elevated one meter above street level in little cages to keep it from being scattered by dogs.

Today the German Mennonite community living in Asunción numbers about 1,400 and growing. The two German Mennonite congregations have almost seven hundred members. So what drew Mennonites to Asunción?

Colony Logistical Office

Initially the rural Mennonite colonies tried to conduct business like buying and selling in Asunción on an itinerant basis. They purchased necessities like flour, sugar, and coffee in Asunción and shipped them to the colonies to be repackaged and sold to members. When Mennonites' production of eggs, cheese, cotton, peanuts, or lumber exceeded their internal needs, the market was in Asunción. Later the colonies needed to deal with Asunción banks and transact business with government offices.

By the mid-1950s the three western colonies each had a *hof* in Asunción. The East Paraguay colonies had not felt this need as keenly, owing in part to their proximity to Asunción.

A Place to Live and Work

Some of the families destined for Neuland or Volendam colonies in the late 1940s preferred to live and work in Asunción. Along with them was a growing number of students from the colonies in the city, the German Mennonite population increased to about three hundred in the late 1940s. That number has increased steadily, as did the reasons to live there. Some now think of Asunción Mennonites as a kind of urban colony, although they live widely scattered throughout the city. Much of their common life revolves around the church.

As German Mennonites became acquainted with Paraguayan business practices and proficient with the Spanish language, they ventured into business. One of the first was Kornelius Walde who, along with duties at Comité Social y Económico Mennonita, (CSEM) developed a thriving import business. In the 1960s and '70s, Juan Neufeld's prosperous travel agency (Menno Tour) and thriving currency exchange was known widely. The number of Mennonite-owned businesses continued to grow and then increased sharply after the departure of President Stroessner in 1989.

In Asunción in 2008, German Mennonites owned more than thirty businesses. They manufacture bicycles, motorcycles, cabinets, and they sell and service electrical components and air-conditioners. There is also a large hardware distributorship. The six largest Mennonite-owned firms had annual sales in excess of 142 million U.S. dollars in 2006. (The largest had sales of seventy million dollars.) They also employ more than two thousand employees; the largest company has more than nine hundred employees.

A Place to Study

From the first years, German Mennonites have gone to Asunción to study. Initially teachers went to learn Spanish at the university. In 1950 Fernheim selected eleven students to study at the university with the expectation that they would return to serve the colony in leadership roles.

To arrange their housing in a Christian setting in the "big city," they purchased a house and installed Fritz and Margarete Kliewer as tutors and house parents. Later David Boschmann, a teacher in Goethe, a prominent German school sponsored by the German government, served in that capacity.

The house was expanded several times until it reached its current capacity of twenty-two residents. The number of students studying in Asunción continued to increase and took a decided upturn in the last decade. There are now more than four hundred German Mennonites in the city, studying teacher education, health-related subjects including medicine, nursing, and pharmacy, as well as accounting, administration, secretarial, social work, and agriculture. This group is obviously far bigger than what can be accommodated in colony-owned housing, and many Mennonite students feel comfortable making their own arrangements.

Medical Treatment

Except for the Mexican colonies, the Mennonite settlements have their own hospitals that can treat most cases, but it was not always that way. In the early years, difficult cases were referred to advanced medical services in Asunción. The Baptist hospital was familiar to colony Mennonites. Patients found shelter with Mennonite families living there, but the need soon exceeded what the Mennonites in the city could provide.

This led to a unique and greatly valued service coordinated with the Mennonitenheim. Rooms are reserved, and a nurse helps colony patients set up appointments, to provide translation if needed, and to help with medications. Staff is also available to help with aftercare that is sometimes

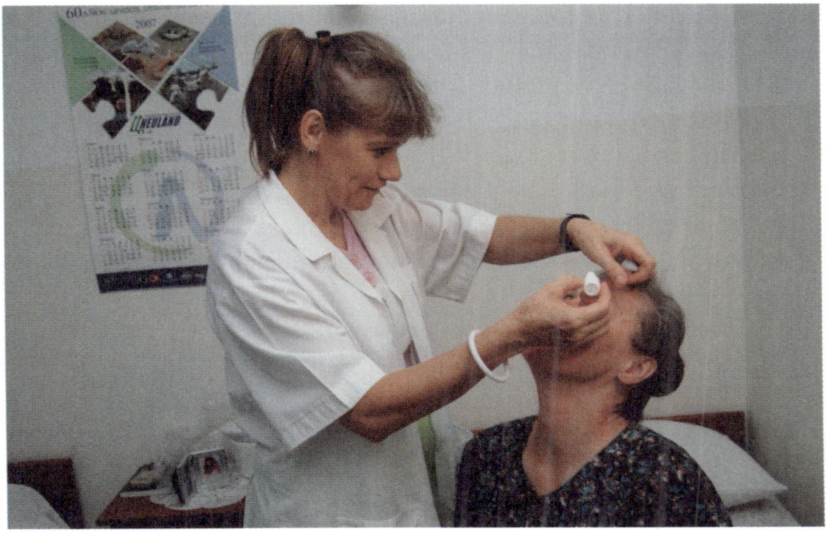

Nurse Rosie Toews administers eyedrops to a resident patient at Mennonitenheim.

several weeks long. In the event of death, staff notify families and help make arrangements.

A Place for Ministry

Both the MG and MB have established mission churches in Asunción. In 2008, there were close to twenty Mennonite churches and outposts (that is, church plants) in greater Asunción. Two large congregations are German-speaking, but the others use Spanish and are comprised predominantly of Latino Paraguayans. Many of these young churches are growing quickly.

The Christian presence is supplemented by the OBEDIRA, an MB-owned radio ministry that blankets Asunción and its suburbs with Christian programming around the clock. It was made possible through the philanthropic generosity of a Winnipeg businessman and former émigré. The ministry celebrated twenty years on the air in 2008.

The success of OBEDIRA led to the 2004 establishment of Red Guaraní, a television station that reaches Asunción and beyond. It seeks to be a Christian alternative to public programming, with a special focus on families. In 2007 more than three thousand people registered for assistance with marriage and family issues on *Confinaza*, one of its most popular and fastest growing programs. In 2005 the station gained a satellite connection, making international transmission possible. The combined OBEDIRA and Red Guaraní programs have 160 employees.

There is also an impressive array of Mennonite-sponsored social service ministries in Asunción. Chief among them is Christlicher Dienst, (Christian Service) with many of its major programs taking place in the city, including the ministry to street children. There is also Tacumbú, a Christian ministry in the national penitentiary.

Arguably the most visible Mennonite ministry in Asunción comes through three schools: Colegio Concordia, Colegio Albert Schweitzer, and Colegio Gutenberg. These serve more than 2,300 children and reach a community of ten thousand people.

Mennonite Guest House

In 1943 Mennonite Central Committee decided that a director should reside in Paraguay to serve the colonies in East Paraguay and the Chaco. MCC purchased a two-story residence a kilometer from center of Asunción that became known as MCC Heim. In October 1980, MCC sold the building to the Mennonites in Paraguay, and it was renamed Mennonitenheim.

Mennonitenheim was for many years the spiritual and social center for Paraguay's Mennonites. It was a guesthouse for visitors, and in its early years a residence for colony women working in Asunción. The CSEM offices are still located there.

It also works as a self-serve post office. Each of the Mennonite colonies and some of the major institutions have a box in the building, located at the far end of the dining hall. A letter deposited in a colony box enters the colony postal system for delivery. "Mennonitenheim Postal 166, Asunción, Paraguay" reaches the entire Mennonite population in Paraguay. It is not always next-day delivery, but all this is possible without a postmaster or postage stamp.

Originally, overnight visitors at Mennonitenheim got little more than a bed with a fly swatter and paper fan. The services increased steadily with the rising standard of living. In the 1970s a few rooms had air-conditioning at an extra charge. Today Mennonitenheim's services are equivalent to an economy hostel with numerous unique features, but no room service. Meals are served family style—Russian Mennonite cuisine with some Latino supplements.

Mennonitenheim came to serve as the unofficial *Treffpunkt* (meeting place). A bonus of staying there is the opportunity to meet and converse with a wide variety of people coming and going. One may be dining with an Oberschulze, an elderly women with a bandaged eye or arm, a Nivaclé man on business in Asunción, or a visitor from Canada or Germany.

Intercolony committees meet in the *aula*, a large meeting room reserved for that purpose. Asunción Mennonites met there many years for zwieback and coffee after their Sunday-afternoon worship services. They gave it up reluctantly when they built a new church in 1985. Asunción youth played many vigorous games of volleyball there, in tight quarters, taking time out occasionally to sweep up window glass.

In 1980, when MCC sold this valuable appreciated property to a body made up jointly of Mennonite churches and colonies, the money was not returned to MCC but, at MCC's insistence, was designated to mission causes within Paraguay. Now a full-fledged hostel, it has sixty-two rooms with 165 beds, most with air-conditioning, and a crowded dining room. In 2006 more than fifteen thousand guests found overnight lodging there; many were medical patients and their families.

Waiting for the call to dinner at Mennonitenheim in Asunción. If these swings and tropical plants could talk, what tales they'd tell of life in Russia, Canada, and Paraguay!

Meeting to Worship

In the early years Asunción's German Mennonites met in members' living rooms. They maintained some semblance of a Mennonite fellowship, but with severe limitations. By 1950 the Mennonite population had grown under the leadership of Ernst Harder, son of a Chaco pioneer preacher, and a church was organized.

The young fellowship leased a church building within walking distance of Mennonitenheim. The lease arrangement required them to meet on Sunday afternoons. They came to like it, and the Asunción congregation continued for many years to meet for Sunday worship in the cool of the early evening. They built their first building in 1963.

Also in 1963, the MB organized separately but continued to meet jointly with the MG for Sunday worship. In 1985 the two congregations built the present attractive and functional edifice, which seats eight hundred. It is conveniently located in the same complex as the Concordia school.

Asunción has become important to the Mennonite community and can be expected to increase as Paraguay continues toward more urbanization. The Mennonitenheim deserves honorable mention in the listing of Mennonite hostels globally as Asunción prepares to host the Mennonite World Conference in 2009.

Centro Familiar de Adoración, the site in Asunción where the Mennonite World Conference will meet in July 2009 for Assembly Gathered.

Part 3
How They Are Giving Back

In Part 1, we saw how German Mennonites came to Paraguay and faced many obstacles. Whether fleeing the advances of modernity or escaping the cruelty of Communist dictators, Mennonites were wonderfully and miraculously led in their quest for a homeland. With ingenuity and persistence, and upheld by the everlasting Arms, they overcame the obstacles and survived, though barely. It is real life drama with few equals.

In Part 2, we saw how Mennonites came to prosper. Under God's blessing and with great human effort, they made the foreboding wilderness into a breadbasket. Some left, and that was sad. There were still stiff challenges ahead, but a new generation emerged. German Mennonites began to feel at home in their Paraguayan surroundings. They were learning to interact with their Latino and aboriginal neighbors, to enjoy manioc and chipa, to start the day with tereré and mate, and to take a refreshing siesta in the heat of the day. They came to see beauty in tropical flora and fauna and in other cultures. The life that at one point seemed so impossible, so absolutely incomprehensible was beginning to make sense. Maybe there was a future for them in Paraguay after all. The tiny mustard seed was growing.

In part 3, we see the fruit of the tree that was planted in part 1 and nurtured in part 2. We see German Mennonites giving back and turning outward in ministries of witness and service. We see them respond to the human needs surrounding them. The result is a mission church with membership exceeding the total membership of their founding churches. Like so much else in this marvelous story, this outward orientation and sharing of the good news of Jesus Christ in word and deed started small—like a mustard seed.

In 2008, Paraguayan Mennonites were doing as much or more on a per capita basis in mission and service than any other national Mennonite body. They have money and a wonderful human resource in their children, for whom they have sacrificed so much. They have vision. Rejoice with me as in part 3, we see this mustard seed grow and bear fruit.

19

Mission

The Fruit of the Church

Mennonites did not come to Paraguay to do mission; they came seeking a homeland. But mission was in their subconscious. The mission seed lay dormant for some years while they were becoming settled, and then it grew and continues to grow. Mennonites are giving back and sharing the Christian faith that sustained them. They are giving the cup of cold water in the name of Christ.

The story is personified in the lives of two remarkable men, Albert Enns and Hans J. Wiens, and their equally dedicated wives. Both Wiens and Enns were born in Russia during the revolution. Their fathers, both preachers, were brutally murdered, Wiens's in Moscow's infamous Butyrka prison. In 1929 seven-year-old Wiens fled with his mother to Moscow. After a temporary stopover in Germany, they were among the single-parent families who immigrated to Fernheim colony. After completing grade ten in Fernheim, Wiens taught in a village school for four years. Then he married Susana Epp, and together they taught in the indigenous school then getting started in Yalve Sanga. They also organized a school for neighboring Paraguayans.

In 1948 the Wienses felt a call to the ministry. They accepted on one condition: that a way could be found to further their formal education. This took them to Argentina, where they spent several enjoyable years studying at the Mennonite Bible School in Bragado. Later they also studied at the International Baptist Seminary in Buenos Aires and the state university in Asunción.

While in Argentina, the Wienses met Albert Enns, who was also preparing for ministry. Enns's family had stayed in Molotschna until 1943, when Albert, together with his mother and sister and brother, joined the Great Trek, retreating ahead of the German army. They arrived in Germany as refugees in the waning days of the war. Albert was drawn into the German army and almost immediately found himself a prisoner of war. While in camp, reflecting on the radical turn his life had taken and uncertain about his future, he had a "serious encounter with Jesus Christ and vowed to serve him" the rest of his life. This he did, with wonderful results.

Enns's mother and sister were arrested in Germany and sent back to Siberia. He and his brother, Gerhard, qualified for passage on the MCC-chartered *Heintzelmann*, destined for Paraguay. In Neuland Enns's natural gift of preaching was recognized and exercised. He too went to Argentina to further his education. While there he met and married Anna Ekert, a Canadian who became his lifelong helpmeet.

The Wiens and Enns couples enjoyed each other's company. They relished opportunities afforded them to minister in Argentina and were thinking of settling there permanently. Then one night, while having devotions together, they felt a strong call to return to Paraguay.

The Wienses returned to Filadelfia, where Hans taught a course to prepare people for ministry. The Ennses, joined by friends from Fernheim, began door-to-door evangelism in Asunción. It was, more or less, a private undertaking; Chaco Mennonites already felt overextended by the burgeoning indigenous mission. A national law that forbade non-Catholic groups from meeting publicly handicapped them.

The Wienses and the Ennses invited the Mennonite Brethren North American mission, later named the Board of Missions and Services (BOMAS), to join them in what they saw as an open door of opportunity. BOMAS assumed responsibility for and financed the early mission work in Asunción. This also included support for the Wiens and Enns families. Some years later, two more couples joined the team. All were filled with joy when in 1956 they had their first public baptism.

By 1964 they felt their next step was a school to train pastors for these growing churches. This led, under Wiens's creative leadership, to the establishment of the Instituto Biblico Asunción (IBA). IBA was and still is an essential organ for the training of future MB pastors and congregational leaders, both German and Spanish speaking.

Mission Collaboration

Nelson Litwiller came to Paraguay in the early 1960s to visit the congregations and survey the fledgling mission work. Wiens and Enns had known Litwiller in Argentina, where he was a missionary under appointment by the (Old) Mennonite Church. Later he became president of the Mennonite seminary in Montevideo. Litwiller was dismayed to find that the historic separation between the MB and the MG conferences was being perpetuated in the emerging mission church. He expressed the hope that missions might go forward united, under a representative committee.

Representatives from both churches liked the idea. They planned to gather for an organizational meeting in 1963, but the MB delegates later announced they would not be joining. Their mission plans were well underway, and while agreeing that some social work might be done jointly, they concluded that the establishment of new churches should be done by individual conferences.

The distraught MG churches, along with the EMB church in Filadelfia and the large Chortitzer Menno congregation, organized the Mennonitische Missionskomitee fur Paraguay (MMKfP). It is significant to note that by this time the Old Colony mindset had relaxed to the point where Menno colony churches were included among the charter members.

MMKfP invited the North American mission boards of the General Conference and (Old) Mennonite Church to partner with them in this venture. In the early stages, these boards underwrote 80 percent of MMKfP's budget.

The work went forward throughout East Paraguay and included church planting emanating from the leprosy clinic at Km 81. MMKfP was also active in the Chaco indigenous camps, but in the late 1980s this work was given over to Menno-Indianer-Mission (MIM).

Congregations came to support the work begun by mission-minded individuals. To complement and expand the congregational efforts, MMKfP commissioned the itinerant evangelistic team of Gerd Dueck, Ernst Wiens, and Jakob Dyck. In addition to preaching and music, they showed a film *Leben Jesu* (Life of Jesus), often in open-air settings that attracted crowds into the hundreds.

These missions efforts emphasized evangelization first, then worked at gathering believers into healthy congregations. This involved recruiting and training pastors and finding a place to worship. It was with much joy that, in 1972, MMKfP was able to install Victoriano Caceres as the first Latino pastor of the newly established congregation in Itacurubi de la Cordillera.

When the Mennonite seminary in Montevideo relocated to Asunción, CEMTA began to train both Spanish- and German-speaking pastors and church leaders. In 1976 MMKfP was incorporated legally under the name Comité Mennonita de Acción Evangélica y Social en el Paraguay (COMAESP).

Establishing a new church is never easy. Though the restrictions prohibiting public meetings in Paraguay were lifted in 1967, it was a struggle for the German-speaking evangelists to address crowds who spoke Spanish or Guaraní. On occasion, they also encountered opposition from the predominant Catholic Church, but the work went on.

MMKfP operated a Christian bookstore in Asunción from 1964 to 1974. It also participated in the establishment of a few primary schools in collaboration with newly established congregations. Financial limitations were constant and exacerbated when the North American mission boards moved from a partnership to a fraternal relationship during the nearly three decades from 1963 to 1992.

Nor was it easy for these emerging Latino churches to find their identity in relationship to the German Mennonite conferences. A painful process came to a head in 1991 when nineteen churches with 890 members joined COMAESP while nineteen churches with 781 members elected to remain with a weakened MMKfP.

MB Missions Expand

Meanwhile MB mission efforts were also moving forward. In 1966, under the visionary leadership of Wiens and with substantial support from Canadian business friends, Colegio Alberto Schweitzer was established in Asunción to provide a high-quality education with a Christian emphasis to children from low-income families. It reached into hundreds of homes and helped to make the public more aware of Mennonites. The school later led to the establishment of the even larger Colegio Johannes Gutenberg (described in more detail in chapter 26).

By 1971 four small congregations had been established in Asunción, with a combined membership of 135, a paltry sum considering the effort invested. The first two Latino pastors, Carlos Chaves and Luis Alum, had been licensed. Driven by passion and vision, they organized themselves into the Convención Evangélica de los Hermanos Mennonitas and adopted an ambitious program of evangelistic outreach.

Wiens was among those who wanted to start a radio ministry to reach the Asunción population. But financial support was hard to come by. Then two former Paraguayan Mennonites who had immigrated to British Columbia and done well in business there rescued the idea by generously offering financial support. In transmitting their sizable gift, the donors said, "When we pass on what God has given us, we do it with great joy and without pain." The resulting OBEDIRA radio ministry still broadcasts Christian programming all day.

An announcer at the OBEDIRA radio, a Christian ministry.

To better equip himself to serve as an evangelist, Enns enrolled in an in-depth evangelism course offered in Costa Rica. He later led a national committee to sponsor a year-long evangelistic campaign. In close collaboration with the MB mission board in Kansas, Enns designed a program of "thrust evangelism," modeled after one that was producing good results in Brazil. Its objective was to start churches in clusters in selected rural communities. Enns accepted an invitation to explain and promote the program in the United States and Canada, helping to raise the substantial funds required. The Paraguay German Mennonite churches also increased their contributions as members prospered.

In the 1980 the Convención Evangélica de los Hermanos Mennonitas adopted a plan to start a new church with at least one hundred members in each of four strategically selected villages. The goal proved to be overstated, but that did not keep them from adopting in 1992 an even more ambitious plan to initiate fifty new congregations in the next ten years. By 2007 the Convención had forty-eight congregations with an estimated membership of 2,500. Most congregations had their own church building. They were served by thirty ordained pastors, over half of whom have studied at IBA.

Facing Challenges

The young Latino churches in both convencións faced similar challenges. One of them is surely to establish its identity in relationship to the German Mennonite identity. The public stereotype of Mennonites was one of austere men with bib overalls and women with long-sleeved dresses, followed by a bevy of children, speaking an unfamiliar language. More recently that public image also includes the positive and negative publicity associated with Mennonites involved in national politics.

Both conventions struggle with relating to their mission parents—the German Mennonite establishment in Paraguay and the North American mission boards. There is genuine appreciation and respect, but moving from dependence to independence to interdependence does not come easy and takes time, especially in a multiethnic milieu.

"Pioneers are pioneers too long—they need to become organizers," wrote IBA director Hartwig Eitzen in a doctoral dissertation. "While the [the North American board] has talked about partnerships for decades, this important missiological term [partnership] does not exist in Spanish."

Finally, these young churches face the challenge of living their own Anabaptist brand of Christianity while surrounded by Catholics and Pentecostals. Most were raised Catholic, though the number of members who've grown up in Mennonite/Anabaptist is increasing.

Both conventions appear to be doing well, but the German and the Latino churches remain separate. Yet there is collaboration and mutual understanding and respect. This can be expected to increase as they unite with Spanish as their common language. The relationship with the Catholic Church is passing through a crucial phase and will test the ecumenical spirit.

Evangelical Mennonite Brethren

In 2008, Paraguay had one Evangelical Mennonite Brethren (EMB) church, located in Filadelfia. It is deeply committed to mission and was a founding member of MMKfP. Its pioneer pastor, Gerhard Schartner, was MMKfP's first chairman. It has maintained a supportive relationship with a sister church in Buenos Aires.

In 1992 the EMB elected to initiate its own outreach program, apart from MMKfP, and established five mission churches around Asunción. The combined membership approaches four hundred, with attendance at about six hundred.

Bergthal, Sommerfeld, and the Mexican Colonies

The Old Colony settlements do not officially engage in evangelism and outreach in the usual sense. Individuals on occasion lend a helping hand to a needy neighbor out of a sense of Christian conviction. Sommerfeld and Bergthal members who felt called to do more outreach separated from the official body and are engaged in a variety of mission activities directed to their neighbors.

Tres Palmas

The small but energetic and mission-minded group Tres Palmas separated from Bergthal Colony in the early 1970s. One of its pioneer members was Agatha Braun, who had studied at the Mennonite seminary in Montevideo and had just retired from Km 81. She started a Sunday school for children from the area that attracted the participation of parents and eventually grew into a congregation.

When they felt the need for a pastor, they extended an invitation to Frank Kroeker, a Canadian missionary from the Evangelical Mennonite Church who was working with the indigenous Sanapaná in the Chaco. Kroeker brought with him EMC support that led to an ongoing partnership. Kroeker led out in an active outreach ministry that blossomed into a network of fifteen small congregations and a medical clinic serving people from the area. They also joined with the Sommerfeld Evangelische Mennonitengemeinde in sponsoring Radio Mensajero, broadcasting a strong evangelical message in five native languages to the surrounding rural communities.

Radio ministry was not new to Kroeker. He had a major role in the 1965 establishment of Radio ZP-30 in Filadelfia. It is heard throughout the vast Chaco region, broadcasting around the clock in eight languages. It focuses on evangelistic outreach and a variety of community services. Its ownership has been transferred to the three Chaco colonies, and planning is underway to expand to television.

To discover how their radio program was being received, directors of Radio Mensajero invited listeners to an open house. They were overwhelmed when 1,200 children and 800 adults showed up. Manager Chris Kroeker reported that "many listeners in this rural area say 'Radio Mensajero is our only pastor.'"

A Christian bookstore has been established in Caaguazú department. An effort is underway to minister to HIV/AIDS sufferers, and plans exist for an economic development program for low-income *campesino* (small farmer) families. The 2007 EMC mission staff included fourteen Canadian missionaries.

Sommerfeld Evangelische Mennonitengemeinde

This large congregation separated from the Sommerfeld Gemeinde in 1994. It is actively involved in numerous outreach ministries including serving a noon meal weekly to hundreds of needy neighbors, operating a daycare program for fifty children, and participating in other outreach ministries, including Radio Mensajero.

One of the largest and most visible projects began when Albert and Mary Hildebrand sold one of their two farms. Undecided what to do with the proceeds, they felt drawn to build LUZ Y Vida, a twenty-five bed hospital to serve their Paraguayan neighbors. The Sommerfeld Evangelishe Mennonitengemeinde runs the completed hospital. In 2006 a staff of forty-six workers and Paraguayan doctors conducted 38,012 consultations, admitted 6,310 patients, assisted with 544 births, and performed thousands of laboratory procedures, eye examinations, and surgeries.

Swiss Mennonite Mission Initiatives

The Amish, Beachy Amish, and Eastern Mennonite Conference, like the Russian Mennonites, are conservatives who came to Paraguay expecting to support themselves through small-scale farming. Their mission intentions and methods vary, but mostly they conduct worship services for themselves while engaging in friendship evangelism. As converts come, they are invited to join in the fellowships, some of which have also led to new congregations.

A worship team leads a Sunday morning service at the La Roca congregation, one of numerous mission outreaches to Paraguayan Latinos in Asunción.

The Future of Mennonite Missions

Mennonite missions in Paraguay can be likened to a medium-sized house with many small rooms in a Catholic neighborhood populated by many poor people. What a new generation will be doing under this roof remains to be seen. Will these multiple interests merge into a strong, unified Mennonite church with a clear Anabaptist orientation? Or will they continue to exist alongside each other in a spirit of mutuality? Will they merge into the evangelical landscape and lose their Anabaptist roots?

Paraguayan pastors representing both the MB and the MG conferences expressed optimism about the Mennonite future in Paraguay. Of the three Mennonite church entities in Paraguay, the Latino churches are clearly growing the fastest. They are impatient that the Mennonite church is today represented in only eight of Paraguay's seventeen departments (provinces). They want to be identified as Mennonites, the many cultural differences resulting from their multiple ethnicities notwithstanding. They look forward to working together with the German and indigenous conferences to host the Mennonite World Conference in 2009. Like a mighty wind, the Spirit of God is at work in Paraguay in many ways, visible and invisible. Mennonites are no longer cowering in isolated colony enclaves. They are actively engaged in a variety of outreach ministries. In unison they say, "Jesu geh voran. Jesus delante de mi. Jesus, lead the way."

20

Indigenous Missions

Neighbors Become Friends and Heirs with Christ

German Mennonites were uncertain why God had led them into such a difficult setting. From an almost storybook existence in Russia to Paraguay's forgotten wasteland in one generation—it made no sense. Then they saw the indigenous people and some said, "Ah ha! That's it. God sent us here to evangelize the Indians. It all makes sense now!"

As we saw in chapter 9, Ältester Isaak sent out a call for the Lord of the harvest to send forth reapers. The Chaco War delayed these efforts, but they resumed on the first day after the war.

The workers could not have known what this interethnic encounter would require of them or how it would change their lives. But they responded to the inner call. Ninety-eight families, who had just a few years earlier been homeless refugees, organized Licht den Indianern, which initiated services to address the four objectives they had identify at their founding: schools, churches, health facilities, and economic self-sufficiency.

Schools

Already in 1937, two years after the founding of Licht den Indianern, missionaries Gerhard and Katharina Giesbrecht were conducting a provisional school in Yalve Sanga with six Enlhet children. Materials were woefully lacking, but the Giesbrechts sang with the children and began intro-

Susana, an Enlhet teacher of the school at Tarso Amyip, tells a story.

ducing them to numbers, the alphabet, and Bible stories. They were feeling their way when suddenly one day no children appeared.

The Giesbrechts were puzzled but undaunted. Later they discovered that the children were interested only until their curiosity was sated. Gradually indigenous parents came to see the advantages of reading and writing.

Initially it was thought that indigenous intellect was capable of comprehending only lower-elementary levels of classroom learning. They were, after all, first-generation literates. Soon indigenous scholastic capacity and appetite for book learning exceeded what Mennonite missions could provide.

Education came to be seen as the key to a better life. Classrooms were added to respond to the growing demand. Settlement plans called for a school in each village. The school year was lengthened and the curriculum broadened. More grades were added as indigenous students proved their scholastic capability. By 1986 mission leaders proclaimed enthusiastically that 95 percent of the indigenous children had access to at least the first three grades—a claim few rural Paraguayan communities were able to make.

A secondary school with a dormitory was later built at the Yalve Sanga campus, where pastors were also being trained for the growing indigenous churches. The demand for indigenous graduates was strong. Schools, medical services, churches, German Mennonite employers—all were anxious to employ indigenous people who had mastered basic literacy.

The role of German Mennonites continues to recede as the indigenous take more control of their education. In recent years, mission leaders have appealed to the Paraguayan government for school accreditation and increased financial support.

Churches

Indigenous people were slow to respond to the gospel message. Church was foreign to them; it belonged initially to the missionaries. But the first

Students Enrolled in ASCIM Schools in 2006

Grade	Male	Female	Total
1	459	382	841
2	325	351	676
3	343	318	661
4	249	244	493
5	219	202	421
6	173	175	348
7	109	106	215
8	80	59	139
9	70	60	130
Total	**2027**	**1897**	**3924**

baptism occurred in 1946, and indigenous pastors were eventually trained and installed. After that the number of churches grew rapidly. The church became the first institution the indigenous community claimed as its own.

Mission leaders wanted the new believers to be able to read the Scriptures in their own language. Two gifted and dedicated men came forward to undertake what became a life-long work for them and their families. Dietrich Lepp translated the Bible into Enlhet and Gerhard Hein into Nivaclé, assisted by their wives and indigenous helpers.

In Menno colony, a similar mission dynamic led to the organization of Menno-Indianer Mission (MIM). In 2008, there were more than three hundred indigenous pastors serving thirty-nine community-based congregations containing eight thousand members. Average Sunday-morning attendance is estimated to be twice the membership. A gathering of the indigenous community may attract as many as a thousand people.

The Indigenous and Mennonite Relationship

Indigenous and German Mennonites share part of the Chaco. They care for and have come to respect each other. Intellectually they recognize each other as brothers and sisters in Christ, and yet they remain separate. The familiar words "In Christ there is no east or west, in Him no south or north, but one great fellowship of love, throughout the whole wide world" are more easily sung than lived.

Distribution of Indigenous Membership 2007

		Nivaclé	Enlhet	Guaraní	Ayoreo	Total
Churches	LdenI	10	7	7	1	25
	MIM	N/A	14	N/A	N/A	14
	Total	10	21	7	1	39
Members	LdenI	2100	2200	300	300	4900
	MIM	N/A	4200	N/A	N/A	4200
	Total	2100	6400	300	300	9100
Pastors	LdenI	60	100	15	6	181
	MIM	N/A	130	N/A	N/A	130
	Total	60	230	15	6	311

Key: LdenI=Licht den Indianern; MIM=Menno-Indianer-Mission (Menno Colony)
Source: Jakob Lepp. (2007)

When long-time mission worker Jakob Lepp asked a gathering of indigenous pastors how they felt about their relationship to the German Mennonite churches, one response was, "We wish the relationship could be closer. Although we have the same faith, and we pray to the same God, we sometime have the feeling we are here and they are there. We are happy when people from the German-speaking churches visit us. We don't feel different, because we preach the same Bible. We are happy that the missionaries have helped us to know the Bible, the Savior Jesus Christ and the almighty God so we can have eternal life. We also pray that we can work together more closely with the German-speaking churches."

Health Facilities

When the German Mennonites first arrived in the Chaco, "coping" might have been the best word to describe the state of the health of the indigenous people. They had their herbal concoctions and traditional remedies, and the people were hardy, but their readiness to embrace "white medicine" suggests that their needs were not being met. Never was this more evident than in the years following the Chaco War, when everyone stood by helplessly as nearly a generation of indigenous children died of small pox introduced by soldiers.

When Abram and Anna Ratzlaff became the first Mennonite missionaries, one reason they were chosen was that Anna had completed three years of medical training in Russia. The indigenous came to draw heavily on her services. Helping them deal with matters of life and death and surviving primitive conditions served to knit these two cultures together.

Difficult cases were referred to colony hospitals, where indigenous people were always welcome. Some colony hospitals report that as many as 30 percent of hospital bed days are filled by indigenous patients. Gerhard Dollinger, a long-term Fernheim physician in the 1950s and '60s, reserved a day each month to consult in indigenous villages. The most common diagnoses were stomach parasites, tuberculosis, and childhood illnesses, many related to respiratory problems due to inadequate shelter.

A 1968 survey found that an alarming 10 percent of the indigenous population was suffering from tuberculosis. By 2007 this has been brought down in the department of Boquerón, where most of the ASCIM indigenous live, to 157 per 100,000. This is still intolerably high and compares to 38 per 100,000 in the rest of Paraguay. In 2008, Gertrude Hiebert and others were seeking support for a comprehensive expanded program that will include a nutritional emphasis.

A Sunday Drive

A visitor driving through the flat Chaco countryside on a quiet Sunday morning may see sesame fields on both sides of the road, with decoys to protect the harvest against birds. Dotting the expanse are *chacras* (small farms) shaded by deep-green grapefruit trees. Along the way young families can be seen on their way to church. Most are walking; sometimes a small family is on a motorbike. Occasionally a family is on a horse-drawn wagon, and aboriginal Mennonites are streaming to an indigenous church.

The state of the health of indigenous people took a decided turn for the better in 1964 when Hans Epp was appointed to serve as the first full-time doctor to the indigenous. The young doctor soon concluded that trying to service sixteen regional clinics, often arriving too late to be of much help, was not the best answer. He was convinced that more emphasis should be given to prevention. To prepare himself to lead such a program, Mennonite Central Committee helped Epp earn a master's degree in public health from Harvard University.

When he returned in 1968, Epp directed his concentration in three areas. To address the hookworm problem, thought to plague 80 to 90 percent of the population, Epp instituted a deworming program, along with a slogan: "Every yard a latrine."

With the incidents of tuberculosis near epidemic rates, Epp started a program that administered more than four thousand inoculations, along with other preventive measures. He also addressed the high infant mortality rate with a series of well-baby clinics.

An unidentified Enlhet plowing his field with a team of horses in the 1970s. Today most of the heavy fieldwork is done by tractors.

Yalve Sanga serves as a hub for about twenty community healthcare promoters, all indigenous. A hospital built there in 1952 now has a twenty-five-bed capacity and treated more than twelve thousand patients in 2007. A major emphasis remains reducing intolerably high levels of tuberculosis.

The results of these efforts have been dramatic, although still short of the ideal. The sharply reduced death rate, improved health, and the discontinuation of infanticide have resulted in a population explosion that has led to an expansion of family planning and maternal childcare programs.

Economic Self-Sufficiency

As Mennonite mission efforts entered their third decade, the indigenous were embracing Christianity and joining the church. They were mastering book learning and enjoying the benefits of modern medicine. But progress on the fourth Licht den Indianern objective, becoming self-sufficient economically, was slow in coming. Indigenous lived in deplorable conditions in worker camps surrounding the three Mennonite Chaco capitals. Hunting and gathering had been largely replaced by seasonal work for Mennonites, some of whom took advantage of the absence of pay standards in a barter economy and paid indigenous workers with food or used clothing. In one incident, a German Mennonite offered an indigenous person a large pumpkin for hoeing a row of cotton. The worker smashed the pumpkin at his feet and departed with a string of angry words.

A Nivaclé woman weaves a warm blanket on a primitive loom with wool shorn from her flock. Weaving and other native crafts are being lost as the indigenous adopt modernity.

During the off season there was no work and therefore no food. Hungry indigenous people appeared regularly at Mennonite kitchens, asking for food. It was for them a new form of hunting and gathering, since their *Supermarkt*, the bush, was no longer available to them.

A new generation of indigenous leaders called what amounted to a timeout: "We are doing all the work and look—Mennonites are getting rich. See how they are enlarging their houses and fields, and we continue to live on the ground like our parents did. We eat on the ground; we sleep on the ground. What is the secret Mennonites refuse to share with us?"

It would have been interesting to listen in as indigenous people discussed this subject around their campfires. The Mennonite secret, they concluded, was land. German Mennonites had it; the indigenous did not. So they demanded land and their own chacras. Some German Mennonites welcomed this initiative, seeing it as freeing them from an increasingly worrisome obligation. Others opposed it, not wanting anything to interfere with their labor supply. Many doubted that indigenous people were capable of becoming farmers.

Mennonite doubts seemed to be substantiated by research. Transforming nomadic indigenous people into productive farming communities had seldom succeeded. But indigenous appeals for land were so persistent that Mennonites felt obligated to respond. Several experimental settlement programs were undertaken, all with disappointing results.

The loudest cries for land came from the Nivaclé, beginning in 1960. This built up to an ugly incident that threatened to become vio-

At a farm near Yalve Sanga, indigenous workers harvest sesame for export.

lent. "Our ears hurt," they chanted angrily. "Enough of your promises. We want land." Mission and colony leaders faced a dilemma. They knew land was available, but Mennonites knew from experience that a successful settlement program required much more than land.

A Call for Help

Mennonite leaders appealed to MCC, which lacked experience with a resettlement program of such a scale. It concluded wisely that a better understanding of indigenous culture should precede any major undertaking. Jacob A. Loewen, then a young professor at Tabor College in Kansas, was invited to perform an anthropological evaluation. For nine fast-paced months in 1962 the indomitable Loewen walked in indigenous moccasins. He gained a working knowledge of both the Enlhet and Nivaclé languages and the aspirations of the indigenous people. When asked what the indigenous people wanted, the Plautdietsch reply was, "Nivaclé vel wel Mensch vohre woare" (Nivaclé wants to be a person).

Loewen explored numerous settlement alternatives. Should the indigenous scheme be predicated on a communal or clan model that they knew or the Mennonite model based on individual family plots in village clusters? What criteria should be used to select families from a pool far greater than the resources available? How much and what kind of support would these predominantly young families require beyond bare land? Who would pay for it?

Though helpful in many ways, and strikingly impressive from a professional anthropological perspective, Loewen did not leave a clear blueprint. After much prayer and searching, mission leaders resorted to basics. Land was what the indigenous people wanted, and it was available. With faith and yet with fear and trembling, they adopted a scaled-down version of the Mennonite model. It was another critical step in this faith journey.

In 1970, after a long evening planning session among Oberschulzen of the three Mennonite colonies in the Chaco and a visiting MCC representative (Edgar Stoesz), plotting how all this should proceed and where the money would come from, we had gathered our papers and were preparing to adjourn. Before the closing prayer Neuland Oberschulze Peter Derksen said reflectively, "We have said A, B, C. How far we are along, no one knows but this is certain—we are far from X, Y, Z." After a thoughtful silence, another member added prophetically, "And the road is too narrow to turn around. We must continue to look to God to show the way."

A Settlement Plan Emerges

An oversight committee with representation from all three Chaco colonies devised a three-year experimental plan in 1961 to settle two hundred indigenous families on plots of 5 hectares (12 acres). Each village of twenty families was provided with four wells and five wagons. Each family got a hand plow, a hand cultivator, help purchasing a team of horses, wire for fencing, and food until the first harvest. The total budget was 80,000 dollars, 400 dollars per family, the value of land not included. That seems like a paltry sum now, but it quickly multiplied into a substantial budget, as many young families were waiting for chacras. It is significant to note that this help, minimal as it was, exceeded the help given to Mennonite families when they settled in the Chaco.

MCC supplied 75 percent of the budget of the resettlement program in its early years. The remaining 25 percent came from the sponsoring colonies and was divided between cash and in-kind contributions. Mennonite families donated more than one thousand head of cattle to populate the newly established chacras.

There followed what seemed to be an endless list of ancillary needs—

schools, clinics, churches, and extension services—to help these little chacras become productive. Advisors were needed to help indigenous with a variety of problems related to food production and community organization. Mennonites and indigenous people alike shared the vagaries of Chaco weather. Some years were good; in other years the fields were distressingly bare and the winters long. Some families succeeded beyond expectation; some fields were overgrown by weeds. While some preferred day labor, the demand for chacras continued to exceed what was available for settlement.

Indigenous musicians provide dinner music for a tour group visiting Yalve Sanga.

Reorganization

The settlement program was placed under the direction of Indianern-Beratungs-Behoerde (IBB), with representation from all three Chaco colonies, the indigenous believers community, and MCC. The program grew and in 1978 was reorganized into the Asociación de Servicios de Cooperación Indigena-Mennonita (ASCIM). The work is now under the direction of an annual meeting consisting of sixty-two representatives, thirty of whom belong to the Enlhet and Nivaclé communities. The remaining thirty-two are from the three Chaco colonies.

The program was initially funded largely from the outside, much of it from MCC, sometimes serving as a conduit for Canadian International Development Agency (CIDA), the International Mennonite Organization (IMO—Europe) and from a Dutch relief organization known as ICCO. As the Mennonite economy strengthened, more of the budget came from the Paraguayan German Mennonite community, which underwrote 41 percent of the 2007 cash budget of 2.2 million U.S. dollars. The remainder came from government and foundation grants. Additional funds are being solicited to sponsor new settlements.

Indigenous participation in all levels of the program continues to increase. Initially the indigenous people were involved in low-skilled work, such as weeding and harvesting cotton, chopping wood, and erecting endless kilometers of fence. Through mentoring and formal education they came to demonstrate their diverse capabilities. Some became expert bricklayers and tractor drivers. Some qualified as teachers, preachers, nurses, and technicians. Gradually the role of German Mennonites has diminished until it is now mostly advisory or supervisory.

Today

The indigenous population in the Chaco has increased exponentially from less than one thousand when Mennonites arrived in 1927 to 12,597 in the official program ASCIM program in 2006 (7,229 Enlhet, 3103 Nivaclé, 1428 Sanapaná, and 837 Ayoreo). When educational and training programs that are extended to communities not in the official ASCIM program are added the total number of indigenous people served by Mennonite-sponsored ASCIM programs is in the range of twenty-four thousand. The population continues to increase rapidly as the result of a

A Nivaclé cowboy proudly displaying his prize bull at the annual Rodeo and Livestock Exposition. The indigenous grow herds of quality cattle.

Indigenous ASCIM Land and Cattle as of 2003/4

Settlement	Population	Land Ha	Pasture Ha	Cattle head
Nivaclé	2,067	13,313	677	844
Yalva Sanga	1,727	5,965	1,780	1,880
Campo Largo	799	8,195	1,399	1,608
Campo Alegre	1,600	24,642	2,084	1,948
Casuarina	519	8,282	435	433
Pozo Amarillo	1,446	16,459	2,922	2,107
Paz del Chaco	893	10,909	1,600	1,854
La Esperanza	656	13,000	500	621
Nicha Toyish	583	10,520	760	896
Nuevo Promesa	787	7,435	227	229
Armonia	372	4,700	925	832
Ebetogue	500	1,875	270	84
Total	**11,949**	**125,295**	**13,579**	**12,938**

Source: ASCIM Newsletter

3.5-percent birth rate, a 1-percent death rate, and continuing immigration. Growth of the indigenous economy can be seen in the above table.

By 2007, the settlement program had secured 170,000 hectares (420,000 acres) of land for indigenous settlement use. Even this is not adequate; the children of the original settlers are now asking for land to build their own chacras. In 2007, 255 families were on a waiting list for land.

Conclusion

What transpired in the Chaco in these years is best described by the German word *einmalig*—unique, never to be repeated. It is hard to imagine two culture more different than the Russian Mennonites and the Chaco indigenous people. But the two groups met peacefully, as God's children, on the common ground of their humanity. Each had its claim to the territory. Each was threatened, and in the end each was helped by the other. The experience is even more striking when we stop to consider how indigenous people were dealt with in the United States, Canada, and other Latin American countries. What transpired in the

Chaco, with all its human imperfections, has few equals anywhere in the world. It emanated from people who took Jesus' commandment to love our neighbors as ourselves to heart.

Yet the future is far from certain. Can these two cultures continue to coexist in a symbiotic relationship in a rapidly changing environment? The destiny of both hangs in the balance.

21

Leprosy Mission

How Mennonites Say 'Thank You'

Paraguay had been inordinately generous to Mennonites. When some Canadian Old Colony Mennonites were seeking a homeland in 1926 and again in 1948, when several thousand Russian Mennonites refugees faced deportation from Germany in 1929, when Mennonite Central Committee needed to resettle four shiploads of refugees after World War II, Paraguay received them all. *Mennonita bienvenido* (Mennonites, welcome), no questions asked.

Consider how extraordinarily generous that was. These refugees were undocumented, able-bodied and disabled alike, young and aged, skilled and unskilled. Argentina was reluctant even to permit them to overnight on its shores. The generosity displayed by Paraguay should, some felt, be acknowledged appropriately.

This concern was resident in Fernheim colony as it anticipated its twenty-fifth anniversary in 1955. Though still uncertain about their future in Paraguay, the Mennonites had received what they wanted most—freedom and land! Paraguay had become their new "home in the distance," the meaning of its German name, Fernheim. How should the grateful Mennonites thank Paraguay appropriately? How should this gratitude should be expressed? A plaque in a public place? The world has enough bronze plaques that tarnish with time. A monument? Asunción is dotted with statutes of sword-wielding generals on horseback. At meeting after meeting, more urgent matter intervened. Then an answer emerged, and all knew this was it.

An Answer Emerges

The Disciples of Christ Mission took an interest in the state-run leper colony at Santa Isabel. They called it to the attention of the American Leprosy Missions (ALM), on whose board MCC executive secretary Orie Miller was serving. A survey commissioned by ALM concluded that as many as thirty thousand people in Paraguay suffered from leprosy, an estimate later found to be overstated. The subhuman conditions at Santa Isabel moved Eugene Kellersberger, head of ALM, to pledge fifty thousand dollars for an expanded ministry. No one remembers who thought of it first but in some spirit-led way the idea emerged to thank Paraguay by offering to undertake a ministry to the poorest in the country, those suffering from leprosy. Mennonites could not have known what it would require of them, or the hope it would bring to thousands.

The idea of a hospital for treating leprosy found favor in Fernheim colony. A committee with representatives from the three churches in Fernheim was formed to bring the vision to reality. Somewhere along the line, Menno, Neuland, Friesland, and Volendam colonies joined in the effort.

Leprosy in the Bible

The Bible contains many references to leprosy, though the word as it's used in Scripture means something different from its meaning today. In the ancient world, many dermatological conditions were called leprosy. Associating leprosy with uncleanness or divine punishment, as some do, adds to a stigma that can be as painful as the disease itself. Leprosy is no more a curse than any other disease.

Someone with leprosy should never be referred to as a leper.

The government of Paraguay welcomed the Mennonite initiative and offered a large tract of land near Concepción, far from any population center. This was not unusual at the time; Paraguay followed the model used the world over: get leprosy's victims out of sight.

A Mennonite delegation visited the government-run program in Santa Isabel and was shocked by the subhuman conditions there. This added urgency to their task. Full of hope and expectation, Mennonite leaders inspected a tract of land the government was giving them. They were dismayed to find it occupied by about one hundred squatter families; some had lived there many years. When Mennonite leaders expressed surprise, a Paraguayan official assured them that, if need be, the military would remove the squatters. This left the Mennonite surveyors uneasy. They knew the plight of homelessness.

When residents of Concepción became aware that a "leper colony" was about to be imposed on them, they reacted as communities in the United States or Canada might after learning that a nuclear waste dump was being planned for their backyard. The search for an appropriate site resumed.

Despite the clarity of vision and support, the project stalled. Apparent progress at one meeting was cancelled by developments before the next meeting. A revolution intervened in 1947. Those on the committee were frustrated. In a low moment, one asked, "If this is really God's will, why is it so difficult?"

The Mission Gets a Home

In the midst of all this uncertainty C. J. Dyck, then MCC director in Paraguay, had a dream in which he saw a small hill alongside one of Paraguay's few roads. A few days later, Dyck was on that very road en route to visit the newly established Bergthal and Sommerfeld colonies.

The road marker on Highway 7, from which the clinic and internationally renowned leprosy hospital and general clinic takes its unofficial name. The hospital, established in 1952, is located 81 kilometers (50 miles) from Asunción.

To his astonishment, near the town of Itacurubí, 81 kilometers (50 miles) from Asunción, was the very hill he had seen in his dream. The next day he sent an agent, who learned that a choice tract of 1,148 hectare (2,837 acres) was for sale.

Dyck asked MCC for immediate funding, which Orie O. Miller, who had been waiting impatiently for this day, approved. The land was purchased in 1950, and a volunteer family agreed to live on it temporarily to secure it against squatters. A herd of three hundred cows was also purchased to make use of the pastures and provide a stream of income. The thank-you project had found a home—and a nickname, "Km 81."

The Mission Gets a Director

When the Mennonite delegation visited the leper colony at Santa Isabel, John R. Schmidt, a doctor who was then completing his term at Fernheim, was with the group. The memory of what he had seen stayed with him. Unknown to Schmidt and his wife, Clara, God had been preparing them to become directors of the new leprosy mission.

The Schmidts had returned to the United States and were comfortably situated in Mountain Lake, Minnesota. Curious to know what was transpiring in Paraguay, they addressed an inquiry to MCC. Years later, Clara said, "We stuck our foot into it."

To shorten the long story, the Schmidts closed their practice and prepared to depart with their five children. Before doing so, however, John had an urge to visit Carville, Louisiana, where some groundbreaking work was being done on the treatment of leprosy. In Carville he learned what had not yet been announced publicly. Researchers believed they had found the long-awaited cure for leprosy in sulfone, a chemical compound. Research had also shown that leprosy was not as contagious as previously believed. Leprosy mission leaders were beginning to imagine treating patients in their homes, not incarcerating them in dead-end colonies.

The Schmidt family arrived in Paraguay in October, 1951 and took up temporary residence in Asunción while their house was being built on the sight that was soon to become the base for this ministry. One Sunday afternoon, while John was acquainting himself with leprosy work in Brazil, Clara was inspecting progress on her future house when some very angry neighbors visited her. It seemed word had gotten around that a leper colony was about to be erected in their midst.

Clara tried with limited Spanish to explain to these Guaraní-speaking Paraguayans the difference between a colony and the ambulatory program they were envisioning. She added that the facility would also be a clinic to serve the general public. Sensing that she was not getting through, she served the neighbors coffee and cookies. They eventually departed, quietly leaving behind the bricks they had planned to rain down on her unfinished house.

Residents lodged a formal protest against construction of the facility in their neighborhood. President Alfredo Stroessner, not known for his democratic ways, reportedly replied, "I wish the Mennonites would build a leprosy hospital in every corner of Paraguay."

Surprise—No Patients

It was widely assumed that patients would line up to be cured of their dreaded disease. But such was not the case. After three years, Schmidt and his staff had treated only fourteen leprosy patients. Supporters of the project felt betrayed. Had they fallen for a hoax? In an emotional speech, Schmidt said to his impatient critics, "They are out there. We must go find them!"

In a four-wheel-drive, army-surplus Jeep, or more often on horseback, Schmidt and his staff scoured the virtually roadless countryside, sometimes sleeping in the open or on church benches. He was right; the patients were hiding out there, often ostracized by well-meaning but frightened families.

What Is Leprosy?

According to the Infectious Disease Research Institute, leprosy, or Hansen's disease, is a chronic infectious disease caused by mycrobacterium leprae, a bacterium related to the organism that causes tuberculosis. Leprosy bacterium is transmitted through droplets from the nose and mouth of infected people. The bacterium grows primarily on cooler areas of the body, such as skin, limbs, eyes, and nasal cavity. Damage to the nerves in leprosy lesions leads to muscle weakness, atrophy, numbness, and loss of sensitivity to touch. It is this nerve damage that leads to the deformities often associated with the disease. The stigma attached to leprosy has often caused those who contact the disease to be shunned by family, friends, and society.

Leprosy is still a public health problem in twenty-four poverty stricken countries. Despite the success of multidrug therapy, about 300,000 new cases are found each year.

When the Km 81 staff asked community people if they knew of people with skin problems, the more vehement their denials, the more certain they were that people with leprosy were out there. Locating them was the challenge.

Controversy

All the while an internal controversy was raging. Schmidt came to Paraguay so convinced of the new ambulatory treatment method that it hardly seemed deserving of further discussion. He was greeted by supporters of the project who could think only in outdated colony terms. Even the initial project holders, MCC and ALM, were still on the old tracks. The ensuing dispute reached such intensity it threatened the Schmidts with an early termination. Then the former director of the Santa Isabel leper colony weighed in with a fourteen-page letter to the Paraguayan minister of health giving a ringing endorsement to the ambulatory treatment approach.

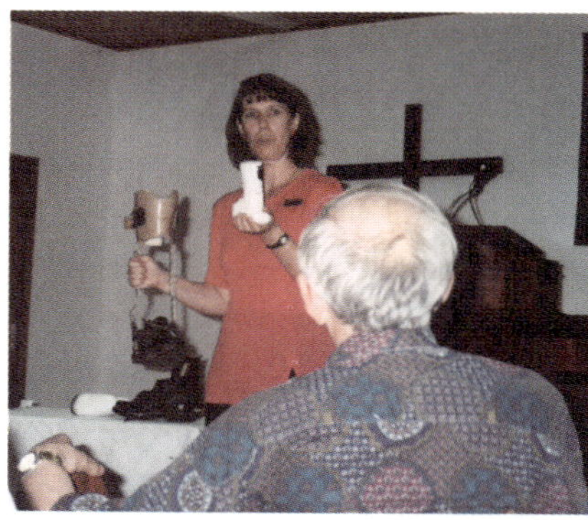

Anneliese Friesen, Km 81 Hospital administrative manager, explaining a prosthesis to victims of leprosy.

Time proved Schmidt right. Between 1953 and 1955, the Km 81 records show that 516 patients were treated, a number far greater than would have been served under the outdated approach of segregating victims in colonies.

As Oliver Hasselblad, the long-time president of ALM who was well acquainted with the treatment of leprosy worldwide, noted, "Doctor Schmidt was the first one to start a program to treat leprosy patients in their homes instead of in colonies."

Even today, search teams composed of a doctor, a pastor, and a helper still scour the countryside treating people in their homes. They take some to Km 81 for corrective surgery or other medical problems. In 2006, there were 11,343 consultations at Km 81.

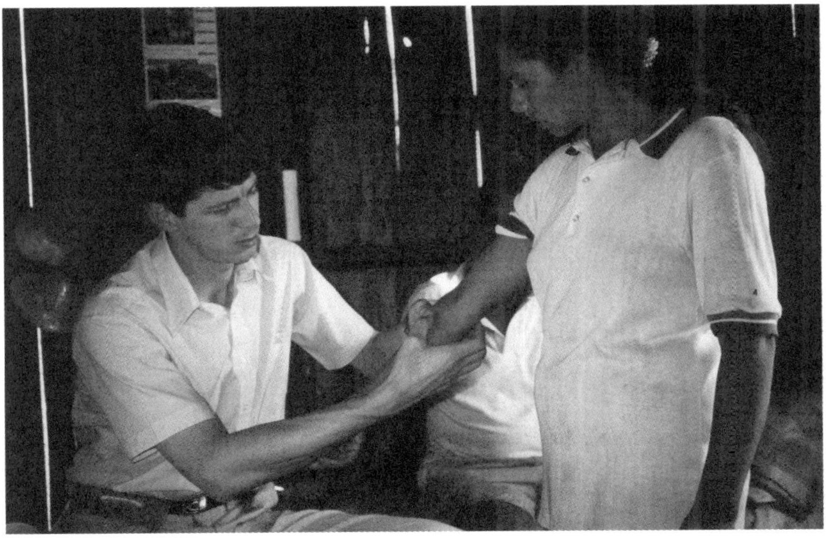

Carlos Wiens examines a patient at Km 81 Hospital Mennonita.

Ministering to Body and Soul

Since its beginning, Km 81 has ministered to both body and soul. Testimony and treatment go hand-in-hand. Services are conducted in a beautiful chapel on the grounds. A number of patients have said they found Jesus through their treatment at the clinic. The first baptisms were conducted in 1959. Because many patients take a newfound faith with them when they return to their home communities, the extension work emanating out of the Km 81 base has also resulted in the establishment of network of churches.

Schmidt insisted from the outset that the Km 81 project should belong to the Mennonite churches

Carlos Wiens, Medical Director of Km 81

Carlos Wiens was born at Km 81 while his father served there as chaplain. His birth was attended by John Schmidt, and he grew up on the Km 81 grounds, playing with neighborhood children and becoming conversant in German, Low German, Spanish, English, and Guaraní. He graduated number one in his class at an Asunción medical school. To the surprise and disappointment of his teachers and classmates, he chose to specialize in treating leprosy.

Wiens served as medical director and resident surgeon at Km 81 from 1988 to 1991, and again from 1994 to 2003, when he took a post as Paraguay's Director Medico del IPS under President Duarte.

of Paraguay, not to the funding agencies. The churches not only own it, they also have supplied much of the staff. They support it financially through an offering taken one Sunday each year in all German Paraguayan Mennonite churches. Very few if any leprosy missions anywhere enjoy such a strong support base.

A Second Feature

Within this story is another beautiful story. Schmidt had a two-fold objective in mind. While serving as Fernheim's first resident doctor he observed large families on little farms. Hardly aware of the world around them, they seemed provincial and self-centered, he thought. While in Kansas in the early 1950s he became aware of a voluntary service program that was capturing the imagination of U.S. and Canadian youth. This led him to the idea to staff Km 81 with volunteers from the colonies.

The idea took root, and from year one a steady stream of colony people have served at the clinic. Some serve a year or two; others join the permanent staff. Three generations of Paraguayan Mennonites have been enriched through a term of service at Km 81. In addition to pioneering a new leprosy treatment program, Km 81 gave rise to the Christlicher Dienst program (described in chapter 22).

In 1971 the Schmidts retired from Km 81, but they remained active in a variety of service roles for many years. John died in 2003 at the age of ninety-two and is buried in the Fernheim graveyard; Clara is receiving lov-

The Km 81 hospital staff and their families in 2007.

ing care in the Fernheim retirement village, surrounded by friends and family. A succession of Mennonite and Paraguayan doctors followed Schmidt as medical director, beginning with John's protégé Frank Duerksen.

I was privileged to be at the 2001 celebration that marked the fiftieth anniversaries of the leprosy mission and its Christlicher Dienst twin. The grounds had been beautifully manicured for the all-day celebration. Attending were dignitaries from the Paraguayan department of health, and leaders from the Mennonite colonies and churches. MCC and ALM leaders, whose organizations have contributed million of dollars of support, were also present.

Mostly it was a reunion for many of the more than one thousand workers who have served a term of voluntary service. Some of the nearly fifteen thousand who've been treated there were also at the celebration.

Still Saying 'Thank You'

The hardy *Mycobacterium leprae* bacillus that causes leprosy developed resistance to the sulfone drug. In the 1980s, the World Health Organization helped develop the long-awaited cure with what is known as multidrug therapy. Km81 was among the first clinics to adopt it. Now patients could be cured—but they still needed to be found. Deformed feet still need to be fitted with custom made shoes. Anxious and troubled souls still need to be ministered to. In 2006 the Km 81 clinic treated 425 patients for leprosy. A staff of more than fifty, one-fourth of whom are volunteers, perform this service of Christian compassion daily. They do so, as the title of the clinic's bimonthly publication says, "in the service of love."

22

Nachbarschaftshilfe

Help Your Neighbor

After years of hard work to clear and fence their land, then populate it with high-quality cattle, Mennonites were distraught to realize that the animals were beginning to disappear. At first when an animal was missing, the colonists assumed it wandered off into the bush. But when these losses occurred with increasing frequency, even the most trusting had to admit the worst. In one year, Friesland families lost six hundred head of cattle. Some families on the rim of the colony lost half their herd in a single night or while attending church. Other Mennonite colonies, especially the Mexican ones, suffered heavy losses as well.

When the Mennonites corralled their herds at night, the thieves butchered cattle right in the pasture in broad daylight, taking the choice cuts and leaving the rest for the owners or vultures. Attempts to intervene were dangerous; it was a scene reminiscent of the wild West. The police responded to Mennonite appeals, but the stealing continued. Some Mennonites wondered if choice steaks were ending up on the tables of police officers.

By the 1990s the Mennonite communities were on edge. They felt victimized and helpless. Some could no longer tolerate the losses; they sold their ranches for what they could get and left Paraguay. Wherever Mennonites congregated, the thievery was a topic of conversation.

A 'Mennonite' Answer

It was a time to think in new ways and examine alternatives. Someone suggested, "Maybe the answer lies not in arming ourselves or in building higher, stronger fences but in establishing better relations with our neighbors. To help them have what we have so they don't need to steal from us. Fertile land, rain, and the sun—it is all there. All we need to do is help them utilize it."

Some dismissed this as naïve and cynically remarked, "If only it were that simple. Rather than plant their fields like we do, these thieves would rather take long siestas in their hammocks."

Others realized the colonists had not done enough for their neighbors. Some of them were very poor, and the Mennonites no doubt looked very rich to them.

Some of the older members recalled how in the 1960s, when Friesland acquired Primavera from the departing Hutterians, a tract was reserved on which seventy-two Paraguayan families were settled in an act of neighborliness. San Alfredo, as the project was called, got off to a promising start. Then Friesland experienced an internal crisis, and the settlement was left to flounder. Some wondered if San Alfredo could be a model for them now.

Hans Theodor Regier, a teacher in the Friesland high school, took an interest in the problem. While a student at the university, he had undertaken a sociological study of development efforts and concluded that many did not succeed because they took a piecemeal approach. One might concentrate on health and another on education, but from the perspective of the campesino, something was always missing. The people stayed mired in poverty.

In 2002, Regier designed a comprehensive program that addressed poverty from the perspective of the campesino families. Organizationally the program was attached to Friesland colony, but supplemental funding was obtained from the European International Mennonite Organization (IMO) and the Swiss Mennonite church. The program was guided by five principles:

1. It must be comprehensive and address the total needs of the family.
2. It must be a long-term commitment, not a quick fix.

3. It must appeal to self-initiative and motivation, not be driven from the outside.
4. It must have support from local and national government but be free of politics and direct church ties.
5. It must be owned by the campesinos and under their responsibility.

The program's focus would be cooperation rather than help, as its name, Cooperación Vecinal en San Pedro (COVESAP) implied. Paraguayan staff member Librada Benitez de Mendoza, summarized: "The human is created by God and deserves [the opportunity] for a wholesome life. Cooperation is the foundation for a better life. Self-administration and personal initiative are essential for COVESAP. Practical education in such matters as health are an essential part of development."

The program involved all nine villages within a 35 kilometer (22 miles) radius of Friesland. That stretched available resources, but they knew that omitting any village would create problems within the wider community.

Program Objectives

COVESAP identified the following objectives:

1. *To select, train and empower local leaders.* This is necessary to counteract and replace the tendency for persons with ability and initiative to migrate to the city. The program can grow roots in the local community and have a future only if it is predicated on local leadership.

2. *To raise the standard of living.* Because it is their biggest resource, families are helped to utilize their land better. Collectively the families in the program are in possession of about 5,000 hectares (12,355 acres) of land, although legal ownership is unclear in many cases. They lack the basic equipment to farm it. Sometimes they are unable to obtain seeds or chemicals, and much land is left idle. Participating families are taught better management practices, including diversification of crops and tree planting. Later, pasture and herd improvement were added.

Part of the program is directed to women, who maintain about four hundred gardens in the COVESAP zone. Though many women do not have a good command of Spanish, their role in family and community formation is crucial.

3. *Purchasing and marketing services.* COVESAP helps villages organize cooperatives and in so doing gain an advantage for its members on both ends. They pay less for the seeds and chemicals they purchase. They get a better price for what they sell. On top of that, any profits that accrue in the transaction remain in the cooperative instead of in the pockets of unscrupulous middle-persons.

4. *Improved roads and bridges.* With help from the Paraguayan government and using Friesland colony equipment, more than 100 kilometers (62 miles) of road have been built and are being maintained within the COVESAP zone. This helps with marketing their products and contributes to a feeling of empowerment.

5. *Better education.* COVESAP enlists teachers of the eight schools within the zone, which has more than one thousand students. Teachers are supplied with materials and attend educational seminars. Parents are encouraged to take an active interest in the education of their children. A junior achievement program offers incentives to outstanding students.

6. *Improved health.* COVESAP is upgrading basic medical care in each village. Major cases are still treated at the Friesland colony hospital, the only health facility within the zone.

While COVESAP is based on biblical principles and administered with Christian motivation, it is neutral regarding the church and politics. It seeks to serve the entire community, regardless of any affiliations. But there is evidence that area churches reap the benefits when the standards of living of their members are raised.

Regier, the program's visionary leader, has worked in close association with an executive committee that consists of three Paraguayans from the community. In the early years Regier performed this role while continuing to teach in the Friesland school. When elected Oberschulze of Friesland in 2005, he asked to be permitted to continue the COVESAP work. A staff consisting of six full-time and three part-time technicians operate with an annual budget of one-hundred fifteen thousand dollars.

The program is producing encouraging results. Relationships between Friesland colonists and their Paraguayan neighbors are much improved. And the theft of cattle has almost ceased.

Regier calls for continued and increased personal interaction and reciprocity between Friesland colony and its Paraguayan neighbors. He anticipates that Mennonites will continue to assume a strong oversight role for some years, but the objective is always to someday bring the project under the direction and possession of the indigenous people. "Development," says Regier, "is more than sending money and getting reports in return. It is relationships." Christian development is a practical application of Jesus' commandment to love our neighbor as ourselves.

I cannot resist the urge to express the wish that the nations of the world would adopt the COVESAP model for peace building. Not bigger guns or higher walls! Instead, help others get what we have so they will not need to take it from us.

23

Political Engagement

Serving in the Public Domain

In 1992, Heinz Ratzlaff was pondering a decision he knew would define his life. He had been asked to file as a substitute candidate for national deputy in the Paraguayan Congress. A Mennonite politician was unheard of, but Ratzlaff was attracted to the proposition.

Ratzlaff's parents had fled Russia and crossed the Amur River in a daring fifty-six-sled caravan. They lived temporarily in Harbin, China, before ending up with 368 others in Fernheim colony, just in time for the start of the Chaco War in 1932.

When the war was over, Abram and Anna Ratzlaff were the first to volunteer their services under the newly established Licht den Indianern mission. With a deep sense of calling they made a new beginning in Yalve Sanga, where Heinz was born on March 14, 1945, in Filadelfia.

Heinz was educated in Neuland colony schools and was the first Mennonite to earn a degree in psychology from Universidad Nacional in Asunción, Paraguay's state university. He also earned a theology degree while pastoring a Baptist church in Buenos Aires and, later, one in Missiones, Argentina. Later he studied at the Catholic University in Asunción and two years at Mennonite Brethren Biblical Seminary in Fresno, California.

Heinz taught for six years at the Mennonite Brethren seminary in Asunción. This was followed by fifteen years as director of the Chaco-based Servicio Mennonita de Salud Mental, in close collaboration with the Kansas-based Mennonite Mental Health Services. This afforded him ample opportunity to interact with officials in the Paraguay's department of mental health.

Ratzlaff had become known as an effective unpaid pastor of the Neuland MB Gemeinde. He was elected to numerous MB conference leadership positions and was in demand as a speaker. He looks back on these years with a lot of satisfaction.

Mennonites Benefit in the Stroessner Era

Heinz was nine years old when Alfredo Stroessner seized power in a coup in 1954. He held the presidency for thirty-five years. Stroessner proceeded to stabilize the economy and improve the infrastructure. Between 1962 and 1982 Paraguay's population grew from 1.8 million to 3.0 million. Arguably the most significant economic achievement of that era was completion of the hydroelectric plant Paraguay shares with Brazil at Itaipú. This made electricity Paraguay's major export at a time when many of its people could not afford a light bulb.

Internationally, Stroessner's strong-fisted opposition to Communism at the height of the Cold War endeared him to the United States despite flagrant human-rights abuses and Paraguay's reputation as the continent's

President Alfred Stroessner (far right) received a Mennonite delegation in his office in 1954. From left: Abram Hiebert, Jakob N. Giesbrecht, Peter Derksen, Heinrich Dürksen, and Kornelius Walde. Stroessner was favorable to Mennonites during his 35-year dictatorship.

smuggling capital. As the opposition to his regime increased, priorities shifted from development to preservation.

Stroessner became acquainted with Mennonites while serving in the Chaco War. When Mennonites held a special celebration, Stroessner often made an appearance. He visited Mennonites in the Chaco twelve times from 1954 to 1989. At Fernheim's fiftieth anniversary celebration in 1980, forty-one cattle were butchered to feed the official guests. Stroessner repeatedly stated, "My door and the doors of my ministers are always open to you." Mennonites found this access comforting and reciprocated by addressing the dictator warmly and receiving him willingly.

Stroessner was for German Mennonites an embarrassment but a much-needed friend in high places. He was corrupt and a dictator, but his German ancestry predisposed Mennonites favorably toward him. The close relationship led critics to see Mennonites as Stroessner's "lap child" and to view him as their "protector."

Ever mindful of their Russian experience following the 1917 revolution, many Mennonites feared what would happen to them in a post-Stroessner era. They preferred not to think about it. Stroessner was overthrown in a bloody coup in 1989, and his name was expunged from public places. He was exiled to Brazil, where he died in 2006. Instead of the blood bath many predicted, the coup opened the door to what became known as *democratización.*

Creating a New Paraguay

The formerly subjugated Paraguayan people began to dream of an open, democratic government. Their slogan was "Root out corruption and give voice to the people."

Mennonites were tiring of the accusation that their increased prosperity was due to privileges afforded them by PL 514, the 1921 law that allowed the first Mennonites to relocate to the Chaco under conditions permitting them religious freedom and exemption from military service. With revolutionary fervor in the air, Mennonite leaders mounted a national interchurch initiative that resulted in a historic four-point resolution that became part of the national constitution adopted in 1992. The four points were separation of church and state, preservation of marriage and the family, religious freedom, and release from military duty for reason of conscience.

It was a precedent of sorts. Mennonites were coming out of their isolation and finding a voice in the national life.

A Fork in the Road

The prospect of replacing a ruthless and corrupt government with a transparent democracy drove the euphoria of these historic days. The new constitution, among other things, gave more authority to provinces, which are called departments. Paraguay has seventeen departments (provinces) and a bicameral Congress, with eighty deputies in the Chamber of Deputies, and forty-five senators in the Chamber of Senators. A term of office is five years.

The department of Boquerón consisted mostly of Mennonites, indigenous people, and a few ranchers. Its capital was Filadelfia. Mennonites found it hard to imagine or accept that they would find themselves under the authority of someone other than a Mennonite *governador* (governor).

Cornelius Sawatzky had just completed his term as Oberschulze of Menno colony when he took the historic step of running for governor of Boquerón. The timing seemed fortuitous. Mennonites could have their own governor in a new administration committed to root out corruption and operate by democratic principles.

If there could be a Mennonite governor, then why not also a Mennonite deputy? Jakob N. Giesbrecht, another former Menno colony Oberschulze, ran for deputy in the new Encuentro Nacional party.

One day before filings closed, Heinz Ratzlaff was asked if he would allow his name to stand as an alternate candidate. The thought of participating in a new Paraguay interested him, but overwhelmed him too. To be able to influence social welfare projects on a national scale excited him. But there was no precedent for a Mennonite serving in a national political office. He wanted to consult with his family, church, and friends, but he had just twenty-four hours to decide. He consoled himself that he was only filing as an alternate candidate. Ultimately, nothing would come of it, he thought.

Before the ink was dry on the papers Ratzlaff had filed, Giesbrecht was disqualified because he had been born in Canada. Word of Ratzlaff's filing had not even reached the far corners of the scattered Mennonite community when Ratzlaff was whisked into office without even engaging in a public campaign. Also, Sawatzky was elected to be the first

Mennonite governor of Boquerón. Mennonites and non-Mennonites alike found it all hard to believe.

"As governor," said Sawatzky, "I am in a position to help the poor and powerless." He did not find politics as governor of a department dominated by Mennonites so different from being Oberschulze of a Mennonite colony. "Both involve politics," he said. Sawatzky enjoyed the support of his MG church and Menno colony. He completed his five-year term then was elected to serve as deputy. Months before completing his five-year term as deputy, he was reelected Oberschulze of Menno colony.

The path ahead for Ratzlaff was not as easy, because he was a licensed minister, though not ordained, in the stricter MB. After a painful and drawn-out process, his right to preach was withdrawn, and he was removed from all church committees. His wife described those days as being wounded by the side of the road without the help of a Samaritan.

It was with a heavy heart that the rookie deputy tried to find his way into his radically new world. He drew up six foundational principles to guide him in the process: to be a Christian witness, to obey the voice of God above party, to not engage in slander against opponents, to be restrained in public pronouncements, to refrain from using alcohol, and to be transparent in all his dealings.

Ratzlaff also resolved to conduct himself in a manner that would not embarrass his wife or disturb his family relationship. "Even if the church does not come with me," said Ratzlaff, "I will take [the values of] the church with me."

Ratzlaff completed his term in 1998. When asked in a 2007 interview what he considered his most noteworthy accomplishment, he said, "To be seen by my fellow deputies as a man of faith and integrity, interested in the welfare of the land." He returned to the Chaco, where he owned a small cattle and horse ranch, and he once again pastors the Neuland MB Gemeinde.

Processing the Implications

Paraguay Mennonites are still processing the implications of this sudden entry onto the political scene. Some admired the courage of the new politicians and shared their enthusiasm for a new Paraguay. Others see parallels to the Mennonite undoing in Russia. Few are without an opinion.

Other than being a topic of conversation over innumerable rounds of tereré and mate, the diverse Mennonite community was not in a position to take definitive action. After all, the two men had acted on their own and within their legal rights, though there were far-reaching implications for the wider Mennonite community.

It was not until May 2000, two years after Sawatzky and Ratzlaff completed their terms of office, that the colonies held a two-day conference called Mennonites in Paraguay: At the Threshold of the Third Millennium. One hundred and fourteen representatives of the wider German Mennonite community (except the Mexican Colonies) participated. Participants presented well-reasoned papers on a variety of subjects affecting the future of Mennonites in Paraguay, including the disputed subject of political engagement. The deliberations can be summarized under three headings:

Theologically, many drew from Martin Luther's two-kingdom theory separating church and state and quoted renowned Mennonite theologians. Their Bibles were often open to Romans 13 and the admonition to pay taxes, give honor to whom it is due, and be subject to governing authorities. Some were attracted by the example of Joseph using his influence as a member of Pharaoh's court to feed his brothers while others built their case on "seek ye first the Kingdom of God, and his righteousness; and all these things shall be added unto you" (Matthew 6:33 KJV). Both supporters and critics found Scripture to support their position.

Historically, some held to the historic perspective of "the quiet in the land," a position to which the conservative Mexican colonies still adhere. Others suggested that a more careful reading of history suggests that Mennonites have not been altogether that quiet! They cited Russia, in year 1800, when Mennonites recognized the government of the czars by negotiating the *priviledgum*, which became the basis for their existence in that country for more than another century. Mennonites similarly negotiated terms with the governments of Canada, Mexico, and Paraguay before moving there in large numbers. In 1905, when confronted by an aggressive program of Russification, Mennonites elected two representatives to the Russian Duma to look after their interests. Mennonites also served as mayors in Russia.

Examples were cited from Canada, where Mennonites have served as members of parliament and in cabinet positions. Even in Paraguay, they were reminded, Mennonites have benefited from the political process. The invitation Paraguay extended to Mennonites in 1921 followed days of debate and political maneuverings that resulted in the adoption of Public Law 514. The Paraguayan president greeted Mennonites—in German—and wished them well as they passed by Asunción en route to their home in the Chaco. Mennonites created Comité Social y Económico Mennonita to coordinate their dealings with the government.

Both those who favored Mennonite engagement in the political process and those who opposed it found historical examples to support their point of view.

Pragmatically, the debate finally came around to considering the practical advantages of involvement in politics. Is it a net gain or net loss for Mennonites and for Paraguay? What difference has it made? Here too the house was divided. Already there were casualties as some Mennonite politicians had been drawn over the threshold of acceptable Mennonite lifestyle. The political process on occasion spilled into the congregational and colony dynamic. Some wondered how the involvement will affect young Latino churches planted by the Mennonites. Others feared backlash from political opponents and the pervasive Catholic Church.

Though an excellent airing of the issue, the conference did not conclude the issue "once and for all." And it is doubtful that anyone changed his or her position. Most left by the same door they entered.

The Duarte Years

In 2003, Óscar Nicanor Duarte Frutos was elected Paraguay's fifty-fifth president on a pledge to root out corruption. To make good on his promise, he appointed Mennonites to important posts in his administration. Among Mennonites, there were varying degrees of enthusiasm and resistance, but Duarte convinced most with his appeal that "honest government is possible only if honest people are willing to serve. Help me level the playing field."

Ernst Bergen, industry, commerce, and finance minister during the Duarte presidency.

One after another, several Mennonites accepted cabinet-level positions: Ernst Bergen became minister of industry and commerce, and later, of finance; Andreas Neufeld became vice minister of finance; Carlos Wiens became director of the Instituto de Prevención Social and Carlos Walde became financial adviser to the president.

In another Mennonite connection, the president's wife, Gloria, is a member of the Raices MB church.

The men who were asked to serve in the cabinet each processed the invitation in his own way. They all resisted it initially but came to see it as their Christian duty and an opportunity to work for social justice. Some saw it as an opportunity to repay Paraguay for the open door it extended to Mennonites over the years.

All four Mennonites were regarded as honest and effective. But there were several accusations of corruption and falsifying résumés by a press that does not always stay within the bounds of truth. Neufeld and Bergen resigned their office in 2007, after four years. Neufeld moved to Loma Plata and in late 2007 was elected Oberschulze of Menno colony. Wiens and Walde also resigned as Duarte's term was ending in the summer of 2008.

During Duarte's administration, according to an interview with Bergen, income from exports doubled, tax revenues and subsidies to schools doubled, appropriations to social services increased by 180 percent, and healthcare expenditure tripled—all this while balancing the national budget.

Orlando Penner succeeded Sawatzky as governador of the Boquerón in 1998. Penner had already won national fame as a three-time champion rally car driver. He was later elected to the Senate but resigned in 2005 amid accusations concerning his personal and family life. Though he was a man of great ability and promise, Penner's political record was spotty. He divorced and has remarried; his first wife and children have moved to Canada.

David Sawatsky became the third consecutive Mennonite governador of Boquerón in 2003.

Judgment of History

What has the involvement of Mennonites at high levels of the government accomplished for Paraguay? What effect has it had on the Mennonite community?

Corruption is reportedly down at national levels, though it remains rife at lower levels. Paraguay's standing with international financial organizations was strengthened during Duarte's term, and the macro economy is performing well. Bergen's one regret when leaving office was that he was unable to reverse a dynamic of the rich maintaining their wealth at the expense of the poor, a dynamic by no means unique to Paraguay.

If Mennonite service in government has been a net gain for Paraguay, which many but not all concede, what has been the effect on the Paraguayan Mennonite church? Here too there have been gains and losses. Mennonites have doubtlessly gained national visibility, although not everyone is comfortable with the image of politicians that has emerged. Some fear revenge from the Catholic Church and political parties. The loss of political neutrality brings with it both gains and losses, depending on who is in power.

Mennonites have lost the services of some of its most talented leaders, some permanently. Not all officeholders have remained related to the church. Not all families have remained intact. Some say the church and the colony are becoming politicized.

The Mennonite discussion is now becoming more nuanced. In a paper presented to the Third Millennium conference, Heinrich Dyck, then president of CSEM, said, "The question today is not yes or no to political engagement but rather where and how." Should Mennonite involvement be at the federal, provincial, or community levels? Should Mennonites aspire to elective offices involving public campaigns, or should they limit themselves to appointed offices that do not involve public campaigns?

Surely one of the most difficult questions is the one of party affiliation. The relatively short history Mennonites have had in Paraguayan political engagement has demonstrated that it is in the party caucuses where major issues are hammered out. This is also where often major compromises and trade-offs are exacted.

While there is value in recalling Mennonite participation in government, the question here is whether this is the time and place for Mennonites to be involved in politics. Those who were drawn into politics in 1993 obviously thought it was. Likewise those who jointed the Duarte administration in 2003 thought it was. It may have been. Some times are more propitious than other times.

Political engagement also varies by country. What is appropriate in Canada may not be appropriate in the United States. The United States has come to assume a different role in the world, including its use of the military. Paraguay has a turbulent political history and an unsavory reputation, both internally and internationally. (The 2007 Report of Transparency International gives Paraguay a ranking of 2.6 out of a possible 10, up from 1.6 in 2003.) Should God's servants put themselves and their church in a position in which they are dragged through the mud? Or in which they drag others through the mud while not always staying within the bounds of truth and civility?

Some say this is exactly where the Christian message is needed. Jesus, they remind us, died in the market place, not in some holy temple. If there is consensus on anything it is that political engagement should be detached from official endorsement by Mennonite institutions, especially the church.

There Are Alternatives

In his Third Millennium conference paper, Dyck reminded his brethren that the political arena is not the only way, and maybe not even the best way, to be good citizens of Paraguay. Good citizenship, he noted, begins with obeying the laws of the land, something Mennonites have not by their own admission always done. It includes avoiding such common abuses as smuggling, bribery, and tax evasion.

Dyck also reminded colony and church leaders that there are other ways to be a Christian neighbor and to build the nation besides party politics. After acknowledging that much good is being done on a person-to-person level and through the programs discussed in Part 3 of this book, Dyck says boldly "Mennonites do much but by far not enough." He warned Mennonites against excusing themselves, as the disciples did when Jesus fed the five thousand, by saying what they have to offer is insignificant. "Unless more is done on the personal level," Dyck said, "our word will carry little weight in the political arena."

Duarte was ineligible for another term after August 2008, so an unsavory campaign was soon underway for his successor. The campaign was hard fought; Duarte's long serving Colorado Party resorted to tactics that embarrassed even his friends. The election was won by Fernando Lugo, a left-leaning Catholic priest. It is doubtful that Mennonites will be given a similar opportunity for influence at the national level.

It is too early to say how history will assess the contribution made by Mennonites. The critical question is if things will revert to their former state.

In chapter 7 of Matthew's Gospel, Jesus warns against false prophets, who often come dressed in sheep's clothing but are ravenous wolves. The warning may be as applicable in Paraguay as anywhere else. Look at their fruit, Jesus exhorts. "Every sound tree bears good fruit, but the bad tree bears evil fruit. A sound tree cannot bear evil fruit, nor can a bad tree bear good fruit" (verses 17-18 RSV).

24

Chaplaincy

Mission in the Marketplace

When Mennonites came to Paraguay they were, with few exceptions, *Bauern* (farmers). That is all Paraguay offered them. Their lives revolved around their farms and ranches.

But not everyone was a Bauer at heart. A few were preachers or teachers, and they found an outlet for their gifts. Others were gifted businesspeople. They were unfulfilled and restless as they struggled with uncooperative oxen and the unpredictable elements.

Private business opportunities were almost nonexistent in the early years. What little business there was in a Mennonite colony revolved around the cooperative to which everyone belonged. So a few gravitated to Asunción. Cornelius Walde and Juan Neufeld were among the first. Walde, joined by his sons, grew a small importing business into one of Asunción's largest diversified enterprises, while Neufeld operated a large travel and currency exchange business known as Menno Tour.

As Mennonites became more comfortable operating in a Spanish-speaking environment, more ventured to make a modest beginning in Asunción. Business blossomed after the Stroessner government was toppled in 1989. Existing businesses expanded, and new businesses capitalized on increased purchasing power throughout the country.

As their businesses grew, a new dynamic was injected into the church community. The church sought to minister to businesspeople as they tried to do what was right in an atmosphere rife with corruption and ethical dilemmas.

A chaplain visits with workers as part of the Capellania Empresaril program.

Finding Mission in Business

When Mennonite-owned businesses began to prosper, it felt good to people who had suffered the humiliation of poverty. Before long, Mennonite businesspeople were not satisfied with getting rich but wondered if they were fulfilling their Christian vocations. They gave generously to missions, but was that enough?

Many struggled to find mission in business. They sought to run their businesses according to biblical principles and principles of social responsibility. Some became leaders in Pacto Ético Comercial, an initiative of business leaders with the Paraguayan-American Chamber of Commerce that encouraged ethical business practices.

The Christian treatment of employees was a popular topic of discussion; it led business owners to become more sensitive to their employees. Initially Mennonites employed Paraguayans who were unskilled, sometimes illiterate, and from poor families. Arriving at a clear understanding of their responsibility as employers was not easy in a setting of high unemployment, few government regulations, and no labor unions. Employees were powerless and expendable.

Good owners knew that their businesses were only as healthy as their workers. Their business instincts told them that the proper treatment of employees was not only right and Christian, it was also good business. They knew the biblical admonition to give everyone his due. The question was how to do that in a marketplace where the Sermon on the Mount did not inform ethics.

A Modest Beginning

In 1992 four Mennonite businessmen from Mennonite congregations in Asunción organized Mision Empresarial de la Iglesia Menonita Concordia, later named Capellania Empresarial. It could be thought of as a chaplaincy with functions similar to an employee assistance program with a Christian emphasis. The group said its objectives were

- to preach the good news and awaken an interest in the person of Jesus Christ, so that people declare themselves for Jesus and follow him faithfully;
- to lead new converts to congregations where faith in Jesus Christ will be nurtured;
- to help believers live a life of discipleship and help them witness to their friends, relatives, and fellow workers.

Paul Amstutz, a former Mennonite Central Committee worker, was hired to be the first part-time chaplain. He remained the sole chaplain until 1996, when a second chaplain was hired and more businesses participated. The idea of a Christian ministry in the workplace was catching on. Chaplains were able to help employees with personal and work-related problems without interfering in employment relationships. Some encounters led to conversions. Families were drawn into meaningful church relationships.

Work Becomes a Mission Field

Between 2000 and 2003, the number of businesses participating in Capellania Empresarial increased to fifteen and the number of chaplains to five. Other businesses were attracted, and the numbers doubled again in a few years. By 2008, thirty-five businesses were participating, most Mennonite owned. There were thirteen full-time and seven part-time chaplains, all male.

From early to late, chaplains circulate in and out of these businesses, never knowing what ministry opportunities will present themselves. They carry with them a Bible and other Christian literature. Their prayer is always to be in the right place and to speak the right words.

Weekly chapel services conducted in these businesses reach nearly two thousand employees, and hundreds attend weekly Bible studies. The chaplains conduct more than one thousand personal counseling sessions monthly.

Some worker needs are job related, like dealing with the pain of a dismissal. The counselee may be a production worker or a supervisor experiencing the stress of management. Counseling related to marriage or other family problems may begin in the workplace and shift to the residence, where the spouse and children can participate. Chaplains are available to help with grief counseling or to share the joy of a family wedding.

In 2007 Capellania Empresarial extended services to entire families. Five *campamentos* (retreats) were conducted with more than 2,500 spouses and children participating. It was a time of relaxation and fellowship as families were entertained with music and games. All this was unprecedented in Paraguay. Another innovation was lunch or breakfast meetings with supervisors to help them apply Christian values in their relationships with employees.

Capellania Empresarial is a spiritual ministry, not a "company congregation." Efforts are being made to strengthen collaborative relationship with pastors of evangelical churches. New converts and special needs are referred to pastors or mental health professionals for more in-depth and sustained counseling. The objective is always to have people give their life to Jesus and live in accordance with biblical principles.

Capellania Empresarial is underwritten financially by the participating businesses. Chaplains, however, are free to concentrate on the needs of the workers and are not paid advocates for management. Participating businesses have identified positive results, such as increased productivity, greater employee loyalty, greater stability in the workforce, increased profits, better morale, fewer complaints, and an ability to plan more confidently. Employers and employees have the inner satisfaction of knowing they are living out their Christian faith in the workplace.

Plans for the Future

Impressive as the program is, its leaders are constantly on the lookout for ways to improve and expand it. Chaplains daily face their limi-

Families at a retreat conducted by the Capellania Empresaril program which provides a spiritual ministry to the workplace.

tations in time and ability. To help chaplains grow in their professional capability, the seminaries and the evangelical university offer a three-year study program leading to the Diplomado Capellania Empresarial.

Capellania Empresarial has collaborated with Mennonite Economic Development Associates and sponsored a congress for German-speaking business owners and managers in Asunción since 2004. The program addresses topics such as using the Bible as a guide for leadership and living by Christian principles every day.

All this is happening without the need to construct a church building or mount a fundraising campaign. Hugo Berthold Friesen, the enthusiastic leader of Capellania Empresarial, says, "Sometimes it is stressful working in the crossfire between congregations, businesses, and workers. It is at the same time a privilege and deeply satisfying to see people come to Christ and live by Christian values."

25

Voluntary Service

It Is in Giving

The Schmidt family had left what appeared to be a dream life to minister to people suffering from leprosy in Paraguay. A choice tract of land had been purchased, but that was all. John Schmidt knew he'd need residences for his large family and for workers he planned to recruit. He envisioned an ambulatory program, but he'd still need a base clinic. He spent sleepless nights wondering how it would happen with his limited budget.

Then he had an idea. While visiting Kansas between stints in Paraguay, Schmidt had become aware of voluntary service, which had grown out of Civilian Public Service, a compulsory alternative service program created during World War II for conscientious objectors. Youth from the United States and Canada could volunteer for a variety of life-changing social service assignments. The program brought rural Mennonites in touch with the wider world.

Schmidt wondered if something similar could get isolated Mennonites out of their cloistered colonies. He would invite the volunteers to work at the leprosy clinic and, in the process, change the lives of the patients and those who attend them.

He had given little thought to how his new leprosy mission was to be organized. With the support of congregational leaders, including the indomitable Gerhard Schartner, people from the colonies built the first buildings at Km 81. This personal involvement helped bond Mennonites to two emerging missions: the clinic and the service program, which was called Christlicher Dienst (Christian Service). The program's motto was "a place where Christian love is made practical and real." It had a faltering beginning, but by 1957, after just six years, 184 people had volunteered for terms of varying length at Km 81.

As volunteers returned to their communities, their reports often injected new life and enthusiasm into their congregations, inspiring others to volunteer. Church leaders were so pleased that they considered making three to six months of service a "voluntary obligation" for all youth.

Service Opportunities Increase

Mennonites became aware of the deplorable conditions in which hundreds of patients lived at the state-run mental hospital, known by the pejorative name Manicomio ("mad house" in Guaraní). Heinrich Bergen, a single man from Fernheim, felt called to volunteer at the hospital. After arriving and seeing the conditions there, he was tempted to leave unnoticed. But an inner voice said, "Continue. I will be with you." He requested to see the Catholic nun in charge. She was taken aback at his offer of service and didn't think he would put up with the situation, so she sent him home.

Bergen was relieved, but his conscience gave him no peace. After some months he presented himself a second time. This time he was permitted to stay, but he had to discover on his own where he might fit in. With limited Spanish, he gravitated to what he knew and found an unused corner of the grounds that was overgrown with weeds. He cleared it and planted a vegetable garden. Patients came to help, making it a therapeutic experience as well as enriching the common diet. When Bergen's eighteen-month term was over, the idea of *voluntarios* had taken root in a most inauspicious place. Forty years later, a rotation of Mennonite workers was still serving there in 2008.

Mennonite churches have contributed tons of used clothing and blankets, and eventually the garden and physical therapy departments were turned over to Mennonite volunteers permanently.

In the 1980s Mennonite Mental Health Services joined in the effort by helping to upgrade psychiatric treatment at the renamed Hospital Neuropsiquiatrico in Asunción. The hospital's director, Isaac Cegla, said, "The Mennonite contribution made up 95 percent of what the hospital is today."

El Abrigo Shelter for Street Children

Children on the streets like this one led to the founding of a homeless shelter now run by Christlicher Dienst.

In the 1990s, amid the euphoria from democratization, thousands of children were living on the streets of Asunción, some as young as five years old. They were begging, selling newspaper while dodging traffic, stealing, and taking drugs. Many Mennonites felt they could not stand idly by.

Peter and Elsie Dürksen had just sold a large ranch in the Chaco. Their love of children motivated them to draw a support group around themselves. They offered to build a shelter if CD, as Christlicher Dienst was called, would staff and operate it. CD leaders hesitated at the immensity of such a challenge. But the urge to make the love of Jesus real to at least some of these children appealed to people who had themselves known homelessness. They erected a large shelter—and that was the easy part.

The challenge was to attract street children to come live there. Years of living on the streets of Asunción had taught them to be suspicious, and they had learned to enjoy their freedom. CD workers went to the streets to compel them to come, but still the shelter remained empty.

But soon there were more than they could accommodate. The original idea had been to provide a day shelter, where children could come and go. Within weeks, the workers realized that day care was not the answer. The street culture had too much latent influence on the children.

So the program and facilities were expanded to provide sleeping accommodations and supervised care twenty-four hours a day for fifty children, giving them freedom to return to their families on weekends. Still the lingering influences of street life were too distracting; what was accomplished during the week was undone on the weekends. So the children were allowed to leave only every second weekend.

The program formulated several objectives: to surround the children with Christian love; to help them break out of the cycle of poverty by providing a high-quality education and wholesome influences; and to reinforce ties to their natural families, in spite of the accompanying negative influences.

A *Kindertagesstatte* (day care center) operated by Christlicher Dienst in Asunción.

In 2007 the program opened a halfway house to help "graduates" make the transition from an institutional setting to independent living.

The results are mixed but encouraging. Many El Abrigo alumni enter into stable marriages and find good employment. Some have been baptized and at least one graduated from the Mennonite seminary in Asunción.

Other Programs

A daycare program called Kindertagesstätte shares the lot with El Abrigo and serves more than eighty children, aged six to twelve years, during daylight hours. A social worker visits an interested family to determine their needs. Mothers are obligated to attend weekly meetings on topics like child rearing, marriage enrichment, household management, and family planning. Sessions are followed by a voluntary Bible study that fosters solidarity among the mothers.

A private grade school teaches more than two hundred students. Both El Abrigo and Kindertagesstätte depend heavily in CD workers to care for children and help them with schoolwork. In 2006 almost half of the Mennonite CD workers were assigned to the three programs.

Other programs in which CD workers volunteer include Luque, a home for the aged founded in the 1970s. Recognizing a growing need, CD sought to improve a facility where one hundred men and women had been deposited and given minimal care. CD instituted a series of improvement projects, including a dining room, which increased socialization. Weekly the Menno colony dairy donates and delivers 150 liters of milk. Residents also plant a garden. CD workers make sure food and money go to the patients. Luque has not been an easy place to serve, but it has afforded an opportunity for Mennonites to give the cup of cold water in the name of Christ to neglected people.

When Paraguayan Mennonites sought ways to dispose of used clothing, CD helped establish Dorcas Laden, a re-use-it shop in a needy neighborhood. Low-income families can replenish their wardrobe at affordable prices, and the store provides opportunities for social interaction and witness.

Disaster Service Begins

Paraguay is not given to hurricanes or earthquakes, but it is subject to flooding. In 1983 major sections of Asunción were flooded in a once-in-a-century rainfall. There was much loss of life and thousands were made homeless. Members of the Concordia congregations (both MB and MG) set up a provisional kitchen in Puerto Botanico and served seven thousand meals over a five-month period. They also supplied blankets and clothing, and entertained children.

Anni Weichselberger, who helped victims of the 1983 flood in the Botanico district of Asunción. She and others from Concordia congregations were a daily presence and helped many rebuild their lives.

When the waters receded CD workers and Paraguayan soldiers constructed a school, paying for in part by contributions from Bergthal colony. Later they appointed teachers who organized classes for women and children. After five months, things had stabilized enough that the Concordia workers were able to close their kitchen.

The people of Botanico wondered why people they did not know would take an interest in them. The many opportunities to demonstrate and witness to the love of God led eventually to the organization of an MG Concordia daughter congregation with 150 members, with twice that number attending.

Mennonites had founded Katastrophendienst (MKD) in 1960 after an earthquake in Chile. It is organized along the lines of Mennonite Disaster Service in Canada and the United States. One of its biggest challenges came in the 2004 Asunción supermarket fire, in which more than four hundred people died and hundreds more were seriously injured. More than two hundred children were orphaned. Two hundred members from the Asunción Concordia congregations volunteered through MKD.

Much of the ministry in this disaster was in the nature of befriending victims and grief counseling. The victims came from very diverse backgrounds, scattered throughout Asunción. It does not appear that a congregation will result from this effort, but it was doubtless the answer to many fervent prayers.

Christlicher Dienst Matures

The Christlicher Dienst organizational base expanded and adjusted as it grew and matured. By 2008, it operated out of a modern, functional, and well-equipped center in an Asunción neighborhood, and its volunteers were grandchildren of the pioneer volunteers. Its agenda has been broadened to include peace education, working in close coordination with member congregations and under the direction of an intercolony peace committee. Paraguay did not have military conscription in 2008, and there was provision for conscientious objection. But the peace agenda is broader than abstinence from military service. The challenge is to find creative ways to teach and perpetuate the biblical commandment to love our enemies, which has been such an integral part of Mennonite history for centuries.

CD's annual budget is just under seven hundred thousand U.S. dollars. Funding comes mostly from Paraguayan Mennonite congregations, supplemented by Mennonite churches and service organizations in Europe and North America. Mennonite youth continue to volunteer, many in the years between school and marriage. Though CD's resources are substantial, the need continues to exceed available funding.

The final test of a mission effort is always changed lives. By that measure, Paraguay CD rates high. God alone knows the lives that have been touched, the wounds that have been healed, the burdens that have been lightened, the countless who have been touched by the selflessness lovingly given in Christ's name.

The benefits of service accrue also to those who offer them. About six thousand youth have participated since CD's 1951 beginning, and their lives have been enriched as service brought them into close contact not only with fellow German Mennonites from other colonies but also with a variety of Paraguayans. Many have altered their course of study or redirected their life's vocation toward service ministries.

A Nivaclé Christlicher Dienst volunteer serving at a neuropsychiatry hospital in Asunción.

The CD worker base has broadened beyond those of German background to include a sprinkling of indigenous volunteers, Latinos from elsewhere in Paraguay, and youth from Germany, the Netherlands, Switzerland, Canada, and the United States, creating a truly international flavor.

Christlicher Dienst is contagious. Consider the story of Eva Horsch, who came to Paraguay from Germany in 1989 and was assigned to Hospital Neuropsiquiatrico. Eva was so moved by her experience that she return to Germany and completed a degree in vocational therapy before returning to Paraguay for two more terms. Though now married and the mother of four children, Eva has made service at the hospital her life's calling.

CD has also enriched the congregations that send volunteers. Supporting churches welcome the "fresh air" returning workers bring with them. All this helps to keep the CD program young and vigorous. To adapt a phrase, if CD didn't exist, Paraguayan Mennonites would need to invent it.

26

Partnerships
The Value of Collaboration

In the early years of the colonies, Mennonite Central Committee followed its usual principles in sending North American administrators to help the settlers: "First people, then money—never just money." As the Paraguayan Mennonites took on more administrative responsibilities—and excelled at the task—MCC reduced its staff in favor of working through Paraguayan institutions and personnel. MCC closed its Asunción office in 1968 and continued to relate directly from its Akron headquarters.

MCC's partnership model has been adopted by other organizations, and this chapter describes three such alliances.

Colegio Johannes Gutenberg

The MB missions started Colegio Albert Schweitzer in 1966 to serve children from poor families in Asunción. Quickly there were more children than desks. More teachers were available, but money was needed to expand the mission.

At about the same time, a Christian organization, Kinderwerk Lima (KWL), supported by churches and individuals in Germany and Switzerland, was starting a similar program in Lima, Peru. Their Lima school grew quickly and added more classrooms, along with food and health services. The response in Lima and from the supporting churches was so positive that KWL began looking for another setting to develop a similar program.

Their search led them to Asunción. The year 1989 was tumultuous

Entrance to the Gutenberg school, where nearly 1,500 children are taught by about 150 teachers, most of them Paraguayan Latinos.

in Paraguay. The thirty-five-year dictatorship of Alfredo Stroessner had just ended. Government institutions and schools were barely functioning. There were reportedly ten children waiting for every school desk. Too many children ended up living on Asunción streets.

That year KWL reached an accord with MB missions to establish Colegio Johannes Gutenberg. The first class opened with 250 elementary pupils. More classrooms were added until the enterprise grew to include buildings and playgrounds that occupied more than a city block.

The student body had grown to nearly one thousand five hundred students in 2008. Schooling begins with kindergarten, starting at age three, and extends through grade twelve. A key feature of Gutenberg is its technical track beginning in grade nine; it includes advanced study in metalworking, electronics, sewing, and nutrition. Because the curriculum is carefully coordinated with the current needs of industry, Gutenberg graduates have a good employment record in a city plagued by high unemployment.

Gutenberg shows a preference to the poor in selecting students. Half of them come from families unable to pay anything toward education. Qualified social workers verify the family's income and provide other help. The Gutenberg program also provides medical and dental care for all students.

Gutenberg receives as many as ten applications for every available desk. The trophy case overflows with awards in athletics and academics. Many graduates go on to college—one to Harvard University so far. Gutenberg employees 147 teachers and staff, a growing number of whom are alumni. Only six are German Mennonite; most are Paraguayan.

Theodor Loewen has been a leader in this burgeoning work through its first eighteen years, under the direction of a church-appointed board. A bold visionary and a gifted administrator, his walks through the campus show that he is a teacher at heart. His first interest is the children. Loewen knows that much depends on teachers who model the school's Christian values.

"What a fortunate man I am," Loewen said as he anticipated retirement. "I have lived my dream."

It has been said that those who believe in the future plant a tree. At Gutenberg, the trees planted by Paraguayan teachers, Kinderwerk Lima money, and Mennonite management skills will yield a forest of human trees that bear eternal fruit.

Mennonite Economic Development Associates

Many North American Mennonites grew wealthy during World War II and the postwar era but were troubled that their brothers and sisters were having such a hard time of it in Paraguay. Mennonites felt good about MCC's relief work and mission-board church plants, but businesspeople were looking for ways to bring their talents as well as their money.

Unlike the Canadians who came to Paraguay voluntarily, many colonists who came from Russia and formed the Fernheim, Neuland, and Volendam settlements knew nothing about farming. It was not what they wanted to do, but farming was all the Paraguay model offered. Some adjusted, but others longed for the industrialization they had known in Russia.

In 1951, MCC commissioned J. Winfield Fretz, a sociologist at Bethel College in North Newton, Kansas, to visit recent Mennonites settlements in Paraguay, Uruguay, Brazil, and Argentina. He sought ways to diversify the economies of the colonies.

Fretz's findings led to the formation of a diverse group of men who

A plant to process manioc, one of the first projects MEDA Paraguay undertook after its organization in 1996.

wanted to use their entrepreneurial skills and resources to help their struggling brethren. Leading the group was Herbert Schmidt, a Kansas physician. Also included were C. A. DeFehr, a businessman from Winnipeg; J. A. Showalter, a farmer from Kansas; Henry Pankratz, a turkey farmer from Minnesota; Ed Peters, a potato magnate from California; Ivan Martin, a stone quarry and paving contractor from Pennsylvania; and John Thieszen, an irrigation farmer from Nebraska.

These men formed partnerships through which they supplied capital and mentoring to Paraguayan partners with business skills. They viewed their contribution not as charity but as investment with altruistic motives.

A string of enterprises followed: a tannery to convert cow hides into leather for harnesses and shoes, a factory that has made shoes for several generations of Chaco men, a model dairy farm, and a beef ranch.

Mennonite Economic Development Associates (MEDA) joined with MCC in a search for ways to improve things in Volendam colony, then at a critical juncture. Attempts were made at dairying, rice production, woodworking, oil extraction, and a supervised credit program for farmers. These partnerships were not all wildly successful, but some lights were being turned on.

In Uruguay, where another group of recent Mennonite immigrants was floundering, MEDA helped to establish a creamery that became the backbone of their economy.

A model that was working with mixed results in South America was transported to Africa at a time when colonialism was winding down and new nations were being born. The Africa program was predicated on hammermills to replace the historic but labor-intensive mortar and pestle.

Many of these projects were a generation ahead of their time and had to be terminated. Losses were written off as *Lehrgeld* (the cost of learning): North American businessmen were learning how to adapt their entrepreneurial gifts in the third world. It took some years and more than a few failures to perfect these partnerships.

MEDA truly emerged out of the Paraguayan partnerships. Fretz tells its inspiring story in a 1978 book, *The MEDA Experiment.* After several reorganizations and mergers, MEDA grew to have the largest membership of any organization in the Mennonite church, consisting of business and professional people.

MEDA has earned a stellar reputation for innovative development programs in nine countries. It has an annual budget of 17 million dollars, 2.8 million of which comes from its members and the rest from grants and contracts.

MEDA's entrepreneurial businesspeople came to enjoy fellowshipping with each other. They found an outlet for their gifts and deepened their faith and commitment to the church. Each year more than five hundred members assemble for an annual meeting to discuss Christian values in the marketplace.

What Goes Around

In the mid-1990s the Mennonite business community in Paraguay wanted to increase assistance to its needy neighbors. In 1995 Tom and Ruth Friesen were assigned to get MEDA Paraguay going, and before long its membership included 110 businesspeople and professionals.

Its first project was a plant to process manioca into flour for bakeries in Asunción. Producer groups organized and built a processing plant on the edge of Bergthal colony. After three years, the enterprise turned modestly profitable. Reports in the *MEDA Journal* point with deserved satisfaction to more than 3.5 million U.S. dollars returned to campesino producers, benefiting more than 1,800 families.

The manioca plant (also known as cassava) is associated with poverty. Poor people grow it and eat it, but they are not well nourished by it. It is high in starch and low in protein, and it is said you get hungry while eating it. The plant grows to be six feet tall, but the edible part is a brown, root-like tuber that looks like an overgrown potato. In its dried and ground form, manioca is used in baking; it is the main ingredient in tapioca.

In 2008 MEDA Paraguay opened another plant and ventured into the production of charcoal. Some 280 tons of charcoal is purchased from six hundred indigenous producers monthly and packaged for the export market. Like manioca, charcoal benefits the very poorest. Both programs are supported and expanded through a supervised credit program. In 2008 a study was underway for the establishment of an alcohol factory.

Habitat for Humanity International

For months neighbors watched as Marta worked on her house, often with the help of her children. They arrived after their day jobs and worked long into the night under a string of lights. Neighbors wondered how Marta could afford a new house. She was a widow with eight children.

While mixing cement to plaster a wall, Marta explained that a Christian organization from the United States, Habitat for Humanity International, builds simple but decent homes for people unable to afford them, and she was overjoyed to have been selected. The house will have a nice day room, a bathroom, two small bedrooms, and a kitchen with a door to the back yard, where she will do much of her cooking. A small front porch will permit her to visit with her neighbors while doing some handwork at night. The house design, she took care to explain, permits her to make additions for her large family as finances permit.

Seeing the doubt in their eyes, Marta explained that the house was not a gift. She had to obtain a suitable lot, which she was able to do with the help of friends. As down payment, the family is required to contribute 550 hours of "sweat equity" by helping with the construction. When the house is finished, it will be sold to her at cost, with no interest charges. She'll have to make monthly payments (less than the rent she has been paying) for seven years, after which the house will belongs to her.

One of the more than 500 families who have benefited from Habitat for Humanity and have been helped to own their own modest house.

The long-awaited day arrived when the house was finally finished. In keeping with Habitat custom, Marta invited family and neighbors to a celebration of dedication. The Habitat staff arrived in the pickup truck neighbors had become accustomed to seeing during the construction. Now they were dressed to celebrate, not mix cement. Marta's eight children, all neatly combed and dressed, helped arrange the table where food and drinks were set on a brightly covered table.

The Habitat director broke into friendly chatter to welcome everyone to Marta's house celebration. Marta was embarrassed when asked to make some remarks. The thought of owning her own house had been something she would not even let herself dream about. It was too much for her, and words did not come—only tears of joy.

A man she did not know came forward. He addressed her kindly, but Spanish was obviously not his first language. Later she learned he was Heinrich Friesen, a Mennonite businessman who helped to bring Habitat to Paraguay. He spoke a few words of congratulations and gave her the key to the house and a Spanish-language Bible. He wished her and her children God's blessing. The guests lingered for a time and then disbursed, leaving Marta to get ready to spend the first night in her own house.

What Marta did not know was how this all came about. The story goes back to 1994 when I was in Paraguay collecting information for my book, *Garden in the Wilderness*. I was at that time also serving as chairman of Habitat for Humanity International. I had observed how MCC had come alongside Habitat to build literally thousands of modest houses in neighboring Bolivia. So why shouldn't Paraguay be one of the nearly one hundred countries where Habitat was building houses?

I introduced the idea to several Mennonite leaders, including Heinrich Dyck, then president of Comité Social y Económico Mennonita, and it resonated with them. They knew that poor houses contribute to the cycle of poverty: poor houses makes it nearly impossible to live in a healthy and productive way. For instance, children find it difficult to do their homework well.

Dyck shared the idea with some of his socially conscious Mennonite friends. These included Heinrich Friesen, whose Asunción-based business had prospered but no longer required all his time. Dyck and Friesen visited Bolivia to observe Habitat for themselves. They were impressed and proceeded to plot how the idea could be adapted for Paraguay.

Following Habitat guidelines, they organized a committee consisting of seven persons, three of whom were Paraguayans, with Friesen serving as executive director. They adopted a constitution and guidelines, and engaged staff to supervise family selection, construction, and fundraising. Habitat funds came from the tithe North American affiliates contribute for the overseas program. These sources provided 60 to 70 percent of the Habitat Paraguay budget. The rest came from Paraguayan sources, much of it from businesses.

With the best of intentions, wanting for the poor what they have for themselves, the inexperienced committee made the common mistake of using a house design that was too grandiose. In an effort to help more families, the plan was scaled down to a house with all the basics that costs about five thousand dollars. This makes it possible for deserving families like Marta's, many with young children, to qualify.

Habitat Paraguay is a Christian organization that does not proselytize. Friesen observes that Habitat families tend to participate more actively in the church of their choice, and they often appreciate the Christian motivation that undergirds the program.

In 2008, after a decade of work, Habitat Paraguay had helped 568 families make the leap from a substandard shelter to a modest house. It all began with a few people who were willing to interrupt what they were doing to join with other people of compassion to help others have a simple, decent house.

Afterword

Is this a rising or a setting sun?

I attended the Sunday-morning worship service in Neuland on Children's Day 2007. Children and their teachers led the entire service. The neatly dressed and groomed children took turns reciting verses and singing songs—all in German—to an audience that included grandmothers born in Russia.

In 1993, I attended a harvest festival celebration in Filadelfia. The front of the sanctuary was decorated with a huge horn of plenty. Locally grown fruit and vegetables were displayed in abundance. First there was a sermon, then some music. Then youth in their upper teens left to prepare to serve tables for the common meal to follow. I watched them leave the sanctuary, dressed in white shirts or blouses and dark skirts or pants—one after another, handsome, healthy—like a parade of Olympic athletes.

I recall visiting a classroom of indigenous children. They had decorated with artwork, much of it depicting nature scenes. At the cue of their indigenous teacher, they recited Bible verses, first in Enlhet, then in Spanish. Their grandparents, I reminded myself, lived in the bush. Some of their parents were illiterate.

What is ahead for this generation? Civilizations rise and fall. Some are renewed while others float out into oblivion.

First, a Reminder

Before addressing this penetrating question, there is another dimension of this remarkable story that deserves mention. Without distracting from what Paraguayan Mennonites have accomplished, as celebrated and chronicled in this book, they did not do it alone. They also benefited from the support of the global Mennonite community, much of it via Mennonite Central Committee. That too is part of the story.

The Old Colony people of Menno, Sommerfeld, Bergthal, and the Mexican colonies relocated on their own initiative. Those who came from Russia and formed the Fernheim, Friesland, Volendam, and Neuland colonies were assisted in a variety of significant ways. We can only imagine how differently the story would have unfolded if people like Benjamin Unruh, along with his German and Dutch friends, and MCC, often in collaboration with other Canadian and European organizations, had not intervened by

- rescuing thousands of Mennonites from starvation in Russia in the 1920s;
- finding new homes in Canada, Brazil, and Paraguay for refugees expelled from Russia in 1930;
- gathering the European refugees after World War II and transporting them to Paraguay, Uruguay, and Canada;
- standing by these new settlements with moral and practical support during the hard 1950s;
- participating in settling thousands of indigenous families on their own land;

- making the transition from relief and charity to partnership in mission (*Zusammenarbeit*), resulting in the establishment of a national Mennonite church and a string of ministries, including those treating leprosy and caring for the mentally ill and homeless, to name a few.

While almost extinguished in Russia, while wandering refugees in Europe, while struggling to survive in the harsh environment in Paraguay, the global Mennonite community stood by their Paraguayan brothers and sisters with prayer and practical help. It seems appropriate against this background that the multiethnic Paraguayan Mennonite community should in 2009 be hosting the Mennonite World Conference.

What Is Ahead?

Is the sun we see on the Mennonite horizon the dawn of a new and better day, or is it setting on a civilization that has seen its best days?

The Chinese symbol for the word crisis is made up of two characters: one means danger and the other opportunity. Paraguayan Mennonites face opportunity as never before. But that opportunity is fraught with danger. Will the grandchildren of the pioneers retain and build on what they inherited, or will they be swept along with the forces of secularism, materialism, and its antecedent, individualism? Are we witnesses to utopia or diaspora? The seeds of both are present.

Outsiders think of Paraguayan Mennonites as one homogeneous body living in isolated enclaves. Readers know by now that this is not the case. It is now three distinct ethnicities living under the Paraguay canopy—German Mennonite, Latino Paraguayans, and indigenous—each with its own subdivisions. They all confront steep challenges.

German Mennonites in the Old Colony Tradition

German Mennonites in the Old Colony tradition include the six colonies located in East Paraguay, with a combined population of about eleven thousand. They continue with the strong sense of tradition they brought with them from Canada, dating back across the centuries to the Radical Reformation. They feel a divine calling to preserve and perpetuate their beliefs, which are grounded in their understanding of the Scriptures. It is likely, therefore, that the Old Colony colonies will continue largely unchanged. I have identified three challenges facing them.

1. *Land.* Wherever Russian Mennonites have settled, with the possible exception of Canada, within a generation or two high birth rates have caused them to outgrow their land. They have always managed to find another uninhabited corner of the world to retreat to. In the space of one lifetime, some have moved from Canada to Mexico to Paraguay to Bolivia. It is doubtful that this mobility can continue; land is becoming less available and more expensive. And Bolivia, where thousands have relocated in recent years, has become less inviting politically.

2. *Unity.* Changes to Old Colony traditions threaten the unity of the body. Differences are most likely to occur over matters related to the education of children, forms of worship, and technology having to do with farming and communications. Old Colony Mennonites have historically demonstrated a greater ability to divide and relocate than to negotiate differences.

When relocation is difficult, the need to negotiate differences increases. The pressure for land may be temporarily delayed by shifting from extensive to intensive agriculture, but there are few options for emigration, increasing the need to resolve differences that arise.

3. *Neighbor relations.* Old Colony Mennonites prefer to stay aloof from the world. In the Latino context, this is interpreted as unfriendliness, and it is resented. Old Colony Mennonites are considered to be relatively wealthy in the Paraguayan context and, being unarmed, thieves see them as easy targets in a setting where law and order cannot be assumed. Mennonites are willing and able to put up with petty thievery, but grand thievery looms as a threat.

German Mennonites in the Progressive Tradition

The three Chaco colonies of Menno, Fernheim, and Neuland, plus Friesland, Volendam, Tres Palmas, and the Asunción German Mennonites have a combined population of about seventeen thousand five hundred people and can be considered progressive. As the pioneer generation, with its simple faith and willingness to work hard and sacrifice, died off, the second generation ventured ever so cautiously and selectively beyond what they had inherited. The third and fourth generations of German-speaking Mennonites in Paraguay are at a critical juncture. They face complex challenges.

Demographics. Birth rates among progressive Mennonites have declined sharply and are just above the replacement level. Both Menno and Fernheim colonies have in one generation gone from a surplus of labor to a shortage. Mennonite colonies are importing workers from other traditions to staff their growing enterprises. Filadelfia was once exclusively German Mennonite; now German-speaking Mennonites are in the minority. This has huge implications for schools, churches, social interaction, and law enforcement.

Wealth. German Mennonites have within one generation progressed from extreme poverty to what their neighbors see as extreme wealth. Precise figures are not available, but informed sources state that the average per capita income of German-speaking Mennonites is at least seven times higher than the national average; some say ten times higher. In 2008, Mennonite colonies and ranchers owned 13,000 square kilometers (3.2 million acres) in the Chaco, an expanse as large as some small nations. They owned nearly a million head of cattle. Colony and private landholdings in East Paraguay reportedly add another 3,000 square kilometers (741,000 acres). Mennonites are among Paraguay's biggest employers. German Mennonite names will soon—if they have not already—appear on the list of Paraguay's hundred wealthiest families—with Spanish spellings!

Wealth inherently breeds individualism. In a paper presented to the conference "On the Threshold of the Third Millennium," Gerhard Klassen, recently elected Oberschulze of Fernheim, said, "Egoism is on the increase among our members. Our members now seek personal gain ahead of the common good" (reversing the motto "the common good ahead of personal gain").

Mennonites can navigate within the Paraguayan economic system and are poised to grow even wealthier. Will this momentum tip over into greed? As Mennonites enter into the fray of national politics, will their wealth make them objects of jealousy and revenge? They've demonstrated their ability to suffer through protracted poverty. How will they live with wealth?

Assimilation. Progressive German Mennonites are increasingly free to associate with Paraguayans. This generation has gone from clutching their Canadian and German passports to being *Paraguayos*, from speaking German and Plautdietsch to speaking Spanish. Their children attend the state university. They bank at Banco Continental. Some share the same church pew with Latin brothers and sister. A few marry Paraguayans.

Progressive German Mennonites have gone from being ethnic to multiethnic, collectively speaking ten languages.

Mennonite colonies are increasingly coming under the authority of Paraguayan law. Their capitals are becoming *municipalidades* (county seats). Gun-toting Paraguayan policemen stand guard outside Mennonite cooperatives. Paraguayan policemen arrest Mennonites for traffic violations. Mennonites pay millions of dollars in taxes each year. The Paraguayan flag flies in front of the governor's office in Filadelfia.

Outsiders still regard German Mennonites as exclusionary, and by some definitions they are. Will they assimilate further into Paraguayan culture and still remain a homogeneous body, or in another three generations will they be absorbed within Latino culture? And is that good or bad?

Governance. In the troika governance model progressive Mennonites brought from Russia, the church is led by the Ältesten, colony administration is under the Oberschulze, and the school is under a separate committee administered by the headmaster. This system has served them well.

Mennonite colony administration is strong, which it needs to be, and succession is well prescribed by Colony regulations. Historically, Mennonite schools were central to preserving the faith and cultural. But some fear they are becoming secularized. Some ask if the church will fulfill its role in upholding Christian standards and resist the invasive forces of the world. Will the delicate balance in this troika be maintained?

Many ethnic Mennonites are growing up on the rim of colony life. They speak Plautdietsch and they appear in church at Christmas and Easter. They may live moral lives, but the faith of their ancestors has receded in importance. It is estimated that on any given Sunday, only half of the colony members are in church. Behavioral problems, some alcohol-related, have reached a level at which special services are required to deal with them. Secular forces are unmistakably at work in Paraguay, as they are everywhere.

Cooperation. In the pioneer era, distance helped each colony remain self-contained. Differences in culture and history contributed to this too. Modern transportation and communications make intercolony interaction easier, but collaboration is still difficult and limited, even when the benefits seem obvious. Outsiders find it hard to understand, for example, why each of the three Chaco colonies has its own meat-processing plant and competes with the others for a limited market. Why should there be six flour mills in Bergthal and Sommerfeld? Some of the smaller colonies with decreasing populations continue to maintain an MG and an MB congregation, each with its own pastor and mission outreach.

Critics wonder why collaboration comes so hard to people of the same faith.

Patriotism. First- and second-generation German Mennonites were barely Paraguayan. Their frequent travels to Canada and Germany supported prosperous travel bureaus. The present generation has strong Paraguayan loyalties. Young Mennonites cheer on the Paraguayan futbal team with a lusty "Arriba Paraguay!" They are excited for a new democratic Paraguay. Some have entered politics, and not all of these have survived with their faith intact. Some Mennonites are supportive, but others are skeptical.

Mennonites in Paraguay are becoming as Paraguayan as their Canadian cousins are Canadian, as their German cousins are German. Is that good or bad?

Ecology. Seeing that their livelihood depends on the environment, it is ironic that German Mennonites have been slow to recognize a responsibility to be good stewards of God's creation. The first generation regarded the bush as an obstacle, and they removed trees with abandon. First with axes and machetes, then with powerful bulldozers running day and night, they pushed back the bush and in the process destroyed wildlife habitats.

The present generation is increasingly concerned about conservation and sustainability. The bush has become a friend. The nicest houses are now tastefully tucked behind virgin bush. A bottle tree in the front yard has come to be seen as a trophy. Switching from crop farming to ranching has almost eliminated wind erosion, although it was not done for that reason. Volendam colony is now planting trees and foresees wood products as a major source of income. A few Mennonites belong to Fundación Moises Bertoni, one of Paraguay's leading conservation groups working with international support to protect the country's rich biodiversity.

At the same time Mennonite ranchers and foreign profiteers are pressing deeper into what remains of the virgin Chaco habitat, hoping to capitalize on a burgeoning livestock industry.

While driving through the Paraguayan countryside, so richly endowed with sun and wind, one is struck by the absence of efforts to harvest renewable energy. One reason, we are told, is that electricity generated by the Itaipú hydroelectric project is readily available and relatively cheap. Windmills are being manufactured in Menno colony, but they are used mostly to supply cattle with water in locations beyond the reach of power lines. The absence of biofuels, of which Paraguay's neighbor, Brazil, is a world leader, is noteworthy, given the high cost of fuel at the pump.

Chaco Mennonites have gone from praying for rain to living better within Paraguay's weather cycles. An oft-delayed project to pipe water about one hundred miles from the Paraguay River to the colonies may soon be a reality. It is expected to have a significant economic impact, though with ecological implications. Oil companies continue to look with a jaundiced eye at the vast Chaco and the prospect of oil. (Pray they never find any!)

Economy. Mennonites are positioned to become even wealthier, assuming there is political stability and law and order is maintained. Even inflation is less of a threat, given that Mennonite wealth is mostly in land and cattle, which have historically floated with inflation. By 2008, the Mennonite economy that had earlier been diversified was heavily concentrated in the livestock industry. Should their herds become diseased or should meat processed in the Mennonite plants become contaminated for some reason, the results would be catastrophic.

Progressive German Mennonites face daunting challenges, many not unlike those faced by their cousins in Canada and the United States, as documented by two books published in 2007: *Road Signs for the Journey: A Profile of Mennonite Church USA* by Conrad L. Kanagy, and *God's People Now! Face to Face with Mennonite Church Canada* by Robert J. Suderman.

Latino Mennonites

Paraguayans who've become Mennonites are a relatively new addition to the Mennonite mix. Most are not many generations removed from their indigenous ancestors and have a strong Roman Catholic background. Though native Paraguayans, they are trying to win acceptance in a tightly knit German Mennonite culture.

How should Latino Mennonites position themselves in relationship to the German Mennonite church and its missionary past? Hartwig Eitzen, general director of the Instituto Biblico Asunción, observes that Latino churches have moved on a continuum from dependence to independence to interdependence. In an effort to build a separate identity, Latino churches have organized themselves into associations while seeking to retain a relationship with their German Mennonite founders.

Will the three cultures—German Mennonites, Latino Paraguayans, indigenous—learn to love and respect each other? Will they be able to look past differences in economic achievement and standards of living? Will they draw the best from each other and demonstrate that there is unity in Christ? Will it be a multiethnic community or a loose federation, each with its own definition of Mennonite?

The churches of the Latino Mennonite Conferences also must wrestle with how to relate to each other. They inherit distinctions from several groups: MG, MB, EMB, EMC, and Swiss Mennonite. The new Latino groups could maintain these distinctions, or the denominational distinctions resulting from their diverse origins could eventually disappear.

The influence of Catholic and Pentecostal thinking on Anabaptist theology also is in play. The Asunción-based Mennonite seminaries will doubtless have a major role in transmitting the distinctiveness of Anabaptist theology to a new generation of church leaders. The Latino leadership appears to be embracing Anabaptism, with a bent toward Pentecostalism.

Still another challenge is how to carry out evangelization within a context dominated historically by the Catholic Church. Mennonites have, until recently, had a low public profile. More opposition can be expected as Mennonites become more visible. Special grace and restraint will be required to avoid a clash with the Catholic Church that would be detrimental to both and to the witness of the gospel.

Can believers from all these backgrounds meld together into a homogeneous community? This is a huge question, one for which they do not find useful models in the American and Canadian churches, where similar distinctions exist.

Indigenous People

Of more than ninety thousand indigenous people still in Paraguay, an estimated fifty thousand reside in the Chaco. Approximately half of these are in the zone covered by the Association of Indigenous-Mennonite Cooperation Services (ASCIM). The overall health of indigenous people has improved. Consequently, their death rate has decreased while the birth rate has risen, resulting in a population explosion. Some live on small *chacras* (small farms); some are employed by German Mennonites and live in the colony capitals. The indigenous people are still dependent on Mennonites for employment, economic infrastructure, and services. The indigenous have at the same time arrived at the point of rising expectations—they want more. I will note three of the many challenges facing them:

Preservation of tradition. The indigenous have within the space of two generations surrendered their semi-nomadic way of life, heavily overlaid by superstitions and the spirit world, to become what some have too simplistically called "Little Mennonites." They have experienced in the extreme what was captured so well in the title of the 1970 book *Future Shock.* Simply stated, there has been too much change in too short a time. This cultural adjustment is especially evident in tensions between the generations. Will future generations continue along the course adopted by their parents, or will they choose another course and perhaps revert to native religions? This question has huge implications for their interface with German Mennonites.

Economy. Many indigenous families are doing remarkably well on their chacras. Their fields are cleared of weeds; their pastures are populated with growing herds of quality cattle; their standard of living and life expectancy has improved. But indigenous farmers have now reached the second-generation phenomenon so familiar to Mennonites. They need more land for their children, who want to build their own chacras. But finding available and affordable land is proving to be a challenge.

Nonfarming alternatives are limited. Many of the jobs provided by Mennonites are being lost to mechanization. Some unemployed people will drift to Asunción, where they will have to adjust to urban life.

Indigenous-Mennonite relationships. Cultures are always in motion; they are never permanently set. As in the world of investing, past performance is no guarantee of future performance. The answers of the 1960s are not adequate to this generation. The paradigm of Mennonite dominance and indigenous submission is being questioned increasingly. A new generation of indigenous people (and Mennonites) is arriving at its own conclusions. One indigenous leader said, "The question was always, 'what can German Mennonites do for the Indians?' It was not, 'how can we live together?'"

Ernesto Unruh, an Enlhet with a German name, and Hannes Kalisch, the son of a Filadelfia teacher from Germany who married an Enlhet women and has become an advocate for indigenous causes, prepared an address for Fernheim colony's seventy-fifth anniversary celebration.

The address was not permitted into the program but was translated and published in the 2005 Mennonite *Jahrbuch* (Yearbook). It has been distributed widely in Paraguay. Here is an excerpt:

> In earlier times we never knew hunger. We had our fields where we grew sweet potatoes, watermelons, beans, and manioca. We had animals, sheep and goats. We got what we needed from the bush. It was our supermarket. If we needed something, we got it from the bush. We ate honey and bush palms until we were full. If we needed meat we went on a hunt.
>
> The Mennonites came and made this land empty of that which nourished us. They discarded it like garbage. It is like this; they had no respect for the bush. With bulldozers they destroyed our habitat. There are at places still animals and fruit, but it does not belong to us. Our white neighbors have ruined our homeland and now we are hungry, especially the old.
>
> What I say here has the weight of truth. Mennonites know how to keep us small. They call us wild ones. They forget that we cleared this land. They came to us. When we ask them for food they say, "Work." They talk hard to us.
>
> Enlhet express their anger by stealing from the Mennonites. We take watermelon from their fields at night or while they are doing siesta, but we never harmed them. We never used to steal, but we do it now to bring about equality.
>
> Some Mennonites make us happy. In the main, the first ones were good. They gave us gifts and food, in spite of not having much themselves. We worked in their fields, though they paid us no wages. Today things are very different. The good Mennonites have died. The new ones do not greet us, in spite that we are old. They just say, "What do you want?" They tell us to work.

Mennonites shake their heads and say *Stimmt nicht*: it does not square with the facts, and it smacks of ingratitude. And yet it contains truth, however inconvenient, and is the perception of some indigenous people. It is a reminder that the story of Mennonites and the indigenous people is not finished. That story so far has been written from the Mennonite perspective. This rendering gives voice to the discontent that smolders just beneath the surface and could still become lethal.

There is a sociological theory that all human institutions have in them the seeds of their destruction. Healthy systems are able to repress these negative forces by change, while unhealthy systems grow rigid and ensure their demise. It would be an error for Paraguayan Mennonites to assume that the future will be an uninterrupted continuation of the past. At stake is whether the present generation of Mennonites and indigenous people will find an accommodation that serves both communities.

The Mennonite Center

For all their lacks and needs, Mennonites came to Paraguay with a strong center, a sense of history, and an indomitable faith in the providence of God. Their center stood the test of their times. As they work toward a centennial celebration in 2027, will their spiritual center hold, or will Mennonites be victims of centrifugal forces?

So is it a rising or a setting sun? God's plan for this people has so wonderfully led them through a dark valley of human experience and placed them in a position of great influence. How that remarkable story connects with God's universal story and where it is headed is, of course, unknown. Paraguay's Mennonites can submit themselves to God in humility and obedience, or they can become disoriented and worship other gods. Will God's blessing continue to rest upon them?

When Solomon was at the height of his glory, having just completed the mighty house of the Lord, he sponsored a great feast. In the middle of this week-long celebration, the Lord appeared and gave Solomon this conditional blessing: "If my people who are called by my name humble themselves, pray, seek my face, and turn from their wicked ways, then I will hear from heaven, and will forgive their sin and heal their land" (2 Chronicles 7:14).

May it be so for Paraguay's Mennonites.

Maps

Paraguay: "An island surrounded by land"

Mennonite Colonies in Paraguay

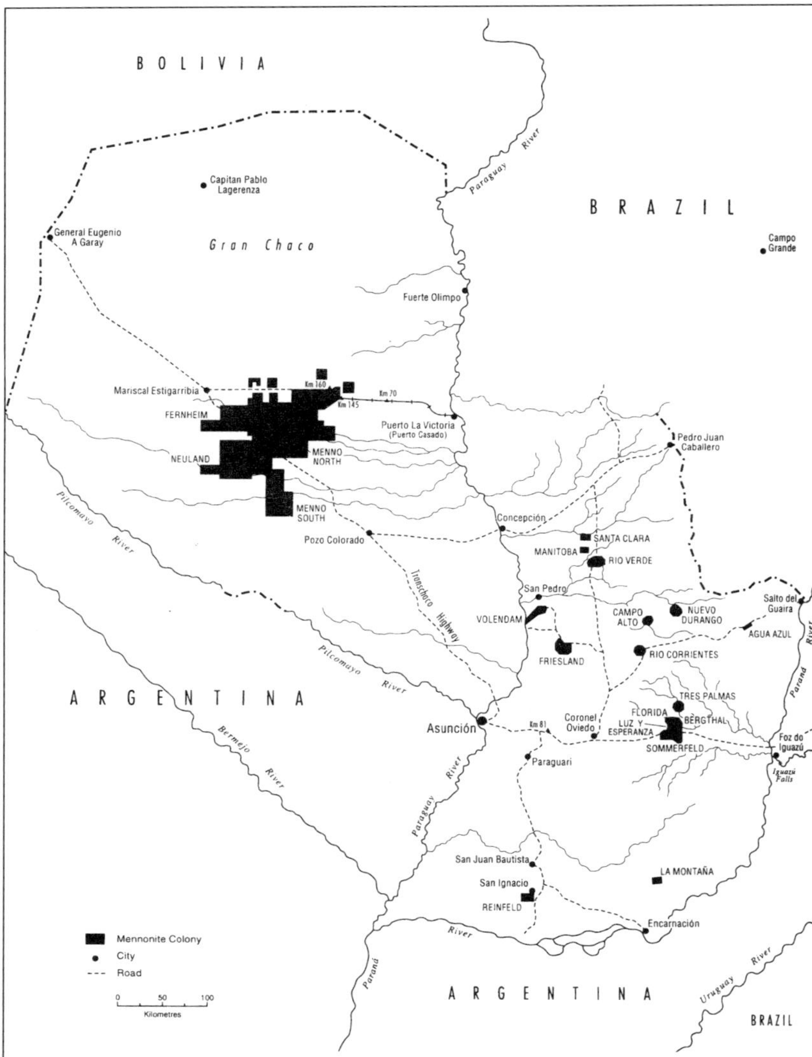

The Trans-Chaco Highway

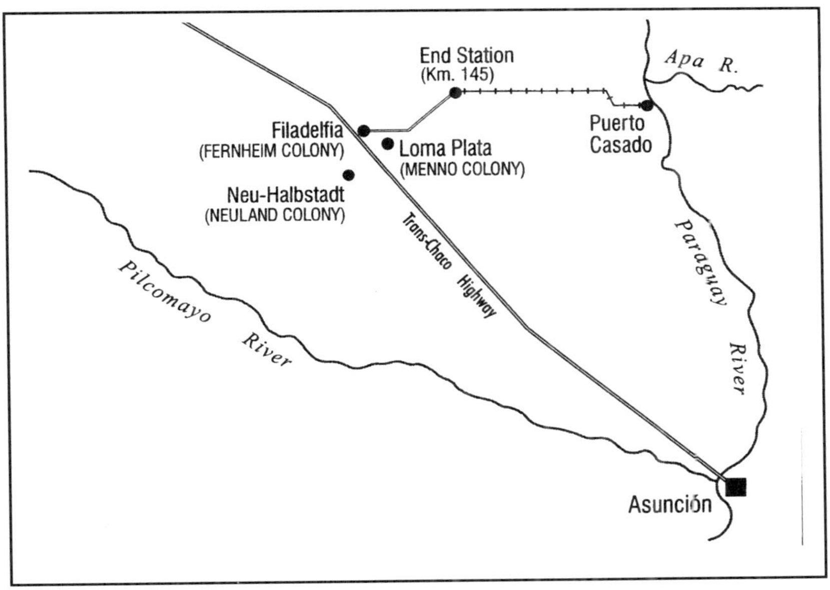

Mennonite Colonies and Indigenous Settlements in the Chaco

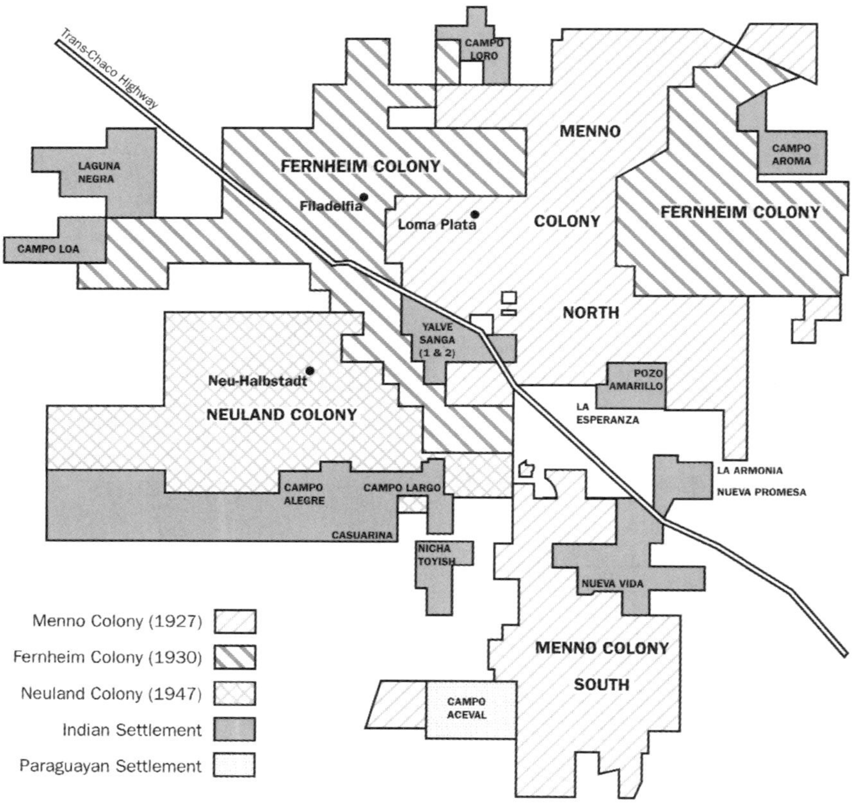

Sources

Chapter 1: Mennonites Search for Paraguay

Friesen, Martin W. *Neue Heimat in der Chaco Wildnis.* Asunción: Chortitzer Komitee, 1987.

Chapter 2: Menno Colony

Friesen, Martin W. *Kanadische Mennoniten Bezwingen eine Wildnis: 50 Jahre Kolonie Menno—erste mennonitische Ansiedlung in Südamerika.* Kolonie Menno, 1977.

Klassen, Peter P. *Kaputi Mennonita: Eine friedliche Begegnung im Chacokrieg.* Filadelfia, Paraguay: 1975.

Colony reports and personal correspondence with Walter Ratzlaff in 2007.

Chapter 3: Fernheim Colony

Fernheim 1930-1980: 50 Jahre Kolonie Fernheim: Ein Beitrag in der Entwicklung Paraguays. Kolonie Fernheim, Paraguay: 1980.

Klassen, Peter P. *Die Mennoniten In Paraguay: Reich Gottes und Reich dieser Welt.* Mennonitischer Geschichtsverein: Bolanden–Weiherhof, 1988.

Thiessen, John D. *Mennonite and Nazi? Attitude Among Mennonite Colonists in Latin America 1933–1945.* Kitchener, Ontario: Pandora Press, 1999.

Ratzlaff, Gerhard. *Vater Abram: Von der Ukraine über Sibirien und China nach Paraguay und Kanada.* Asunción: self-published, 2004.

Chapter 4: Friesland Colony

Ratzlaff, Gerhard. *Auf den Spuren der Vaeter: Eine Jubiläumsschrift der*

Kolonie Friesland in Ostparaguay 1937-1987. Kolonie Friesland, Paraguay: self-published, 1987.

Klassen, Peter P. *Die Mennoniten In Paraguay: Reich Gottes und Reich dieser Welt*. Mennonitischer Geschichtsverein: Bolanden–Weiherhof, 1988.

Chapter 5: Neuland and Volendam Colonies

Dyck, Peter and Elfrieda. *Up from the Rubble*. Scottdale, Pa.: Herald Press, 1991.

Regehr, Walter. *25 Jahre Kolonie Neuland Chaco—Paraguay 1947–1972*. Neuland: Kolonieverwaltung, 1972

Funk, Abram. *25 Jahre Volendam 1947-1972*. Volendam: Komitee für kirchliche Angelegenheiten, 1972.

Chapter 6: Sommerfeld and Bergthal Colonies

Sommerfeld: 1948–1998. Self-published by Sommerfeld colony for its fiftieth anniversary.

Ratzlaff, Gerhard. *Ein Leib–viele Glieder: Die mennonitischen Gemeinden in Paraguay*. Asunción: Gemeindekomitee, 2001.

Interviews and personal correspondence with Jakob Heinrichs, Heinrich Stoesz, and Abram Wiebe in 2007.

Chapter 7: Mexican Colonies

Sawatzky, Harry Leonard. *They Sought a Country: Mennonite Colonization in Mexico*. Berkley, Calif.: University of California Press, 1971.

Global Anabaptist Mennonite Encyclopedia Online (www.gameo.org).

Interview and personal correspondence with Berthold Penner.

Chapter 8: Swiss Mennonite and Amish Colonies

Petersheim, Henry. *Bringing in the Sheaves: The first 50 years of Amish Mennonite Aid*. N.P.: Amish Mennonite Aid, 2005.

Klassen, Peter P. *Die Mennoniten In Paraguay: Reich Gottes und Reich dieser Welt*. Mennonitischer Geschichtsverein: Bolanden–Weiherhof, 1988.

Ratzlaff, Gerhard. *Ein Leib–viele Glieder: Die mennonitischen Gemeinden in Paraguay*. Asunción: Gemeindekomitee, 2001.

Jahrbuch 2000: Verein fur Geschichte und Kultur der Mennoniten in Paraguay. Asuncion, self-published, 2000.

Interview with Harold Good in 2007.

Chapter 9: The Indigenous People

Klassen, Peter P. *Kaputi Mennonita: Eine friedliche Begegnung im Chacokrieg*. Filadelfia, Paraguay: 1975.

Redekop, Calvin. *Strangers Become Neighbors: Mennonite and Indigenous Relations in the Paraguayan Chaco*. Scottdale, Pa.: Herald Press, 1980.

Stahl, Wilmer. *Wer ist mein Naechster? Indianermission im zentralen Chaco von Paraguay 1936–1986*. Filadelfia: Licht den Indianern und Indianer-Beratungsbehörde, 1986.

Chapter 10: Church

Regehr, Walter. *25 Jahre Kolonie Neuland Chaco—Paraguay 1947–1972*. Kolonieverwaltung Neuland, 1972

Ratzlaff, Gerhard. *Ein Leib–viele Glieder: Die mennonitischen Gemeinden in Paraguay*. Asunción: Gemeindekomitee, 2001.

Fretz, J. Winfield. *Pilgrims in Paraguay*. Scottdale, Pa.: Herald Press, 1953.

Personal correspondence with Abram Boschmann.

Chapter 11: Cooperatives

Klassen, Peter P. *Die Mennoniten In Paraguay: Reich Gottes und Reich dieser Welt*. Mennonitischer Geschichtsverein: Bolanden–Weiherhof, 1988.

Mennoniten in Paraguay: Am Tor des dritten Jahrtausends. Asunción: Asociación de las Colonias Mennonitas del Paraguay, 2000.

Interviews and personal correspondence with Berthold Penner and Heinrich Dyck in 2007.

Chapter 12: Roads

Ratzlaff, Gerhard. *Die Ruta Transchaco–wie sie entstand*. Asunción, Paraguay, 1988.

Klassen, Peter P. *Die Mennoniten In Paraguay: Reich Gottes und Reich dieser Welt*. Mennonitischer Geschichtsverein: Bolanden–Weiherhof, 1988.

The Agricultural Impact of the Paraguayan Trans-Chaco Roadway.

Mimeographed reports by Alfred Hecht. 1974 Working paper No. 1. and 2. Wilfrid Laurier University, Waterloo, Ontario.

Chapter 13: Credit

Dürksen, Heinrich. *Das du Nicht vergessest der Geschichten*. Filadelfia, Paraguay: 1990.

Interviews and personal correspondence with Berthold Penner and Alfred Fast in 2007.

Chapter 14: Scientific Agriculture

Ratzlaff, Gerhard. *Robert and Myrtle Unruh: Dienst an der Gemeinschaft mit nachhaltiger Wirkung*. Filadelfia, Paraguay: self-published, 2007.

Chapter 15: Women

Klassen, Peter P. *Frauenschicksale*. Uchte, Germany: Sonnentau Verlag, 2004.

Epp, Marlene. *Women Without Men: Mennonite Refugees of the Second World War*. Toronto: University of Toronto Press, 2000.

Harms, Patricia. "Gott es hiea uck." *Journal of Mennonite Studies*, 22:(2004), p. 39.

Personal correspondence with Edith Neufeld in 2007.

Chapter 16: Health

Dyck, Rudolf. *Aus dem Leben eines Arztes im Chaco: Teils heiter–teils wolkig*. Filadelfia, Paraguay: self-published, 2007.

Klassen, Peter P. *Frauenschicksale*. Uchte, Germany: Sonnentau Verlag, 2004.

Personal correspondence with Ingrid Epp and Jakob Heinrichs in 2007.

Chapter 17: Education

Boschmann, David. *Pioneer Lehrer*. N.P.: self-published, 1989.

Ratzlaff, Gerhard. *Ein Leib–viele Glieder: Die mennonitischen Gemeinden in Paraguay*. Asunción: Gemeindekomitee, 2001.

Stahl, Wilmer. *Wer ist mein Naechster? Indianermission im zentralen Chaco von Paraguay 1936–1986*. Filadelfia: Licht den Indianern und Indianer-Beratungsbehörde, 1986.

Warkentin, Jakob. "Bildung als Herausforderung für Gemeinde und Kolonie." *Jahrbuch*, December 2006, p. 102.

Chapter 18: Asunción

Friesen, Martin W. *Neue Heimat in der Chaco Wildnis*. Asunción: Chortitzer Komitee, 1987.

Ratzlaff, Gerhard. *Ein Leib–viele Glieder: Die mennonitischen Gemeinden in Paraguay*. Asunción: Gemeindekomitee, 2001.

Chapter 19: Mission

Ratzlaff, Gerhard. *Ein Leib–viele Glieder: Die mennonitischen Gemeinden in Paraguay*. Asunción: Gemeindekomitee, 2001.

Eitzen, Hartwig. *Dependent, Independent, Interdependent? A Case Study of Mission Partnership*. Doctoral dissertation, Trinity International University, Deerfield, Ill.: 2003.

Petersheim, Henry. *Bringing in the Sheaves: The first 50 years of Amish Mennonite Aid*. N.P.: Amish Mennonite Aid, 2005.

Hamm, Menno. *Come See What GOD Has Done: The Jubilee Celebration of the Evangelical Mennonite Conference Missions*. Steinbach, Man.: Evangelical Mennonite Conference, 2003.

Interviews and personal correspondence with Hans Wiens, Jakob Heinrichs, and Paul Amstutz.

Chapter 20: Indigenous Missions

Wiens, Hans. *Das die Heiden Miterben seien*. Filadelfia, Paraguay: Licht den Indianern, 1987.

Interviews and personal correspondence with Wilmar Stahl, Edwardo Klassen, Jakob Lepp, Gertrude Hiebert, Edith Neufeld, and Hans Epp in 2007.

Chapter 21: Leprosy Mission

Stoesz, Edgar, ed. *Contagious Compassion: Celebrating One Hundred Years of American Leprosy Missions*. Franklin, Tenn.: Providence House Publishers, 2006.

Ratzlaff, Gerhard. *Hospital Mennonita Km 81: Liebe, die tatig wird: Eine Festschrift zum 50 jährigen Bestehen*. Asunción: Gemeindekomitee, 2001.

Ratzlaff, Gerhard. *Ein Leib–viele Glieder: Die mennonitischen Gemeinden in Paraguay*. Asunción: Gemeindekomitee, 2001.

Interview and correspondence with Clara Schmidt and Werner Jantz.

Chapter 22: *Nachbarschaftshilfe*

Interviews and personal correspondence with Hans Theodor Regier and Beate Penner.

Chapter 23: Political Engagement

Mennoniten in Paraguay: Am Tor des dritten Jahrtausends. Asunción: Asociación de las Colonias Mennonitas del Paraguay, 2000.

Jahrbuch 2000: Verein fur Geschichte und Kultur der Mennoniten in Paraguay. Asuncion, self-published, 2000.

Ratzlaff, Gerhard. "Die Mennoniten in Paraguay." Unpublished paper. 2007.

Interviews with Heinz Ratzlaff, Heinrich Dyck in 2007 and Ernst Bergen in 2008.

Chapter 24: Chaplaincy

Interviews and personal correspondence with Hugo Friesen, Berthold Penner, and Paul Amstutz in 2007.

Chapter 25: Voluntary Service

Ratzlaff, Gerhard. *Ein Leib–viele Glieder: Die mennonitischen Gemeinden in Paraguay.* Asunción: Gemeindekomitee, 2001.

CD Jahresberichte 2006. Annual report.

Correspondence with Ron Rempel in 2007.

Chapter 26: Partnerships

Interviews with Theodor Loewen, Hugo Friesen, and Heinrich Friesen in 2007.

Photo Credits

All photos used by permission from the following sources:

Pages 28, 40, 70: From the book *Neue Heimat in der Chaco Wildnis* by Martin W. Friesen (Asunción: Chortitzer Komitee, 1987).
Page 37: Provided by Menno colony.
Pages 45, 53, 145, 252: From the book *Fernheim 1930-1980: 50 Jahre Kolonie Fernheim: Ein Beitrag in der Entwicklung Paraguays* (Kolonie Fernheim, Paraguay: 1980).
Pages 51, 61, 144, 172: From the book *Im Schweiße deines Angesichts* by Walter Quiring. (Self published, 1953).
Pages 50, 163: Provided by Fernheim colony.
Pages 66, 78, 90, 167, 195, 202, 205, 207, 215, 219, 270, 275, 278, 283, 287: By Matthew Bauman.
Pages 85, 88, 188: From the book *Sommerfeld: 1948–1998*. Self-published by Sommerfeld colony for its fiftieth anniversary.
Pages 97, 237: From the book *Ein Leib–viele Glieder: Die mennonitischen Gemeinden in Paraguay* by Gerhard Ratzlaff (Asunción: Gemeindekomitee, 2001).
Pages 108, 118: By Mary Derksen.
Pages 115, 117: Provided by Licht den Indianern.
Pages 125, 241, 280: By Mark Beach.
Pages 116, 136, 185, 192, 196, 199: From the book *Unter der heißen Sonne des Südens: 75 Jahre Kolonie Menno, 1927-2002* (Kolonie Menno, Paraguay: 2002).
Page 151: Provided by the family of Heinrich Dürksen.
Page 160: Provided by Betty Unruh Leite.
Page 208: Provided by Mennonite World Conference.

Page 226: From the cover of *25 Jahre Kolonie Neuland Chaco—Paraguay 1947–1972* by Walter Regehr (Kolonieverwaltung Neuland, 1972).

Cover and pages 222, 227, 228, 230, 231: Provided by Association of Indigenous-Mennonite Cooperation Services.

Pages 240, 242: Provided by the Km 81 Mennonite Hospital.

Page 257: By Merle Good.

Page 264, 267: Provided by Capellanía Empresarial.

Pages 271, 272: Provided by Christlicher Dienst.

The Author

Edgar Stoesz served for nearly four decades as director of various programs with Mennonite Central Committee, including the Latin American program that served Paraguay. He has made more than twenty trips to the region. He is the author of numerous books, including *Garden in the Wilderness: Mennonite Communities in the Paraguayan Chaco, 1927-1997*; *Doing Good Better*; and *Doing Good Even Better*. Edgar was concurrently also CEO of Mennonite Indemnity Inc. and president of Goodville Mutual Casualty. He served as moderator of the Atlantic Coast Conference of Mennonite Church USA from 2001 to 2005. He and his wife, Gladys, live in Akron, Pennsylvania, and are charter members of Akron Mennonite Church. Edgar was born and grew up in Mountain Lake, Minnesota, the son of Russian Mennonite parents.